SHAKESPEARE'S NEIGHBORS

*Theory Matters in the Bard
And His Contemporaries*

Rocco Coronato

University Press of America,® Inc.
Lanham · New York · Oxford

Copyright © 2001 by
University Press of America,® Inc.
4720 Boston Way
Lanham, Maryland 20706
UPA Acquisitions Department (301) 459-3366

12 Hid's Copse Rd.
Cumnor Hill, Oxford OX2 9JJ

British Library Cataloging in Publication Information Available

Library of Congress Cataloging-in-Publication Data

Coronato, Rocco.
Shakespeare's neighbors : theory matters in the Bard and his
contemporaries / Rocco Coronato.
p.   cm
Includes bibliographical references and index.
1. English drama—Early modern and Elizabethan, 1500-1600—
History and criticism—Theory, etc. 2. English drama—17th
century—History and criticism—Theory, etc. 3. Shakespeare,
William, 1564-1616—Criticism and interpretation. 4. Shakespeare,
William, 1564-1616—Contemporaries. I. Title.

PR651 .C67 2001   822'.309—dc21   2001053079 CIP

ISBN 0-7618-2145-7 (cloth : alk. paper)
ISBN 0-7618-2146-5 (pbk. : alk. paper)

™ The paper used in this publication meets the minimum
requirements of American National Standard for Information
Sciences—Permanence of Paper for Printed Library Materials,
ANSI Z39.48—1984

Contents

Foreword

The writing of Rocco Coronato is *sui generis*, yet it is difficult to imagine who will not be drawn to its remarkable combination of learning, investigation, and wit. Coronato's exploration of Renaissance culture—even when the putative (and final) subject is Shakespeare's *Richard III* or *Twelfth Night*, Christopher Marlowe's Barabas or Donne's "The Extasie"—is what that culture itself most prized: a probing mind, an extensive learning, a rich array of resources in juxtaposition, a passion for learning, the play of intellect. Both the matter and the manner are instructive, and continually attractive, too. Take the chapter on Shakespeare and laughter, for instance. It begins with Groucho Marx ("that other Marx") which turns out to be remarkably apposite for the Renaissance:

> Perhaps I'm not a comic. It's not worth arguing about . . . I'm a pretty wary fellow, and I have neither the desire nor the equipment to analyze what makes one man funny to another man . . . I doubt if any comedian can honestly say why he is funny and why his next-door neighbor is not.

This sounds, at first, like Shakespeare: Keats' natural–born genius who did not worry over the theory of laughter as (for instance) Sir Philip Sidney did. But Coronato places Marx (and Shakespeare) in the Renaissance context of their received Plato and Aristotle and Joubert—and, surprisingly, of the dour–faced Ramus. The object of laughter is deformity, we learn (as they did); its method is unexpectedness; its basis is the division (of genus from species, of fact from another fact; here is Ramus). For Coronato, some of these theories just don't work; others explain laughter away and so don't help. The resilient text is Shakespeare's (in this case, *Twelfth Night*). Coronato's own juxtapositionings always light fires to our reason *and* our imagination, and not the least of his examples is consistently his own thought: "Laughter is a cage—*Twelfth Night* rings with the constant intimation of characters that are, like Viola, temporarily put out of the text and those that conversely are continually framed into a structure of interpretation." (The method, we note, derives from Ramus if the ideas do not.) But no matter what Renaissance text has attracted Coronato's attention and ours and will not let any of us free, the mind at play here—I can think only of Harry Levin as comparable—always illuminates.

Let me illustrate this with another instance, the chapter on Donne's "Extasie." Here a contemporary authority for Coronato is the medical expert Ambroise Paré. Paré finds ecstasy is the basis for procreation and survival, "a veritable miracle of providential pleasure and physiological cogency." Alongside Paré Coronato puts the Neoplatonists, who saw ecstasy as a spiritual state, and Aristotle, who

v

associated ecstasy with sleep and the loss of conscience. He goes to Donne's sermons, too, where ecstasy is associated with the words of St. Paul and St. Gregory, where the womb seems to be a prison and birth "going out to the place of Execution." What is true in the chapter on Donne is true throughout this book—the cultural filiations that Coronato develops out of a text always widen our horizons, and yet always keep the text shadowing the investigation and reappearing at its close. As readers, we can be divided between total submersion into the culture he defines so tellingly and kept distanced, aware that all we read interplays with literary texts in ways that give them original, authentic life.

There is a chapter on Pocahontas as she is redefined from her own culture by that of the English that Coronato enriches through an understanding of Renaissance Aristotelian dialectic; of Marlowe's *Jew of Malta* in light of the scholastic definitions of commutative versus distributive justice; of *Winter's Tale* in light of the myth of the lost island called Perdita (a new cultural source for me); of Viola in light of cultural definitions in the Renaissance of individuation. Different readers will find different chapters enthralling; my own favorite is the discussion of contrition, confession, and grief that he traces from the Church Fathers forward through the age of Richard III (in Catholic England) and of Shakespeare (in Protestant England) in order to understand the scenes of sorrow in *Richard III*.

The thesis of *Shakespeare's Neighbors*, Rocco Coronato says at one point, is his interest in suspension: that notion, growing out of philosophical stoicism, when all things are in balance and there is a moment of respite before decisions are made and future actions ascertained. Surely those moments are central to each chapter and each investigation. But we arrive at them with so much sense of cultural activity and belief that they become not moments of inaction but moments of startling accumulation.

Here is a book to be read with every kind of joy.

ARTHUR F. KINNEY

Thomas Copeland Professor of Literary History

*Director of the Massachusetts Center
for Renaissance Studies*

University of Massachusetts, Amherst

Preface

And those are liked who are clever at making or taking a joke,
for each has the same end in view as his neighbor,
being able to take a joke and return it in good taste.
—Aristotle, *Rhetorics*

Should one wish to go and catch a falling star, at least by sight, Auguste Dupin's theory might turn out handy:

> To look at a star by glances—to view it in a side-long way, by turning toward it the exterior portions of the *retina* (more susceptible of feeble impressions of light than the interior) is to behold the star distinctly—is to have the best appreciation of its lustre—a lustre which grows dim just in proportion as we turn our vision *fully* upon it. A greater number of rays actually fall upon the eye in the latter case, but, in the former, there is the more refined capacity for comprehension. By undue profundity we perplex and enfeeble thought; and it is possible to make even Venus herself vanish from the firmament by a scrutiny too sustained, too concentrated, or too direct. (Poe 1843, 23)

This belief in proximity, in the scrutiny of the radiant purlieus to grasp their contours, naturally calls for a good neighborhood—hardly the type mentioned by Groucho Marx, in the illuminating quotation I report in my last chapter, when he dismissingly notes that not even the best comedian would be able to say why he is funny and his neighbor not.

Shakespeare's "neighbors" were definitely much less dull. Many a Feste does live by his church: hidden Jesuits and outspoken Protestants, masters of Ramist rhetoric and popularizers of mongrelized Aristotle, Church fathers on edenic lovemaking and Renaissance doctors on postcoital discontents, theologians and merchants on just profit and philosophers, ancient and new, on the transformation of matter—those "neighbors" are my authorities. If we turn our vision to the theories encircling concepts such as confession, ecstasy and laughter, Shakespeare's works radiate a different, slightly attenuated lustre that affords legibility or, at least, the inception of a "more refined capacity for comprehension" of the connections between the Bard and his neighbors.

Yet why should one wish to abstain from Shakespeare? While the Bard has been often relocated in Freud's Vienna or Lacan's Paris, one would raise no objection to taking him to his own London just for a change. For most, if not virtually all the sources, or at least their analogues, I have surveyed here were accessible to the Bard in variably divulged ways. Yet my lateral approach is only a momentary pause before more decided engagement with the shining star, rather than a respite into a proliferation of possibilities that may deter interpretation.

In a sense, Shakespeare is not enough—again, because of too much light. Ignorance is our lot, especially this writer's: the text is insufficient in its very proliferation of meanings embedded in apparently quotidian words and concepts such as 'confession', 'laughter' or 'ecstasy'. One has to choose between two directions: either focusing on the star to analyze the texts as unchangeable records of *the* human being *ab aeterno*, or highlighting the social body surrounding the Bard. My own proximity method, if any, revives the latter interest in broader frameworks of interpretation, without, however positing the literary author as a translator of wider social forces. Nor does it vindicate a pococurante sense of antiquarianism, an ill-fated belief in the myth of the sources as a perfect Baedeker to the Renaissance mind.

To quote a lyric sung by Joy Division, there is a hope—"touching from a distance." For distance does not necessarily prevent plenty of touching. In fact, the texts are copious, too. The very proliferation of sources, the plethora of authorities and references, make comparison virtually inescapable. All the concepts I have considered here, most notably millennial theories such as the tradition on confession and laughter, live off a principle of saturation: references pile up in the effort to saturate the already said and thus dispel any further doubts, nonetheless bringing to light new illuminating questions in the process. Much like confession, all theories aspire to the status of *summa*, to the impossible union of all that has been said and denied on a given subject. Just as confession is a discourse to be delivered *ante januas,* before the gates of Paradise and the comprehension of God's radiant grace or, more profanely, as Viola always awaits at the gates before reception, my liminal walk through these whereabouts tries to tread upon the very last compound close to (*juxta*) the text.

Theories, I have said, not "discourses." For this book partakes of the school of ethnic studies, evoking as it does Renaissance Italians' trust in theory. A sense of intended hierarchy differentiates theory from discourse, in the pre-eminence afforded to the rule as handed down by the sources, rather than to the peripheral observation of the subject. By repeating the same story all over again, the sources outline the contours where the literary text, neither resulting from them nor producing them in its turn, offers comprehension in its usage of the same concepts. Set respectively against the backdrop of the theories on confession and laughter, weeping in *Richard III* and diversion in *Twelfth Night* have more stories to tell. Theory as a form of hierarchy, I have said: yet theory is not binding. One is faced with plenty of authorities on the subject, yet none of them says what laughter or ecstasy indeed are—they evoke the purlieus of what they might have been. The second sort of naivety I have tried to push out of sight is the attempt to prove that Shakespeare (as well as Marlowe, Jonson and Donne) *must* have come into contact with at least a parcel of this or that theory. While I have tried to conjecture, especially in the notes apparatus, how the factual relation might have been established, this is none of my business here. Instead I have pursued a play of possibilities, rendered quite likely by the copious consistency and structured redundancy of the theories.

Hence, my essays have no point to make, no thesis to defend, no relation to prove. A "Catholic" Shakespeare is not of the essence here, nor is the contention that Marlowe was familiar with scholastic economy and classics on matter transformation or Donne with the manifold notions of ecstasy (not very unlikely, though). I object to the belief in *the* proof, the falsely positivist faith in a thesis to be proven—Shakespeare conversant with confession, Marlowe with Plato and Aristotle on destruction, and so forth (not very unlikely, though). On the other hand, while resting on theories, these chapters ultimately try to reach a point where theory itself is absent, a place of suspension where the interrogation of the words enhances how the literary text may be read through the partially fading connotations of those self-same words. This kind of reversion between literary and non-literary texts does not strive after a straightforward relation, but mutual illumination, a protracted indwelling on the shining outskirts of the star. "In investigations such as we are now pursuing, it should not be so much asked 'what has occurred,' as 'what has occurred that has never occurred before'" (Poe 1843, 24). Or what might have occurred, one may add: I am not interested in what did indeed occur, but what might have occurred and how this serendipity illuminates the text.

Most recent criticism reveals a sonata structure: the literary text triggers off a network of meanings related to a cluster of non-literary texts; the latter group garners an even more connoted nebula of meaning; lastly, the reinsertion of this cluster into the text unveils the author's rephrasing of the concept. The musical simile is well worth pursuing. Shortly before his death, Kurt Cobain had self-deprecatingly pointed at the typical Nirvana in-house style, "This thing of going from quiet to loud," starting with the verse and then going into the chorus: "I'm getting so tired of the formula. And it is formula. . . . It is a dynamic style. I'm only using two of the dynamics." Cobain conjured up the possibility that new forms might have been created if—"I want to learn to go in between those things, go back and forth, almost become psychedelic in a way but with a lot more structure" (1994, 66, 68). I also have tried to "go in between those things," following the almost musical structures that the authorities seemed to suggest. Since going psychedelic was not my aim, I have decided to specify the underlying forms just to foster clarity, not to unearth recondite parallelisms.

"A Descent into Richard" (Chapter 1), is organized as a *rondo*, an alternation of episodes each focusing on a head of confession theory (its genesis, the importance of tears, orality and the heart, and so forth) and its counterpart in *Richard III*, trying to shed light on Shakespeare's vision of the spoken word and its relation to the heart. In Chapter 2, "What The Matter Is With Barabas," the reader is offered a *suite* of several movements all set in the same key, the transformation of matter along the lines of philosophy and the debate on the legitimacy of trade. "The Invention of Perdita" (Chapter 3), tallies with the structure of the *aria dal segno*: the first section deals with the topic of travel and loss in the Renaissance; the second reprises the theme in *The Winter's Tale*, while the concluding section gets back to an element (not its beginning) of the first section temporarily left on the margins—chance and its representation. The *fugue* is the overarching structure of Chapter 4, "Inducting Pocahontas": the exposition of the topic of geographical discovery in the Renaissance paves the way to a new episode on the same theme, the sense of alterity, followed by other episodes such as the negotiation of otherness through Aristotelian dialectic and the representation of discovery in Ben Jonson's masques. Also the other chapter on Aristotelian dialectic, "The Likes of Viola" (Chapter 5), may be likened to a *fugue* in its succession of episodes on similarity in Aristotle, Ramus and *Twelfth Night*. For Chapter 6, "A Poem on the Tube," the fast-slow-fast structure of the *concerto* comes to one's mind: the material is grouped by starting from an overview of the concept of sexual ecstasy in theology, philosophy and medicine, reaching the central locus of suspension, the absence of consciousness and speech, and then heading on to Donne's "Ecstasy" under the light shed upon the concept by the preceding movement. My last essay, "Shakespeare in Laughter" (Chapter 7), presents the form of a *sonata*: the exposition presents a reasonably undersized survey of Renaissance theories on laughter, briefly hinting at the element of unexpectedness; the development expatiates on the topic of diversion at the core of the Renaissance interpretation of laughter; the recapitulation juxtaposes the theory of laughter as diversion with *Twelfth Night*.

As Feste says, the ideal pursued here is that of a "voyage of nothing"—no code, no authority except *the* authorities. Perhaps this is the essayists' lot, a tribe wryly depicted by Ben Jonson in *Timber* as those who "in all they write, confesse still what bookes they have read last; and therein their owne folly, so much, that they bring it to the *Stake* raw, and undigested: not that the place did need it neither; but that they thought themselves furnished, and would vent it" (*BJ* 8:6.725-9). Benign acceptance of the ensuing eructations is welcome.

Acknowledgments

§ All quotations of the works of **Plato** and **Aristotle** are reprinted by permission of the publishers and the Trustees of the Loeb Classical Library from:

Plato. Volume I. Transl. H. North Fowler. The Loeb Classical Library. 1982 (1914). *Phaedrus.*
Plato. Volume IV. Transl. H. North Fowler. The Loeb Classical Library. 1977 (1926). *Cratylus.*
Plato. Volume IX. Transl. R. G. Bury. The Loeb Classical Library. 1981 (1929). *Timaeus.*
Aristotle. Volume III. Transl. E. S. Forster. The Loeb Classical Library. 1978 (1955). *Of Coming-to-Be and Passing-Away.*
Aristotle. Poetics. Transl. S. Halliwell. The Loeb Classical Library. 1995.
Aristotle. The Organon. Volume II. *Posterior Analytics* (transl. H. Tredennick). *Topica* (transl. E.S. Forster). The Loeb Classical Library. 1966 (1960).

The Loeb Classical Library ® is a registered trademark of the President and Fellows of Harvard College.

§ Quotations from **Marlowe** refer to *The Jew of Malta*, edited by Richard W. Van Fossen. 1964. The University of Nebraska Press. Reprinted by permission of the publisher.

§ Quotations from the works of **Jonson** are taken from *Ben Jonson.* Eds. C.H. Herford, P. Simpson and Evelyn Simpson. Oxford: Clarendon Press. Reprinted by permission of Oxford University Press.

FROM *Timber.* In *Ben Jonson.* Eds. C.H. Herford, P. Simpson and Evelyn Simpson. Oxford: Clarendon Press.Vol. 8. *The Poems. The Prose Works.* 1947.
FROM *The Staple of Newes.* In *Ben Jonson.* Eds. C.H. Herford, P. Simpson and E. Simpson. Oxford: Clarendon Press, vol. 6. 1938.
FROM *Christmas His Masque.* In *Ben Jonson.* Eds. C.H. Herford, P. Simpson and E. Simpson. Oxford: Clarendon Press, vol. 7. *Masques and Entertainments.* 1941.

FROM *The Vision of Delight*. In *Ben Jonson*. Eds. C.H. Herford, P. Simpson and E. Simpson. Oxford: Clarendon Press, vol. 7. *Masques and Entertainments*. 1941.

§ Chapter 4, "Inducting Pocahontas", was originally published in *Symbiosis: A Journal of Anglo-American Literary Relations* 2.1 (1998), 24-38, University of Plymouth, U.K. Reprinted by permission of the publisher.

* * *

Chapter 1, "A Descent Into Richard", is a revised version of a paper given at the Warburg Institute, London, in May 1999, as a part of my Francis Yate Fellowship. I hope the chapter encapsulates not only the rich comments and objections I received, but also what truly makes the Warburg so close to Renaissance ideals: an insatiable quest for knowledge and its sharing, matched with the reconcilement between the overall vision of the period and the scholarly zest for the revealing detail. While I am not sure my chapter ultimately complies with such demanding criteria, I am quite certain that I have been happy to meet "good neighbors," intending not only the original shelving principle of the immensely endowed library, but all those scholars and colleagues who have always been eager to contribute illuminating comments from their own neck of the woods. One can bravely face the discomfort of finding some kind of edible, reasonably prized food in Bloomsbury when sure to stage later on a debate on internal will in Aquinas. Our talks were usually much more mundane, though.

Natascia Tonelli managed to keep quiet at my extempore objections and interruptions while sharing with me the office and a wondrous heap of scholarly substantiated comments as well.

I would especially like to thank Nicholas Mann, the Director, for his paternal support to young scholars—*cosa rara*. A Renaissance *bottega* must have been quite something of the ilk.

My stay at London would have been considerably less memorable without Laurent Milesi. What with experimenting new treats in Oriental cuisine, chatting about antivirus programs and dropping (de)constructive remarks on Derrida, those were really *les beaux jours*.

The Biblioteca Comunale of Senigallia and the treasures of the Biblioteca Universitaria of Bologna, with their behest from the munificence of enlightened popes and cardinals, have been a valuable support in this and other fields of inquiry. The Andover Theological Library of Harvard University provided an idyllic setting to the first version of this essay, offering the book-lined bliss of monastic peace in the warmest of havens away from Boston wind-chill.

Chapter 2, "What the Matter Is With Barabas," is based on a lecture given at the University of Florence during my postdoctoral fellowship under the guidance of Professor Guido Fink, whom I thank for giving me unforgettable classes in my undergraduate years and vigorously introducing me to the very idea of graduate studies.

Chapter 3, "The Invention of Perdita," was given as a paper in Lisbon, 1998, at the International Conference *"Discovery, New Frontiers, and Expansion in the Iberian World,"* organized by the Mediterranean Studies Association, University of Massachusetts Dartmouth and Arizona State University. The material for the research was the result of a happy periplus through the branches of the University of Amsterdam Library during a Visiting Scholarship. Dominic Baker-Smith marvellously united Erasmian frankness with encouragement and friendship. Paul Gabriner at the English Department offered warm support, as well as informed, humorous directions to life in the Netherlands. Teun Van Dijk has always offered me an outstanding example of self-motivation, incessant quest for new directions in research and sincere interest in the work of the youngest generation.

I thank the *Symbiosis* staff for their illuminating remarks on an earlier version of Chapter 4, "Inducting Pocahontas", as well as for granting me the permission to reprint the article. Raffaella Baccolini also contributed some good advice on the paper, providing me with friendly encouragement and support when things were quite tough.

Chapter 6, "A Poem on the Tube", was originally presented as a paper at the Conference on *Procreation and Poetry* organized by the Connotations Society at Halberstadt, Germany, in 1999. The persuasive love for literature lavished by Inge Leimberg, coupled with the steady impulse administered from Matthias Bauer and the sincere participation of all members of the Society, managed to create a niche virtuously immune from all reasonable distaste for academic, compartmentalized conferences. I am happy to thank John Russell Brown, Yumiko Yamada, Leona Toker and Arthur F. Kinney for their friendly remarks. Donald R. Dickson kindly read a version of this chapter, sharing with me his unique perception of the world of Donne. He also treated us to a fully-fledged version of the story of the seventh Kaiser sleeping in the mountain den—or was it the sixth? Problem is, that German liquor we were sipping at his invitation, I can't recall its name . . .

The outline for Chapter 7, "Shakespeare in Laughter", came from a postdoctoral fellowship I spent in 1996 at the Folger Shakespeare Library, whose wondrous resources amazingly helped me etch out the contours of my research on laughter.

A proverb from Lucania, a region in Southern Italy, can be thus transliterated: *The louse dipping into the flour thinks to be the miller.* Well, something like that for me at Harvard. Chapter 7 is mainly based on a paper given at the Department of English and American Literature of Harvard University, where I was the happy recipient of a Fulbright Visiting Fellowship in Fall 1998.

Truly falling into that flour escapes description. One should learn to convey the thrill of crossing the campus green early in the morning, greedy with expectations, on the way to the Widener Library and the Houghton Library and their unbelievable stock of treasures on any and each particle of the universe. One should also have to convey that vigorous sense of participating, though imperfectly, to incessant research that braces up the shrill air at Harvard. Simply walking through that green—that was huge. Thinking of laughter *there* was unbearably good.

The more so when it was time to cross the green and have a talk with my sponsor, Stephen Greenblatt. He added the constructive pleasure of mindboggling advice, given with a sense of *kind presence,* of being there with *you,* talking to *you* about what *you* are researching, sharing his impressions with *you,* without ever letting you receive any more than justified slight from his enormous eminence in scholarship, without ever dodging the question or uselessly praising "other mens provisions," to quote Ben Jonson.

I would like to thank Marco Lenci for introducing us to a representative slice of Manhattan nightlife and, as it was on the way, to some lesser known resorts in New Jersey. The scene in the taxi center at New Brunswick, late night, a rerun of E.R. on the telly, with the guy coming in and, while constantly saying "hey man" to his girlfriend, ordering a taxi for two, only to be answered by the bewildered man behind the counter with "for*d*y-two?", will be always carved in my memory. Corrado Bacchiocchi (drums) and Lapo Boschi (rhythm guitar) were splendid chaperons all the way through, especially when they let me unashamedly maul Simon LeBon's falsetto on *Rio* in a jam session at their Somerville flat.

Before our stay at Medford we didn't yet know we had a second family over there. Anthony and Anna Repole have been the kindest of "American" parents to us, spoiling us beyond decency. Anna (no chance she actually shares my mother's name) welcomed us like a long-lost duo of son and daughter; her faked quarrels with Anthony, good man, husband, father and friend, were exceptionally warming scenes. And their own kids were brothers and sisters to us: Michael and Cindy with Aaron and Noah, two terrorist children if ever there were any, and Rosanna and Paul with the twins, Johnny and Anthony, whom I did manage to tell one from the other shortly before the end of our stay, were also extraordinary friends. Joe, Marianne, Sal, Babetta and

Stephen further spiced up the adventure with their unflinching friendship. I wonder why I am using the past tense, for they are still parents, friends, brothers and sisters to us.

During my stay in London, Lucia Boldrini renewed her huge heaps of boundless friendship and literary competence into a unique combination of assets beyond counting. And the Victorian-looking wine bar near Charing Cross Station, with the moldy vaults and the casks of Amontillado, how on earth would I have ever discovered it?

One stage of revision of these articles occurred while sharing the office at the University of Florence with Mario Domenichelli. Mario taught me memorable lessons in the art of competently interrogating literary texts and calmly listening to students' needs and questions, without taking too much for granted.

A further stage of revision took place during a Visiting Scholarship at Brown University, Providence, RI, thanks to the good offices of Karen Newman, my providentially munificent sponsor.

Henry Paul Monaco has also offered illuminating remarks and unobtrusive suggestions on the format of this book, as well as a nice chance to talk about major artists the likes of the Clash and Joy Division.

In a bar where angels like Kurt Cobain and Jeff Buckley leave much too soon and sickening jocks still linger on, the presence of what we dare call "animals" makes this place a more humane place to live in. Chopin, my black cat, simply saved me before exiting. Pettona arrived on Christmas Eve, and truly she was a much more human present than all the rest. Even the simple mention of Jumper-Miciaccia, the most egotistic of all cats, still imparts joy and happiness. And Mohini's divine humanity defeats many self-appointed members of the human race.

Artù uniquely bestowed on me his loyalty and friendship, managing to reach a compromize with Chopin—what a bargain for a German Shepherd. And Ginger—here's the picture of us in the other place: I am walking you out on Sunday mornings to the lake, always comforting you when it thunders, always teasing you when you climb upstairs to see where I am hiding myself, always taking you out to your favorite walk around the block—in all those beautiful American mornings you will be forever cocking up your ears at the magical words *wanna go bye-bye*?

Amongst a heap of things that usually take a life to tell, Anna and Nicola, my parents (the ones I would have chosen in a thousand million), gave me a first name (my sarcastic, Norman-looking grandfather's) I have grown to respect, despite all my juvenile whining about. They have been as always completely supportive of my efforts, avoiding to raise their eyebrows every time I was about to pack my bags for some new location, even though they sometimes would have had plenty of reasons for doing that. But then they should have checked this a long time ago, when I would listen for hours to my brother Tony introducing me to Greek sophistry (yet if there is any in this book, it is my entire fault), Django Reinhardt and Jimi Hendrix. For he has always been ahead of me, and he keeps being so.

There should be a sort of *valediction: forbidding dedicating* books to wives. Ill omen, or their abusive diminishment to clerical workers or spiritual companions, invariably loom large. The hard facts, then. Paola has often enjoyed the dubious privilege of listening to half-baked, listener-unfriendly raw versions of the present material. For she was always out there when eelish harlequins were having their day, Hope had left the building and Plutus was running away. For Paola and the author have seen things neither of them believed could be existing synchronically—all those small things: listening to 1980s hits while Mohini would sleep for hours in the perfect bliss of the Jordaan; Ginger actively trotting at their side on the snow-clad alleys of Medford; a walk to a painter's studio off Prinsegracht on a Sunday afternoon; a morose promenade on Bankside and a dazed stroll through St. James's Park; unbearable vertigo atop the Empire State Building; the whales off Cape Cod; the piper playing the *Narcisetto amoroso* in the Louvre main yard, that flowered dress coming out of nowhere in Rue du Bac, the ride on the Grande Roue—yet all this was quite small when compared to the first time they listened, courtesy of medical instruments, to the throbbing heartbeats of a peaceful star whimsically descended from the sky above San Gimignano—

All this was conceived while living off the pretty songs left by Boddah's friend, the only one who could ask "hello how low" and shout out aloud for me. Without him, not only the writing, but also the living would have been past hope in this pit. "Don't know what it means," but I do.

"*Good night, sweet prince, / And flights of angels sing thee to thy rest.*"

References and Abbreviations

§ All quotations to the English translation of the **Bible** refer to the "Geneva Bible" (*The Bible: that Is, the Holy Scriptures Conteined in the Olde and Newe Testament.* 1587. London)

§ **Cicero**. 1536-7. *Opera Omnia.* Venice. **Lucretius**. 1583. *De rerum natura. Libri vi.* Ed. D. Lambyn. Frankfurt. **Plautus**, 1511. *Menaechmi.* In *Comoediae XX recens ex collatione multorum codicum.* Venice. **Ovid**. 1618. *Metamorphoseon.* Antwerp. **Seneca**. 1514. *Tragoediae pristinae integritati restitutae.* Paris.

§ Works frequently cited have been identified by the following abbreviations (titles of Shakespeare's works are abbreviated as in C.T. Onions, *A Shakespeare Glossary*, rev. and enl. by Robert D. Eagleson, New York: Oxford University Press, p. x).

BJ   *Ben Jonson.* 1925-52. Ed. C.H. Herford, P. Simpson and E. Simpson. Oxford: Clarendon Press. Vols. 11.

ERR   William Shakespeare. 1983. *The Comedy of Errors.* Arden Edition. Ed. R.A. Foakes. London and New York: Methuen.

EXT   John Donne. 1921. "The Extasie". In *Metaphysical Lyrics and Poems of the 17th Century.* Ed. H. J. C. Grierson. Oxford: Clarendon Press.

JM Christopher Marlowe. 1964. *The Jew of Malta.* Ed. R. W. Van Fossen. Lincoln and London: Univ. of Nebraska Press.

LLL   William Shakespeare. 1968. *Love's Labour's Lost.* Arden Edition. Ed. R. David. London and New York: Methuen.

PER   William Shakespeare. 1986[4]. *Pericles, Prince of Tyre.* Arden Edition. Ed. F.D. Hoeniger. London and New York: Methuen.

PG   *Patrologia Greca.* Ed. J.-P. Migne. Brussels 1849-

PL   *Patrologia Latina.* Ed. J.-P. Migne. Brussels 1849-

R3   William Shakespeare. 1981. *Richard III.* Arden Edition. Ed. A. Hammond. London and New York: Methuen.

ST   Aquinas, St. Thomas. 1594. *Summa Theologiae.* In *Divi Thomae Aquinatis Doctoris Angelici Opera Omnia.* Venice.

TIT   William Shakespeare. 1985. *Titus Andronicus.* Arden Edition. Ed. J.C. Maxwell. London and New York: Methuen.

TN   William Shakespeare. 1975. *Twelfth Night.* Arden Edition. Ed. J.M. Lothian and T.W. Craik. London and New York: Methuen.

WT   William Shakespeare. 1988. *The Winter's Tale.* Arden Edition. Ed. J.H.P. Pafford. London and New York: Methuen.

§ I have decided to avoid the "he/she" convention for various reasons. First, most of the times the original reference is to explicitly male figures like the confessor or the male being in procreation; in many other cases, the original text I am quoting is modulated on the male gender—the "he/she" tag would entail weird transformations on the way; furthermore, more often than not the impersonal being the text is referring to plays hardly pleasing roles such as the sinner, the lascivious being or the immoderate laugher—nor would impartiality compensate for the cluttering of the text with the tag.

1

A Descent Into Richard

Water is my eye
Most faithful mirror
Fearless on my breath
Teardrop on the fire of a confession
—Massive Attack, "Teardrop"

One should not report the words said by others.

This proviso may hardly befit the inception of a book entirely devoted to interpreting such multifaceted words as confession, ecstasy and laughter in the works of Shakespeare and his "neighbors." Yet, under some circumstances, reporting someone else's words can be a sin. For there are words that are to be delivered to God and never unbosomed to our neighbors.

A prominent aspect of the sacramentality of auricular confession is the unswerving precept of absolute secrecy over the words exchanged between priest and confessant. Not even the Pope could ever be granted the divine privilege to dissever this sacramental bond. Despite the peripheral fallacies occasioned by either forgetful sinners or untrained priests, confession delivers a perfect speech to God. Even the most blatantly canonical attestations of sacramentality and dogmatic knowledge, however, imbricate with a more mundane description of the spoken word. By way of introduction to this study on *Richard III* and confessional language, I will single out some instances of the primacy of the spoken word in confession theory: the secrecy rule in Aquinas's interpretation, the importance of shutting and opening the right gates as glossed by a medieval treatise on confession, a massive manhunt for missing corpses in *Richard III*, a lenient version of the secrecy seal circulating among Italian priests, and present-day confessions broadcast by US chat-info shows.

The secrecy precept was vested with the adept symbol of the seal, the *sigillum* that decreed the inviolability of the oral message much as a written transcript. One practical reason was that venting such dangerous secrets might go to the detriment of moral conduct, teaching and then putting into practice novel sins, as well as to the material undoing of one's partners in crime. All Renaissance authors of handbooks on penance indefatigably strove to circumvent this contagious possibility. On a theological level, the seal derives from the status of confession as divine law. Aquinas thus explains its logical genesis. Confession is to be concealed (*celanda*) from the eyes and ears of third parties because it is a sacrament. Laying down a dogmatic cornerstone that would be most willingly dislodged by the Protestants, Aquinas argues that the precept of compulsory sacramental confession is no invention of ours: for no human being could wield the authority to impose secrecy in such absolute terms and to reinforce them in practice. On the other hand, since the obligation of making a sacramental confession is of divine law, no one can be exonerated from absolving it: God awaits our personal confession. Yet, granted the self-accusing nature of this sacramental act, no one can be forced or authorized to divulge the secret of confession (*ST* 3.11.1.2).

Confession theory perpetually alternates between dogmatic absoluteness and individual privilege, in an interplay between the judiciary constraint to tell the truth and the pursuit of personal freedom. However, the secrecy seal has often attracted fewer theoretical interpretations than satirical ones. Satirical literature fleeces those confessors who, spurred by their own unconfessed lechery, want to prevail over their confessants' rights to secrecy, especially when they are attractive *madonne*.[1] This would be yet another token of "inclusionism," or "elevation," whereby non-literary genres are subsumed under the status of literature as an illustration of a wider thesis (Colie 1973).

Yet my intention differs from the study of confession "in" literature, just as the following chapters refrain from the analysis of a topic as included in literature. I will now turn to the *Weye of Paradys*, a popular Middle English analogue to the influential *Voie de Paradis*. The three days mentioned in this treatise on the almost miraculous virtues of confession refer to God's calling out the Israelites to a three-day journey away from their captivity in Egypt (Ex 5.3). Since the captivity of Israel is interpreted by Christianity as a figure of the sin that entrammels all of us, confession is likewise compared to a three-day journey. The number "three" is not mentioned by chance. The general act of penance, which includes oral confession, consists of three parts: contrition, confession and satisfaction. Contrition, or heartfelt repentance, represents the first route in this journey; oral confession covers the second tranche in the path to salvation; satisfaction redeems the practical consequences of sins, thus achieving the liberation of the sinner.

In particular, the words one uses to confess one's sins are bestowed with the absolute power purchased by Christ's sacrifice. As soon as the sinner pronounces the word *confiteor* ("I confess"), he causes the opening and closing of opposite gates: the word both "schittyth the [g]ate of helle the whiche was open to the synner er he schrof hym" and "openyth the [g]ates of Paradys that arn schet to synful man er than he seith 'I me schryue'" (Diekstra 1991, 60.151). For the Psalmist had celebrated confession as the material act of opening up the gates of Heaven: "*Introite portas eius in confession[e]*. 'Entreth the [g]ates of Paradys by confession" (63.153). In the double bind between absolute power and freedom, confession by word of mouth entails in fact an opposite condition of muteness on the other side of the contract: the priest's mouth cannot prevail over this act of self-accusation. As well as opening up the gates of Heaven, the *confiteor* also seals the confessor's mouth, so much so that he cannot report a single word from the confessant's speech: "La bouche du confesseur et du prestre est clouse" (58.148). Such is the power of divine prohibition against any disclosure that there is no fitter cove where the sinner might want to lock up his secrets safely—once stored in confession, not one thing will be ever seen or found again (*point seüe ne trouvee*).

The practical side to this device is evident in the sources of Shakespeare's *Richard III*. Where are the Princes' bodies? A priest took charge of their overhasty burial "in such a place secretely as by the occasion of his death (which was very shortely after) whiche onely knewe it the very trueth could never yet be very wel and perfightly knowen" (Hall 1548, 27v-28r).[2]

Perhaps in compliance with our laid-back times, it is just the case that young Italian priests are often chaperoned into the secrecy rule by an admonitory *ficta causa* (I owe this titbit to a dear friend who is a great master of this art of discretion). A new parish priest listens to his first confession, contritely delivered by an attractive woman who cheats on her husband. Then he joins the welcoming party, where he voices his first impressions to the Mayor: "Oh, I couldn't begin any worse. I heard the confession of an adulteress." The Mayor nods his head sympathetically: "O tempora!," then he genially summons his wife: "My dear, do please come here. Let me introduce you to our new priest"—"Oh darling, I have already enjoyed this privilege. You know, I was his first confessant."

Indeed name-dropping should be avoided. Therefore, I will not mention the identity of a young American woman who was recently enmeshed in an affair with a powerful man occupying a very high position in public office. Going public for the first time during a highly-rated TV show, the young woman was asked to debrief the audience on oral sex, which had spread the biggest buzz in the media. And the sinner's mouth hardly failed to attract the attention of the cam throughout the two-hour long public confession. Yet it was no big deal:

a wide conspiratorial smile, and she was through in a debonair fashion. Later, the discussion rolled on to the relatively safer topic of phone sex. She was simply lost. Her cheeks turning the same tinge of red as her copious lipstick, she muttered something like "well, you know." She could not go on, at a loss for the words that might express how one makes sex with words alone.

The commodious terminology of auricular confession might have eased off such a harassing predicament. An absolute secrecy rule that nonetheless praises and extols the value of the spoken word; a three-day journey that discloses the realm of salvation and closes up what may be inconveniently uttered; a heightened status of the word, whereby sinners may be taught how to perform a complete mnemonic report of past sins and to spell it out in a rhetorically satisfying form—confession is one of the most detailed theories of the spoken word. Taken at face value, confession theory may seem a descent of authorities where repetition has virtually no negative place, since no originality was ever intended. Indeed, the *summae*—a term that does not leave much room for innovative endeavors—were often characterized by their brevity and their elementary nature (Michaud-Quantin 1962, 10). Yet I intend to bear testimony precisely to this overarching sense of repetition, where a single sentence or canon is frequently hoisted completely unaltered across the centuries. Repetition and accumulation serve the enormous task of making communication perfect and complete because of its sacramentality. Confession offers an unmatched portal to the study of the volatile status of the spoken word, especially when proffered by a deformed Duke "that had his teeth before his eyes" (*R3* 4.4.49).

Richard III advances a serious claim to the status of "confessional" work among the Shakespearean canon, together with the adamant case of *Measure for Measure.* How can one abstain from the boundless sympathy for Richard's efforts as a budding comparatist: "And thus I clothe my naked villainy / With odd old ends stol'n forth of Holy Writ" (1.3.336-7)? A more scholarly reason is that the play unmistakably teems with religious language, a fact variously interpreted by scholars who surmised that Shakespeare was refreshing the obsolete genre of religious drama in the light of the controversies generated by the Reformation (Richmond 1984; Faure 1970). This reference is enriched with the *vexata quaestio* of the providentiality of history—for providence must truly abound in this Shakespearean sinner, granted the numerous references to the Biblical examples of troubled conscience (Shaheen 1989, 77).[3]

Yet I intend to analyze the religious language of the play as religious language. And with a denominational attitude as well: for the evidence is lop-sided in terms of inescapable references to the old religion, in clear excess of the Catholic context of maneuvering and conspiracy that the rise of the Tudors would providentially curtail. Indeed the text thrives on the sacramental presence of Catholic dogmatism. Good angels are invoked both by the Ghost of Clarence and by the Princes (*R3* 5.3.139, 157). In her mourning, Anne invokes the almost saint-like ghost of Henry VI (1.2.5). Richmond is assuaged by the Ghost of Prince Edward, who addresses the souls of butchered princes (5.3.122-3) ready to take arms on his side. Then he beseeches the prayers of holy saints, and after the battle grants a pardon to the soldiers who fled (5.3.242, 5.5.16).

Richard III sedately recoups confession theory. Clarence repeatedly adducts his murderers' redemption from sins (the release granted by confession in our quotidian life) as a reason to wrest piety from his murderers (1.4.178-9). In the *Mirror for Magistrates* (18:370-71), Clarence thus prefigures his place of burial: his brother "in a butte of Malmesey standing by, / Newe Christened me, because I should not crie" (cf. *R3* 1.1.50). Ominous punning aside, crying is explicitly linked with the nature of confession. Accordingly, when Richard attests that such is his descent into sin that "tear-falling pity dwells not in this eye" (4.2.65), he denies the possibility of redemption from sins. Confession was defined by Jerome as the *secunda tabula*, the second table sent to us after baptism (*Epistulae* 84.6, *PL* 32:748). To use the words of the English translation of the Jesuit Vincenzo Bruno's treatise on confession (1597, 3), "loosing by new sins this first Table of the grace of Baptisme, we returne miserably to our owne drowning: our most benigne Redeemer, vnwiling to leaue vs without remedy, hath provided for vs this Sacrament of *Penance* as a second table, whereby we may be saued, and deliuered fro the danger of euerlasting death." Yet Clarence is occluded from a proper confession: nobody is allowed to have private conference with him (*R3* 1.1.86). Richard's maimed etiquette abruptly trims down Clarence's penitential journey from its original three-day scansion to a short "path" on the way to Heaven (1.1.117, 119).

Confession threads the text of *Richard III*. One of the devices used to hammer home the importance of voluntary confession was the display of confessional images (*figurae*) in paintings, which conveyed the absolute meaning of sacramental confession as well as its etiquette (Rusconi 1996; Nichols 1986). The anything but small portion of Shakespeare's audience still familiar with confession according to the old religion would probably have sensed its connotations in the events befalling Hastings. In Hall (1548, 15r), the meeting between Hastings and a priest serves some sarcastic innuendo: "Sir Thomas Haward . . . brake the lordes tale, saying to him merely, what my lord i pray you come on, wherfore talke you so long with that priest, you have no nede of a priest yet, & laughed upon him." In *The True Tragedy of Richard the Third*, roughly coeval (1594) to Shakespeare's play, Richard abruptly clinches the question: "Go fetch me a Priest, make a short shrift, and dispatch him quickly" (D4r). In Shakespeare, the episode is a visual symbol of interrupted confession—an occupation often pursued by Richard. Hastings first throws a purse to a homonymous pursuant and then exchanges a short talk with a priest. He even whispers in his ear, an act that vividly fleshes out the Protestant satire of the Catholic practice of auricular confession. Only later will Hastings realize that he preciously needed that priest—now he is entrusted to a short shrift, all but unfit to be tossed down into "the fatal bowels of the deep" (*R3* 3.4.101).

Richard's longer "confession" virtually encompasses the whole play. The confessional language is especially vibrant in the first wooing scene. Richard begs Anne to lend an ear to his confession of these "supposed crimes," which purports to be duly articled with the circumstances of the sins committed ("by circumstance, but to acquit myself"). Anne receives it as a self-accusation for his notorious crimes ("known evils," 1.2.76-7, 79). Although Anne spits at Richard, an act that evokes the description of confession as an act of vomiting the poison we ingest with our sins (149), she will eventually rejoice for his conversion since he has become so penitent (224). While fully conversant with the niceties of religious confession, Richard will not be able to rid himself of his faults: "All several sins, all us'd in each degree, / Throng to the bar, crying all, 'Guilty, guilty!'" (5.3.199-200). Let no one call for mistrial: Richard can handle sin and report it by the same metaphors that the millennial tradition on confession had carefully parsed and made viable to all sinners.

Now, does the juxtaposition of confessional language and *Richard III* imply a direct relationship between the two domains? Does one need to posit Shakespeare's (and his neighbors') direct or indirect knowledge of the rudiments of religious confession?

The investigation of the Catholic background of Shakespeare's early years has informed recent endeavors in the academy (Wilson 1997).[4] And yet this is not my hunting ground. Nor is it my aim to probe into any direct bond between Shakespeare and the persisting niches of Catholic tradition in Elizabethan England. While the Reformation endorsed the importance of general confession of sins during the Sunday service and laid an antagonistic emphasis on heartfelt, continual repentance, rather than on the practical application of penance, many private chapels continued to adhere to Catholic tradition. The presence of Jesuits in Elizabethan England also led to a change in the penitential customs of the Catholic gentry, who had to forsake the annual confession at Easter and instead practice the daily *examen* and amendment of their lives in the light of the sins of the mind as well as of the body (Bossy 1976, 268). With the arrival of the Douai missionaries in 1574 and the Jesuits in 1580, anti-Catholic writing instanced the Jesuit confessor as the corrupter of women through the malicious practice of auricular confession.[5] In 1597 Henry Garnet, the Jesuit superior who was to be sentenced to death for his participation in the Gunpowder Plot and his refusal to break the seal of confession, secretly printed in London the translation of Vincenzo Bruno's treatise on confession that I have already quoted, a concise work which virtually encapsulates all the points on auricular confession I will be examining in this chapter.[6]

I assume that the proliferating diffusion of both Catholic and Protestant doctrines on penance and their iteration foisted upon all levels of society, from learned disquisition on points of pure theology to practical, handy manuals for going to confession, surpass the problem of ascertaining the specific points of contact. Confessional language elicits a theory of the spoken word that illuminates otherwise unnoticed avenues within the text of *Richard III*. Not to leave matters in the vague, *Richard III* is not about confession. Nevertheless confession theory retrieves some of its otherwise volatile nuances, such as the report of past crimes and its internalization in the speaker's body. Although the image of Shakespeare at confession is highly fascinating, we will have to make do with Richard.

The Bible presents a relative paucity of direct sources on the subject (Watkins 1920, 3-7). The major foundation is the passage where the Apostles receive from Christ the commission to remit and retain sins. Another concurrent passage, which was to fuel the contention between Papal authority and the Reformed brethren, was the pericope in which Christ promised that whatsoever they should bind or loose (*lusete*) on earth would be repeated in heaven (Jn 20.23). In the Catholic interpretation, the priests had the absolute power to decree which sins could be remitted and which instead (the reserved cases) required intervention from the higher ranks in hierarchy (Mt 16.19).

Words are of the essence in religion not a whit less than in literary querelles. In this case, the diatribe primarily verged on the interpretation of the *exomologesis*, the act of penance explicitly cited by the early Fathers of the Church, as either mutual correction or sacramental confession (Manns 1984). The Apostle James had recommended reciprocal confession: "Acknowledge your faultes one to another" (Jas 5.16). The *Didache*, an early second-century composite document generally referred to the teaching of the Twelve Apostles, prescribed that the acts of repentance had to be mutually exchanged: "In the congregation thou shalt confess [*exomologese*] thy transgressions . . . On the Lord's day come together, break bread and hold Eucharist, after confessing your transgressions that your offering may be pure" (4.14, 14.1). In Tertullian's vivid depiction of the belabored practices appended to *exomologesis* (*De Poenitentia 9, PL* 1:1243-4), the sinner lies in sackcloth and ashes, plunging his soul into sorrow and exchanging sin for suffering (*illa quae peccavit tristi tractatione mutare*).

Words and their prepositions make the matters even worse. Let us take the case of *exomologesis*, reciprocal confession, and *metanoia*, the inward change experienced by the repentant sinner. A first tier of ambiguity concerns the difference between the personal confession of sins and the related concept of the *confessio fidei*, the act of confessing Christ before humankind. In fact, the prevalence of *exomologesis* as implying the confession of sins became overwhelming in the fifth and sixth centuries, until it gradually overshadowed the confession of faith (Valgiglio 1980, 9-10; Cochrane 1977). The Reformed Churches precisely acclaimed the general profession of faith as the only confession that exceeds our innate frailty thanks to the supererogatory grace acquired by Christ. Quoting James's precept of mutual confession, Fulke (1583, 388) questioned the naive (Catholic) believer's dependence on the actual words spoken in confession, as if the act of confessing one's faith should depend on such a material emission: "Does acknowledging signifie any other thing than confessing? You want then nothing else, but the sound of confession, which among the ignoraunt would help you litle, whiche terme your Popishe acknowledging rather shrifte than confession."

Another widely diverging interpretation relates to *metanoia*. The first occurrence of the word is in Rv 2.4-5, concerning the repentance that the church of the Ephesians must offer for forgiveness. Luther interpreted it not as penance, as translated by the Vulgate, but rather as a coming to one's senses which implies a change in our hearts in response to God's grace.[7]

Such interpretative cruces, obfuscated by indulgences and pardons, may have fuelled Erasmus's doubts about both the explicitness of the Biblical foundations of the sacrament and the overweening confidence that sinners like his famous soldier in the *Confessio militis* might experience after confession (Delumeau 1990, 45). After his copious plunders and sacrileges, the soldier should sink under the heavy burden of sin. No *metanoia* to be found yet: far from having to go directly to Rome for complete forgiveness, he will go to the Dominicans and strike a bargain with them. Even if he had robbed or beheaded Christ himself, their indulgences would be expedient enough. As soon as he finds an easygoing confessor, he will dump the dregs of his sins into his cowl. And he will know he has been absolved when the priest resorts to his usual ceremonial words, placing his hand on the unrepentant soldier and mumbling something incomprehensible, *admurmurans nescio quid* (Erasmus 1972a, 950-51, 1027-28, 1035-36, 1039-44).

The diatribe extended to the whole doctrine of sacramental confession. The Reformation questioned the Biblical foundations of the sacrament and gradually moved confession from the individual sphere to the general confession and absolution that was delivered during the service and other public prayers (Cameron 1991, 132). Luther (1520, A2r-B1r) watered down voluntary confession to a good form of brotherly advice. Confession intends rather to appease than vex conscience (*ad quietandam, non perturbandam conscientiam*). Since it contains Christ's promise of forgiveness (*venia*) to the confessants, Luther contends that the true glory must be granted only to this promise and its certainty, rather than to the dignity, let alone sufficiency of our confession. Instead of addressing the confessor as a mediator, confession must be primarily directed to God, since nothing can escape His eye. Sacramental confession is to be scourged as an instrument for inflicting slaughter on conscience (*carnificina conscientiae*), since it transforms the Gospel into strict law and thus denies our contrite heart the solace that derives from the consideration of grace (Balduin 1654, 831). Confession is a *ritus utilis* only if deprived of sacramentality and used as an indifferent ritual (*adiaphoron*) for exploring the communicants to the service (346). As for outward penance, it serves either to recompense the neighbor we have offended or to seek counseling from a minister. For it offers great solace to hear from the minister's mouth (*ex ore ministri*) the words of remission that Christ spoke for all sinners, being locally and personally applied to us in a special application of grace (829).

Calvin (1559, 3.4.3) voiced the harshest indictment of confession as a Catholic ruse to harass the believers. His rebuttal rests both on the impossibility of the complete report of one's misdemeanors, since our innate corruption defeats all enumeration, and on the fictitious quality of the confessional act, which can be counterfeited at will. Since complete report and remission are both unattainable, the only aim of Catholic sacramental confession is either to lead souls into despair or to lure sinners into mimicking the outward accoutrements of contrition. Calvin defiantly asks his Catholic opponents to show him a single sinner who has not experienced utter despair or conversely made do with the *simulationem doloris,* a succinct display of contrition.

The Church of England solicits longer investigation.[8] The main policy seemed to be simply to retain the ritual without calling it a sacrament (Osborne 1990, 150-5; Denis 1983). The Anglicans recognized in voluntary confession an instrument that "engraffeth in us a certain humility, submission and lowliness of mind" and "bringeth us to knowledge of ourselves" (Becon 1990). Once enfranchised from the clutches of the Catholic cachet of circumstances, provisos, exceptions and all similar pretexts for poaching into the unassailable realm of conscience, confession was still kept by the canonical texts of the Anglican Church for those cases where an enormous overload of anxiety could endanger the believer's moral well-being, or in limited provisions such as the rules prescribing the visitation of the sick (McNeill 1951, 210). The 1536 *Articles About Religion* still described the sacrament of penance as "institute of Christ in the New Testament" and therefore as a thing "necessary for man's salvation." It consists of contrition, confession, and the "amendment of the former life."

Contrition embraces both "the filthiness and abomination of his own sin" and "a certain faith, trust, and confidence of the mercy and goodness of God." Auricular confession is considered "a very expedient and necessary mean, whereby they may require and ask this absolution at the priest's hands, at such time as they shall find their consciences grieved with mortal sin." Far from being reprimanded, these precepts should be "taught and inculked into the ears of our people" (*Formularies of Faith*, xx-xxiii, xxv). The 1543 *Necessary Doctrine and Erudition for Any Christian Man* defined penance as "an inward sorrow and grief of the heart for the sins by us done and committed, and an hatred and detestation of the same, with an earnest desire to be purged from them." The confessant must prostrate himself in front of the priest "as deputed of God" and then proceed to the "remembrance of his sinful life past . . . and the same before the priest, God's minister, he declareth and uttereth with his mouth" (257, 259).

Then something changed. In a trenchant denial of the sacramentality of confession, the *Thirty-Nine Articles* (1854, 6.255, 257) attacked four elements of note within the Catholic doctrine of penance: matter, form, minister and effect, "whereof none of them is truly grounded upon the word of God." In fact, "no man is, or can be, sufficiently contrite for his sins. To confess all sins, and that one after another with all circumstances, unto a priest, as it is impossible, so is it never enjoined by God, nor hath ever been practised by any of God's saints." The *Second Prayer Book* tends to make confession a fairly exceptional case for those instances where conscience cannot be ordinarily appeased by the awareness of God's grace. One may note the omission of any reference to secrecy, which constituted the pith of the medieval system of confession, as well as to the auricular and secret confession to the priest.

Yet confession—in its muted forms—can be still efficient. It is explicitly kept "only for them that feele their conscience troubled with any waighty matter, that they may receive counsaile, and comforte by the minister" (Fulke 1583, 389). Analogously, it is generally remarked that personal confession, if discretely used, without any superstition, is not to be reproved (Randolph 1911, 20-1). Its practice was still attested in the Canons of 1604, and the evidence for the use of private confession is equally pervasive (Pusey 1878, xxxix). The spread of sacramental confession, especially among the nobility, was also endemic during the Caroline period (Belton 1949, 6-7). Confession defended its minimized status as an activity of counseling, a choice instrument that might be likened to modern conflict-solving (Thomas 1997, 157; Ingram 1984).

Confession is embedded in another kind of conflict, at least in modern criticism. It will be remembered that Becon granted voluntary confession the virtue of infusing some degree of self-knowledge and gracious humility in us, poor sinners. For modern historiography, confession has been preferably associated to little humility, less knowledge and more submission. Even if it is impossible to provide a hard-and-fast survey of the overall debate, many scholars have repeatedly seen in the precept of individual, annual, general confession promulgated by the Fourth Lateran Council in 1215 the dawn of a history of oppression.[9]

While I do not intend to trespass on the ground of historiography, a florilegium of the divergent opinions might contrastively enhance the literary aspects of confession. According to the oppression school, the *summae* on confession became instruments of social control, as the tendency toward decreasing severity was spuriously reconciled with the intellectual effort to guide the conscience (Tentler 1974). Confession was reminiscent of the scholastic structure of an interrogation, in a simplified version of the dialectical method that dovetailed with the scholastic fondness for subdivision (Delumeau 1983, 225). It was also a negotiation between the seller and the purchaser of fair penance, almost the picture of the relationship between a lawyer and his client (Little 1981, 98-9).[10] Such a commercial nature should not, however, make us oblivious to the *carnificina conscientiae*—for we are told that confession elicited hostility not just to sexual indulgence, but also to all kinds of concupiscence (Briggs 1989, 282).

More lenient forms of interpretation have been proposed, and the evidence looks just as persuasive as the one buttressing the other front. As Mansfield (1995) proved in her wonderful study on the rituals of public penance in Medieval France, penance also imported on the creation of privacy and individualism; nor was the passage from public rituals of cleansing to individual penance a linear development. Mansfield aptly comments: "the terms 'communal' and 'social' should only be used with great caution; too often they serve to conceal an assumed functionalist model of ritual and religion" (292). Let me couple these words of wisdom with the remark that a moral "sociography" can dangerously arise from the "notion of a central medieval penitential revolution '1215 and All'," appending social comment to penitential theory (Biller 1998, 18, 30). Owing to its universal usage, confession also refrained from being tagged to specific social classes. While the elites could have tried to employ it as a way of marshalling the behavior of their subjects into obedience, they were not exempted from control: one of the signs of distinction among wealthy laymen was the presence of a personal confessor in the household (Minois 1988; Cameron 1991, 12-3). Perhaps secrecy was more the issue, rather than privacy or the oppression of individual conscience. Quite paradoxically, confession sparked a compromise between the apparently jarring requirements of privacy, the secrecy of confession, and publicity: for it was placed in a sphere where some kind of social control forestalled much too private negotiation or prevarication (Myers 1996, 199-200). As to the *summae*, they already existed before the

Lateran Council, and its Protestant counterparts were well into their heyday in the seventeenth and eighteenth centuries (Wood 1952). They formed a subgenre within the body of *Pastoralia*, the works intended for the cure of souls (Boyle 1982). While they may have seemed formidable specimens of authoritarian control, their most immediate aim was to help priests engaged in the hearing of confessions, especially those who could have no access to specialized writings and commentaries. Their distinctive character was a sense of conformity to the law of God, to which the respect for hierarchy was seen as instrumental (Boyle 1974). On top of that, there seems to be little evidence of contrite sinners flocking to confession in droves: confessors could be chosen, and the ignorance of many priests, mingled with the array of legalist loopholes (hardly ever a scarce commodity in religious questions) could well deter any rise of widespread anxiety (Duggan 1984).

Could it be that confession was also the catalyst for the same anxiety it stands accused of having copiously engendered? Some scholars have in fact seen in confession the dawn of a principle of personal, interiorized discipline for the individual (Bossy 1975, 21). Sinners were exhorted to frequent confessions, but then the self-same Church raised many obstacles to the perfect accomplishment of this obligation (Martin 1983, 119). By investigating the specific sins, confession also discouraged underscoring the endemic corruption of humankind that for Protestants inhibited the very act of confession. The confessional was so much an expression as a cause of anxiety, offering sinners a scrutiny that released them of the fear of a final apparition before God with even a single sin left unpurged (Brouwsma 1980, 221). It might be a reasonable compromise to say that, even in its less attractive appearance as hair-splitting casuistry, with which it often seems to be generally confused, confession both reduced anxieties by offering an instrument of pastoral care and raised other concerns by configuring an epistemology of opacity and contingency in self-analysis (Gallagher 1991, 4).[11]

Even in the thick of the disquisition on oppression and anxiety, confession eminently remains a symbol for speech, a theory of orality that retraces the voices of the dead. Contrasting the Papal institution of the precept of confession, Wyclif (1845, 179) retorted that "no one can believe that a man may be not saved without confession of this kind, because otherwise, all the dead from Christ's ascension to the time of Innocent III are lost—a terrible thing to believe." One can adapt the vast hosts of the dead to the words they uttered in their confession—where are they? Confession theory wrested meaning from the volatile status of the spoken word. It elicited the creation of a discursive sanctuary, a "space to speke," to quote Chaucer (*The House of Fame,* 1054-5), where one could cleanse his sins by duly reporting them (Root 1990).[12] In confession, the sinner could thoroughly grasp his knowledge of sin and articulate it with due attention to motive and self-awareness (Braswell 1983, 12). Arguably the most tantalizing summary of this fascination comes from a scholar who might hardly be suspected of being in close quarters with patriarchal power. Foucault (1980, 59-60) detected the birth of a discursive space in the shift toward "the infinite task of extracting from the depths of oneself, in between the words, a truth which the very form of the confession holds out like a shimmering image." In its penitential obfuscation, confession theory truly offers an iridescent icon of the sinner at talk.

The rise of the *confessio oris,* confession by word of mouth, has been saluted as the inception of a rationalist *statut de la parole* (Legendre 1986, 406). We have seen that Aquinas traced the secrecy rule back to its status as divine law. On the spur of this remark, many Catholic authors argued the sacramentality of confession on the ground of the hiatus between human and divine jurisdictions. Confession covers the most hidden sins in the secret of our hearts (*ad peccata occultissima, & secreta cordis*), where neither human authorities nor even the Church itself can wield any power of obligation or prohibition. Accordingly, the obligation to profess one's sins cannot derive from human law. It must come from God, for the Church (and all human agencies of power) cannot enforce a law if its violator cannot be punished: the Church can punish neither the secret sins, nor the omission of their report. For it is only God, the *scrutator rerum & cordium,* who can intuit the real content of our hearts and scrutinize all things (Eisengrein 1577, 12r-v).[13]

On the other hand, the Protestants used the existence of the *peccata occultissima* to prove the impossibility of such a complete report and thus to hollow out the pretence of sacramental confession.[14] Mentioning the question of hidden sins, Luther (1520, A3v) initially seemed to push it away from his jurisdiction—*extra meum captum est.* The point cannot be proven either by reason or by biblical evidence: is it not just another way of fomenting anguish among the followers of Christ? None of us can fully ascertain all the sins we commit when feeling mortal envy, pride or covetousness. Nor can any priest judge what is actually mortal. How can a man know somebody's else heart when his own heart is yet unknown to him—"alienum cor cognoscet, qui suum non satis novit?" For Tyndale (1548, 80r), the confession of faith is the only oral confession that can be satisfyingly inferred from the Bible: "One foloweth true fayth inseparably—And is the confessynge & knowlagynge with the mouthe, wher in we put our truste and confidence." Another lawful form of confession is the one "whiche gothe before faythe and accompanyeth repentaunce—for one who so euer repenteth do the knowlage his synnes in his herte" (81r). But man's hidden sins definitely bar any reporting feat:

> When I haue told the in thyne eare all that I haue done my lyfe longe, in ordre and with all circumstances after the shamefulest maner, what canst thou do more then preache me the promyses sayeng. If thou repente & beleue / goddes truthe shall saue the for Chrystes sake? Thou seest not myne herte[.] (82r)

The Psalmist had averred that "innumerable troubles haue compassed mee," for his sins "are moe in number then the heares of mine head" (Ps 40.12). Calvin (1559, 3.4.16) polemically offered the example of David who could not number his sins: the sinner who willingly condemns and accuses himself in his conscience by way of a constant, inmost confession to God, will also be naturally ready to declare his praise to God. But he need not go through a detailed report (*ad recensendum catalogum*), for even David openly accused himself of depravity.

The argument of the enumeration of sins often undergirds the Protestant assault on confession (Brown 1948). In the reign of Queen Mary, a woman ironically named Agnes Priest denounced auricular confession as contrary to Scripture (Whiting 1989, 153): who can number his sins? So many are the hidden sins that no sinner can faithfully register and report all of them; therefore, enumeration is impossible (Balduin 1654, 831). Denying that man may be capable of knowing all his sins, the Puritan William Perkins argues that "God indeede requires a particular repentance for particular knowne sinnes; but if they bee hidden and unknown, hee accepts a generall repentance" (Perkins 1966, 60).

The only narration that we are enabled to deliver is the incessant confession of faith that pours forth from the secret of our hearts, a *cantus firmus* on which we have to intone our self-accusation. For Ambrose, one of the main reasons for confessional self-accusation was that all-knowing God awaits our voice (*expectat vocem*) not to punish us, but to forgive us: if we hide our sins, we will be insulted by the devil, who is constantly accusing us (*De Poenitentia* 2.7.53, *PL* 16:510). Sinners must not confess to God with a detailed enumeration (*specifica enumeratio*): they have to acknowledge the general incongruity between their actions and the norms sanctioned by the word of God (Chemnitz 1596, 189b).

Yet narration is still out there. Catholics turned confession into a perfect speech that, provided that it met with the right circumstances and conditions, could completely report the past. The outraged reports from the Protestant front precisely recognized Catholic confession as a human, all too human act of narration. Tyndale (1548, 70v, 81v) excoriated the dispersing nature of the Catholic acceptation of *exomologesis* with words that recall the Hastings episode in *Richard III*: "Shryfte in the ear is verely a worke of Sathan . . . It began among the grekes & was not as it is nowe to reken all a mannes synnes in the preestes eare." Catholics are to be reprimanded, for they resort to "no other door of Mercy, but the Priests Lips" (Goodman 1684, 2). In a revealing inversion of the confessional virtues attested by the Middle English treatise I started with, Becon (1844, 414) leers at the magical powers once attributed to the words of remittance uttered by the confessor: "What affiance did we put in auricular confession, and in the whispering absolution of papists, believing our sins straightways to be forgiven, if *ego absolvo* were once spoken!"

The perfection of a confession duly delivered thus motivated the arresting attention devoted to the details of the act of speaking to the pries, a set of formal requirements that were to be impugned and caricatured by Protestant writers. A survey of the conceitedly imaginative realm of the *selve* and *summae* provides ample leafage of apparently casuistic remarks on the sufficiency of confession, most of them the distinctive contribution of Italian authors.

For style matters as well. To begin with, confession must consist of clear, adamant words and refrain from *verba oscura*. If the confessor does not fully understand which sin is which, the confession is void. The sinner must describe his sins with words dictated by chastity, soberness and honesty (*Angelica* 201). He is warned against the verbiage of the *historiae prolixae*: the superfluity of speech must be curtailed and trimmed down into a concise report (*Sylvestrina* 77v). Those who resort to useless prolixity, often because of their expressive deficiency, become boring storytellers who, instead of reporting one definite sin only, churn out story after story and thus mutate their confessions into enthralling tales for the scandalous solace of their confessors (Scarsella 1592, 175r). God, the ultimate recipient of confession, demands purity of style: the sinner's tongue is shaken up with fear and reverence as if he were attending the very presence of Christ (Gabrielli 1561, 369). Yet this self-same presence need arouse no fear, since the sinner reports his sins, through the proxy of the priest, to Him who already knows them all (*Pacifica* 10r). In Vincenzo Bruno's bowdlerized version of these points (1597, 17-9), confession must be entire, "expressing euery [sin] in particular, in kinde and number: procuring to tell them in such forme, that the confessor may vnderstand the grieuousnes of euery one"; diligent, in that the sinner prepares "him selfe with diligent examination of his conscience"; faithful, "that is plaine and simple, not artificially composed, confessing sincerely all sinnes wythout excuse, or couering or diminishing any thing at all"; and obedient, in that the penitent promises to "haue purpose of dooing whatsoeuer shall be imposed him by his Confessor."

As in a formal contract, both sides must be competent and well-formed to render a truthful, valid statement. Let us consider the sinner first. Alongside respecting the requirements for stylistic purity, the sinner must not, carried away by his zest, confess sins that he has not committed. This act would entail a veritable mortal sin in its turn, since he would deceive the confessor into granting him an absolution that cannot be conceded—how can one absolve a sin that was not committed in the first place? Sinners must be assured that God is not a sophist, nor does he need any such snares (Eisengrein 1577, 49v). Speaking of sophistry, the academy is not better off. When the Bible says that *scrutabor Ierusalem in lucernis* (Zep 1.12), it portends that the sins of the *litterati* demand more diligent scrutiny, as their fallacies can be concealed with more art (Peter of Poitiers 1980, 10.5-14). As a Jesuit obviously conversant with the higher classes, Vincenzo Bruno (1597, 91-2) bids the sinner "to procure a plainenes and clearenesse in speaking . . . without superfluous wordes, or telling of stories, which make not to the matter."

The act of oral confession cannot be substituted by in-between messengers or written transcripts: for it is an act of revelation of one's sins in front of one's priest (*Angelica* 205). The sinner must confess his crimes by word of mouth—if he can so do (Scarsella 1592, 178v).[15] And this possibility is not a binge of casuistic fantasy. In fact, one should consider the exceptions when the sinner—or the priest, for that matter—is deaf or dumb (De Odendorff 1490, 46v-47r). If the sinner speaks another language, his confession will hold good only if a fitter priest cannot be summoned, a particular danger is approaching, or the sinner has eloquently conveyed his repentance by producing an unmistakable *signum doloris*.[16] Analogously, a foreigner can confess his sins to a priest who does not speak his language only *in articulo mortis*, in point of death: bar this condition, and he will have to send for a suitable confessor. The priest who confesses a Native American, for instance, without the confessor knowing his language or the confessant knowing Spanish, will incur in mortal sin: the confessor may well absolve him on the uncertain grounds of the actual contrition experienced by the sinner and the very sins he committed (De Medina 1584, 243a).

These instances are the gist of the confessor's legitimacy and training for the role. The priest must satisfy no less detailed requirements for perfection. For confession rests on the unicity of representation. It cannot be made to more persons at once, since the priest represents only the same Christ at a time (*Sylvestrina* 79r).[17] If the priest is deficient in any respect, from his ignorance of languages to sleepiness to occasional distraction, confession can reveal nothing at all (*Defecerunt* 16r). And what if the sinner acts *in absentia sacerdotis*, the defective priest either having drifted off to sleep or died suddenly? The sinner will have not committed a mortal sin only if he did not bank on this circumstance, a prophetic act that may defeat any present stretch of the imagination (Gerson 1487, 14v).

Perfect confession must be complete, well-planned in advance and preceded by careful preparation in our memory. One of the reasons for the integrity of confession is that any division would hinder the mnemonic connection between facts (*Sylvestrina* 79r). For the same reason, one cannot resort to two different confessors, one for the hearing and one for the absolving (*Angelica* 223; Azpilcueta 1592, 93r). The sinner must carefully devote his thoughts to the task, having all his misdemeanors precisely fall in place into a detailed account of his past life *in minuto conto* (Gabrielli 1561, 365).[18] The confessor will help the sinner out of predicament by interrogating him on the sins that may have been omitted (De Chaimis 1474, 19v). And the interrogation must be conducted over the whole span of time elapsing between the present moment and his last confession (Savonarola 1496, C1r). Should the sinner remember other sins immediately afterwards, he has to report them in a new confession, provided that the oblivion was not deliberate, in which case all of the former confession would be void (*Sylvestrina* 79r). Analogously, confession must be repeated if he has toyed with his memory by keeping in store some sins or, worst of all, if he has perpetrated the sin of *memoria ficta,* consciously hiding or garbling his crimes or even confessing sins he did not commit (*Defecerunt* 18r). The confessor is exhorted to use "gode dyscrecione" while inquiring about the nature of sins, and downright astuteness when dealing with the penance to compute: "Wayte þat þow be slegh & fel, / To understonde hys schryft wel" (Mirk 1974, 147r).

Confession was eminently an oral act, a perfect tale between the soul and God. This is evident in Augustine's interpretation of the resurrection of Lazarus (Jn 11.39), taken to represent the habitual sinner, buried into the arms of death: "qui . . . peccare consuevit, sepultus est." When the sinner makes his confession, he comes forth (*quando profiteris, procedis*); the confession is effected by God, who cried in a loud voice (*magna voce clamavit*), that is, with abounding grace (*In Ioan. Ev. Tract.* 49.3, 24, *PL* 35:1748, 1756-7).[19] A Renaissance writer thus completes the picture: whereas Christ could make Lazarus come back alive by simply calling him out (*sola vocatio*), now our bonds cannot be solved without contrition, confession and satisfaction (De Odendorff 1490, 32v): the *vocatio* turns into a complete tale. Similarly, Guido de Monte Rocherii traced the ancestry of oral confession back to the question moved by God to Adam soon after the original sin ("Where are you?"), whereby he actually urged him to confession and provided him with medicine for his subsequent sins as well (Tentler 1977, 59). Beneath the didactic sugarcoating—or perhaps saltcoating—confession theory constantly prescribed the need to tell one's tale and thus respond to God's *vocatio.*

The insistence on the orality of confession elicited much vociferous comment from the Protestants. Taken in itself, confession is an indifferent thing (*adiaphoron*) that provokes none of the physical or emotional reactions like the elated or contrite moods alleged by Catholic propaganda. The hypocritical attire of sacramental confession, with its array of outward signs of contrition, only leaves unheeded the marrow of human wickedness. While man's outward glory is vacuously deflated in an instant, the fury of his sins wreaks havoc inside his conscience: "Foris inanis gloria ut Bulla perit. Intra conscientiam truculentior saevit erynnis" (Oecolampadius 1521, A4r-v). Catholics also overestimate the importance of the outward signs of contrition, whose salience for actual penance no Biblical reference ever substantiates. Auricular confession is a private abuse of conscience, an interrogation where confessors rabble up their inquisitorial skills to analyze the *auditorum indicia*, the circumstantial evidence obtained from the confessants (Chemnitz 1596, 195a). For confession by word of mouth results in further disadvantages: any hypocrite can easily report his sins and, at the same time, keep loathing this type of confession in his heart, *in corde suo* (Balduin 1654, 831).

Calvin launched an all-out attack on the doctrine of soul-healing in confession, scourging the *sophistes* and the *glosateurs* on the specific tenet of the salience of crying. It would seem that, for the Catholics, crying away one's sins (*plourer les péchez*, Calvin 1960, 3.4.3) offers a promise both of redeeming past sins and of preventing their future repetition. Far from implying that contrition, confession and satisfaction were the three necessary parts of penance, the Fathers of the Church rather meant to exhort sinners against the repetition of sins. As to contrition and attrition, Calvin underlined the hiatus between the Catholic insistence on self-inflicted psychological distress and its swift remission, whereby the most prostrated hearts were suddenly healed by the aspersion of pomp (*laevi ceremoniarum aspersionem*, 1559, 3.4.1). Contrariwise, contrition is the sinner's perpetual lot, as he can never reconcile himself to the task of the complete remission of his faults. After listless vexation and anguish, our conscience finds no better accommodation than some perfunctory expression of pain, a few tears prescribed by confessional etiquette: "Lacrimas exprimunt, quibus suam contritionem perficiant" (3.4.2). The Catholic model of confession diverts the sinner's attention from the inward voice, the abysm of wickedness deeply lodged into his heart (*le secret abysme de vice qu'ils ont au profond du coeur*, 1960, 3.4.18).[20] For the oral reporting of sins can be materially affected and counterfeited. Unrepentant sinners acquire further confidence and hardiness from the bodily vest of confession: they distort their own mouths (*tergere os*, 1559, 3.4.19) and deny their own sins—"ils estiment qu'ils puvent torcher leur bouche."

Confession ultimately presents itself as a tale fitted into the sinner's body. The magical word of the *confiteor*; the requirement for completeness and perfection on both sides of the oral contract; the bodily purgation of sins through crying and heartfelt contrition; the outward signs of the reporting of sins to God through the disfeatured visage of the sinner and his dissembling actions—as a theory of perfect orality, confession powerfully attracted the liminal signs of its oral utterance. The Elizabethan Jesuit John Gerard (1951, 78) reported in his diary the usage he had made of an opening in the walls of the prison: "I had catholicks praying in the next cell . . . they showed me how I could have freer dealings with them through a hole made in the wall, which they had covered over and concealed with a picture . . . Through this same hole I also made my confession and received the Blessed Sacrament." It is through these corporeal doors that the confession of sins is vented, even in the blasphemous case of *Richard III*.

Since confession hinged on the proper transmission of words from the heart to God, its material aspect received appropriate emphasis. As a sacrament, confession ought to contain both form and matter. The form is represented by priestly absolution, while the outward acts performed by the penitents pertain to the *materia* of the sacrament (*ST* 3.84.1 ad 1; Spykman 1955). In a further subdivision, the matter is either proximate (*propinqua*) or remote (*remota*). The former, most immediate type of matter consists in the material acts that the confessant performs (contrition, confession and satisfaction). On the other hand, the remote matter extends itself to the confessant's sins, which, in their detestable nature, nonetheless offer the matter of sacrament to confession, so that they might be expelled from the body (*ST* 3.84.1 ad 3). The image may be likened to a vector that originates in the heart and is vented outside through the mouth, in a trajectory marked by the outward signs of contrition.

One can thus notice the constant drive towards "placing" confession in the body of the speaking sinner. The confessant's face bespeaks testimony as to his possible sins. Gerson warns that it would be virtually impossible to offer a universal doctrine for confessing. The reasons for this apparent pessimism include both intellectual variations such as the widely differing manners in speaking and learning, and physical differences importing on the variety of men in the nature and complexion of their bodies and consequently the souls that inhabit them (Ouy 1985, 302). The observation of the physical behavior of the sinner may attenuate this over-differentiated continuum. Alan of Lille (1965, 1.20) also instructed the confessor into attentively perusing the gestures made by the sinner, for the inward man can be understood through his outward appearance, and the face is almost a sign and a figure of the soul (*quasi animi signaculum, et figura*). The internal will can be perceived by the visage: a downcast, crying face in dejection will testify to interior contrition and excruciation, whereas an erect posture betraying no signs of sadness will reveal the lack of repentance. Nor must tears be sophistic tools: they must ooze forth from their true source, the heart—"non sophisticae sint lacrimae, sed a fonte cordis manantes" (2.1). Quoting Isidorus, Alan recalls that outward satisfaction and copious abundance of tears (*crebra lacrimarum profusio*) do not suffice in themselves for the sacrifice. Tears can also be shed not out of penance, but of the *inconstantia mentis*, the imperfect mind of the ignorant sinner: by reviving his sins through the mnemonic device of the tears, rather than through the actual reminiscence, the inadvertent sinner commits them again (4.10).

Like confession, tears required astute interpretation. For confession must be tearful (*lacrimabilis*). The pardon granted by the Church requires both compassion and admonition, as the sinner's copious tears administer dutiful example to the brethren: penance stands before the doors of the Church (*pro foribus*), and provides exemplary shame, calling to its assistance the tears of the brethren (Tertullian, *De Pudicitia* 3, *PL* 2:986). The Irish *Penitential of Cummean* (McNeill 1938, 99) listed, among the several types of remission available alongside orthodox baptism in water, "the shedding of tears, as saith the Lord [1Kgs 21.27]: 'Since Ahab wept in my sight and walked sad in my presence I will not bring evil things in his days.'" Early *summae* defined penance as consisting of the act of crying out the past sins and by means of this very act not to commit them again, "mala preterita plangere et ulterius plangenda non committere" (*Quia Non Pigris* 32.221).

A point often reiterated was that confession had to be copiously showered with tears. *Lacrimae lavant delictum*—tears wash sins away.[21] The Psalmist had said that tears were his food day and night in his effort to communicate with God (Ps 41.1, 88.1). Ambrose detected another piece of Biblical evidence for the importance of *fletus* in the conversion of the anonymous woman who silently washed Jesus' feet with her tears. That Biblical hope of pardon can duly inspire the penitent, who has to increase his tears (*fletus augeat*) in his hope for pardon (*De Poenitentia* 1.16.90, *PL* 16:493). In Origen's reading, the Bible lists seven ways of remitting sins in the Gospels: the seventh type is penance, administered through heartfelt contrition, which washes away all sins: "lavat peccator in lacrimis stratum suum" (*Homiliae In Leviticum* 2.4, *PG* 12:417).

Tears lend visibility to sins and to their report. Yet the epithet lacrimabilis does not refer to the outward appearance of confession, an objection that chimes in with Calvin's argument against the outward hypocrisy of sacramental confession. In compliance with this liminal function of crying, Raymund of Peñafort (1500, 116r), the medieval creator of the term "cases" of conscience, introduces two sorts of *fletus*, exterior and interior. In a true confession, together with their outward tears, sinners also release a *fletus interior*, crying over their past sins within their sick hearts (*cum cordis amaritudine*).[22]

Crying both traces the inward excruciation of the sinner and brings sins to the surface. It is also a liminal representation of the working of confession, the mediation between conscience and God. To these recondite mysteries, Paul gave a serene answer (Rom 11.33). Daring to approach the threshold of this mind-boggling secret, as he could not be admitted to interiority (*ad interiora*) through comprehension, he stood in humility before the doors (*ante januas*) by his confession, and he praised from the outside what he could not understand inside: "Quod intus comprehendere non potuit foris timendo laudavit" (Taio Caesaraugustanus, *Sententiae* 1.39, *PL* 80:774).

The crying sinner who confesses places himself at the door of his salvation, and also transforms his body into the door to his heart. To this nexus between heart and tears pays homage the Page's description of Richard's misery shortly before the end of *The True Tragedy* (1594, G4r):

> his looks are gastly,
> Hidious to behold, and from the priuie sentire of his heart,
> There comes such deepe fetcht sighes and fearefull cries,
> That being with him in his chamber oft,
> He mooues me weepe and sigh for company.

Does the abundance of tears in Shakespeare's *Richard III* open the doors of mercy? The text is awash in lachrymose characters. At the outset, tears convey the unspeakable distress caused by bereavement, and as such can conventionally prove a means of self-consumption (Lange 1996).[23]

Yet tears, much like other trappings of woe, can be counterfeited. Enter Richard, the master of faked contrition. In the first wooing scene, he chastely professes he will duly mourn Henry's grave with repentant tears (*R3* 1.2.219). All beset by weeping, he hugs Clarence, who poignantly remembers this scene of farewell, where Richard portends to offer Clarence a solution—and that is final: "He bewept my fortune, / And . . . swore with sobs / That he would labour my delivery" (1.4.234-6). Nor does Richard spare his tears for Hastings, hastily prevented from confession (3.5.24).

Richard exceeds, however, Calvin's attack on dissembling repentance. In the Catholic and Protestant theories of penance and its material performance, confession grasps the very words it conveys from the heart to God. Although Richard is only pretending to be contrite and repentant, for him tears may transcend into a tale: "The liquid drop of tears that you have shed / Shall come again, transform'd to orient pearl" (4.4.321-2). What is placed in the repository of conscience is coming up, and tears offer a perfect narration especially when words fail the speaker. In the contagion of tears, the salience of *fletus* as a revelation of interiority extends to other parts of the body as well. King Henry's wounds are likened by Anne to further "windows" for her profusion of tears, the unmistakable expression of her excruciation (1.2.12-3). According to a well-established topos, wounds bled in the presence of the murderer.[24] The report of past events calls for a revelation from the inside, as his wounds, disclosing a posthumous confession, "open their congeal'd mouths and bleed afresh" (56).

Confessional crying extracts the sinner speaking from his heart, as tears turn his body into a speaking mouth. Richard's magisterial revamping of the Catholic doctrine on contrition does not hollow out the confessional mode of his description: Anne's crying has infected his manly reluctance to lachrymose speaking: "Those eyes of thine from mine have drawn salt tears" (159)—*fletus augeat*. Her crying has caused an unprecedented, if feigned tale, to gush out from the recesses of conscience: "And what these sorrows could not thence exhale, / Thy beauty hath" (169-70). The sinner's sorrows could not provide a tale if the *fletus* did not "exhale" from the confessing soul. By an incessant transformation of speech into its material reality, Richard's confession has approached the source of all words, the heart.

In its emphasis on orality, confession recalls the ancient oral dimension of religion, where the scriptural text is apprehended and communicated by voice (Graham 1993). For Augustine, the human voice, as a *vox intexta*, marked the presence of the body in the text (Nichols 1991, 146). And the voice is often attuned to the task of confession. Our frailty entails constant storytelling: Mannyng (1983, 11348-52) contended that as Christ took on our flesh and thus knew our wickedness without being tainted by it, we are all compelled to "telle oure trespas / Syn he knewe al þat yn man was." But why did Christ leave no writings after him? Aquinas argued that the spoken word of Christ's doctrine is imprinted on the hearts of his hearers and therefore needs no transposition: it is direct knowledge (*ST* 3.42.4).[25] The voice of confession drew its source from the heart, as three examples will show.

The salience of heartfelt contrition is adamant in yet another of the recursive arguments adduced for going to confession. Why confess in the first place? God already knows our sins. But we cannot perceive the burden of our sins until we bring them back to our memory, nor can we fully appreciate the extent of God's piety before such a tremendous feat. The *recordatio* of the past serves to experience the guilt of the present and to praise the scope of the grace granted to us (Eisengrein 1577, 35v-36r).

The second example concerns a seemingly practical point: why is confession is to be made by mouth? Raymund of Peñafort (1500, 130r) quoted Augustine to upbraid those who venture that confession might be written or reported: confession must be delivered *proprio ore*, by one's own mouth, because it is a divine sacrament. Natural law constantly engenders thoughts of accusation and defense inside our hearts (Eisengrein 1577, 34r). The difference between confession and other forms of narration, as well as between confession and simple contrition, is that the former is given as a self-accusation, delivered in the sickness of one's heart, whereby the sinner pores over his sins and execrates them. Therefore, confession must not be a haughty repetition that can geminate further sins, nor does it suffice to deliver a narration; confession must take place *in amaritudine cordis*, in our bitter hearts (45r).

The third example illustrates the saturating principle of handbooks on penance. Here is how Peter of Poitiers (1980, 40.4-26) took one single line from the Bible (*Dixi: Confitebor aduersum me iniustitiam meam Domino*, Ps 32.1—"for I thought, I will confesse against my selfe my wickednesse vnto the Lord") to encompass all the requirements for perfect confession. Confession must be voluntary, not sophistic, since "I said" (*dixi*) means "I voluntarily proffered." As the *confiteor* seals off the confession by word of mouth, the actual meaning is "I put forth in my heart what I will confess by my mouth" (*proposui corde quod confitebor ore*). As to the requirements *perfecta* and *integra*, they portend that I will speak from all my heart, mouth and works, reporting all my sins and their circumstances. And I will speak against myself in the sense that I will confess to you, my God, in the direction of my heart (*in directione cordis*). The requirement of *simplicitas* implies an unabashed survey of all past sins that, unlike Adam's reply to God, neither seeks excuses nor accuses others.

Confession was frequently described as a *corde recitatio*, a report made with and within one's heart. As the Bible says that we will either be condemned or justified by our words (Mt 12.37), confession by word of mouth was deemed good only if sincere and from the heart.[26] Tertullian warns that the sinner should not be ashamed of the external habiliments of penance, the *incommoda corporis*, since they are the signs of heartfelt repentance (*De Poenitentia* 11, *PL* 1:1246). Gregory the Great saw a vivid version of this communication between heart and mouth in the last encounter between Samuel and Saul (1 Kgs 15.14-15, 30). True confession is not received in the mouth but in the heart: in the episode of Saul who, while speaking with false words to Samuel, hears the bleating of his sheep (*vox gregum et armentorum*), Gregory probes the hiatus between false and true confession: the herd of his impurities is crying against Saul. Then he confesses his sins by the mouth: what is in fact the use of affliction and penance if they are not followed by the *vox* of confession (Judic 1986, 170-6)? A similar gap intervened for Augustine between simple speaking and actual confessing: confession is saying what one has in the heart (*dicere quod habes in corde*); if one does not say that, it is only talking—"loqueris, non confiteris" (*In Ioan. Ev. Tract.* 26.6.2, *PL* 35:1607).[27] Gregory adapts this difference to a ternary representation. True confession consists of these three things: conversion of the soul, confession by the mouth and punishment of sins (*conversio mentis, confessio oris, vindicta peccati*). What the unrepentant sinner apparently expels by talking, he actually ingests again by still loving it. In the acme of his affliction, Job had promised not to spare his mouth: he would have spoken in the tribulation of his soul (Jb 7.11).

The return to perfect interiority, which was Adam's lot in Eden, required the complete oral confession of the secret contents of the heart, followed by exterior penance. In the secret of the heart, God freely reads and interprets our thoughts and misdemeanors. No sinner can lay the blame on the Devil or his neighbor: "Let him say from the bottom of his heart, I am he that did the sinne, and all the faulte is wholly mine, because voluntarily and of mine owne free will I gaue consent thereunto" (Arias 1602, 28). Ambrose quoted the penitential example of David, whose sincere pain made him speak faithfully from his heart in an *interioris cordis confessio*, giving vent to all the *secreta mentis* (Ambrose, *Enarr. In Ps. Dav.* 37.42, *PL* 14:1030).

As the disclosure of a latent disease of the soul, confession from the heart materially touches the breast and symbolically ingests our actions. It was a tale to be made with the mouth and even with the heart (*ore vel corde*, Gerson 1487, 14v). Again, it is threefold: it first happens in the internal forum of conscience before God, then in the external forum before his minister, and then in the contentious forum before the earthly judge. Through confession, the latent ailment is opened up to the promise of forgiveness, just as we literally make a clean breast of our sins. Now, our breast (*pectus*) does not open up in the first forum, as it is already open to God; it opens up before the mundane judge, but not because of the promise of forgiveness: only in the second forum, before the priest, does it open up with this hope (*Eruditorium* 1490, B8r-v).

The tripartite structure of penance covered in fact the whole body of the sinner. According to a division established by John Chrysostomus and Jerome, the three components of penance (contrition, confession and satisfaction) matched up with a tripartite, symbolical structure of the sinner's body, whose first two elements have occupied the last pages: heart, mouth and outward workings. Contrition is matched with the heart, confession with the mouth and satisfaction with the workings (*in corde ejus contritio, in ore confessio, in opere tota humilitas*). As we can offend God in those three ways, we must expel our sins by their mirror-like repetition in our penance.

Raymund of Peñafort (1500, 116r) similarly iterated the symbolism of confession as a bodily image. As an effect of the material disclosure of the breast caused by penance, confession is relocated in the body of the sinner. Again, three are the causes of sins that correspond to the tripartite breast (*triplici pectori*): lustful thoughts (*delectatio cogitationis*), foul talk (*turpe eloquium*) and pride (*superbia*). These sins are yoked with the three parts of the breast: lustful thoughts correspond to the contrition of the heart, from which they flowed out; foul talk corresponds to confession with the mouth, as it exuded from that orifice; and pride corresponds to material satisfaction, which sets right the evils we committed. By no means a vestige of the Medieval past, the tripartite theory still recurred in Vincenzo Bruno:

[A]s man in three maners sinneth and offendeth God, that is, with heart, words and deeds: so is it meet that hee submit him selfe vnto the keys of the church, in those verie things wherewith he offended: and that hee force him selfe to pacifie Gods wrath: first, with contrition of heart: secondly, with confession of mouth: thirdly, with satisfaction of workes. (1597, 11-2)

Even the usual means of penance (fasting, alms and prayers) corresponded to such a tripartite division. Every sin stems from a tripartite root (*ex triplici radice*), that is, lust in our flesh (*concupiscentia carnis*), lust in our eyes (*concupiscentia oculorum*) or pride that goads the sinner into sinning against God, himself or his neighbor. Satisfaction offers a triple remedy against this tripartite genesis of sins: fasting tames concupiscence, alms sustain the neighbor, and prayers evade concupiscence from our eyes (*Manuale per confessori* 32v).[28]

All penitential acts, from contrition to confession to satisfaction, were introverted into the sinner's tripartite breast, almost a mnemonic device for envisaging the three kinds of sins the sinner might commit and their retrieval and expulsion through the workings of penance. Tears and heartfelt contrition efficiently bring to the surface all unspeakable sins for expulsion, each dovetailing with their place of origin in the sinner's tripartite body. In confession, the narration of sins is a pure report bolting up from the heart that cannot be reverted or stopped, lest the sinner should seek eternal damnation.

This branch of confession theory sheds new light on the conceits of plangent excruciation deployed by Richard in the wooing scenes. In fact, the latent confessional language adds new flavor to the Senecan sources behind the passages.[29] In *Hyppolitus,* the passage that most resembles Shakespeare's first wooing scene occurs when Phaedra, Hippolytus's stepmother, declares her incestuous love, after Hippolytus has advised her to entrust her anxiety to his ears (608). Her heart is scorched by the fire of love (*pectus insanum vapor / Amorque torret,* 640-1), so much so that Hippolytus's refusal causes her to point a sword at her breast (710-2).[30] Another analogue is provided by the long wooing scene in *Hercules Furens* (329-438) where Lycus indecently tries to win over the favors of Megara, whose family he has butchered: will she really have to touch Lycus's "parentis sanguine aspersam manum" (372)? It is interesting to note that Legge (1979) has his Richard reply to a similar question in terms redolent of confessional language: if her brothers have been slain, he is grieved by the fact (*Doleo facti paenitet*); yet why weep for the dead, if tears avail nothing (*nihil lacrimae valent,* 3.4.5, 32-4)?[31]

Shakespeare's *Richard III* even more adamantly smacks of the penitential coloring of the Senecan sources. I will begin with the second scene, between Richard and Elizabeth. The heart begets the foulest thoughts of pride, covetousness, and lechery. As such, it boasts primacy in a well-ordered confession, whose first requirement is contrition, or what Richard terms the leisure to repent (*R3* 4.4.293). In Richard's adaptation of confession theory, the heart is the house from which sprang out his abominable love for Elizabeth's daughter. As he professes to love her from his soul (256), Elizabeth retorts that there did originate all the passions that eventually brought into being his murders, all material sins which no satisfaction could ever redeem: "Thou dost love my daughter from thy soul: / So from thy soul's love didst thou love her brothers" (259-60).

The closest reflection Richard ever furnishes of the tripartite theory of penance occurs in the first wooing scene, where confession unveils the genesis of the words in the heart. Anne bears testimony to the beliefs of yore. Gazing upon the King's wounds, she duly invokes the tripartite structure of sins, stressing the outward action imported by sin (the hand who killed the King) and the heart which originated the action, as well as the blood that, instead of causing satisfaction, called for further blood to be shed: "O, cursed be the hand that made these holes; / Cursed the heart that had the heart to do it; / Cursed the blood that let this blood from hence" (1.2.14-6). As the sham confession progresses to its inward source, the duo pursues their dialectical feud by cobbling together the paraphernalia of tripartite penance. Richard, the master of verbal equivocations, invokes the powers of the tongue that can articulate further excuses, thus refraining from the excruciation of the Psalmist who made his heart speak against himself. Anne replies by invoking the heart, which, far from being contrite, should lead him into despair, the abyss of damnation that confession purported to deter. Origen had called *vindicta peccati* the satisfaction offered in the last step of penance. For Vincenzo Bruno (1597, 9-10), the last evil caused by sin to the soul is "that always the gate of Gods mercy and pardon is more shut against it"; the more he lingers in sin, the more he is removed from His mercy, "alwayes provoking more his anger for to take reuenge of his sinnes." While Richard seeks some "patient leisure to excuse" himself (*R3* 1.2.82), despair, by which he should "accuse" himself, is the only satisfaction and vengeance he may offer: "And by despairing shalt thou stand excus'd / For doing worthy vengeance on thyself / That didst unworthy slaughter upon others" (86-8).

Vincenzo Bruno (1597, 4-5) claimed that self-accusation had been instituted as an antagonist remedy "opposite vnto our euil disposition": as Adam, "after he had sinned, did hide himselfe, & excuse his sinne before God: so if a man would returne into grace, he should manifest and accuse himself before men." But Richard never accuses himself. Again, Anne retorts, it was his "bloody mind, / That never dream'st on aught but butcheries," who prompted the workings of pride, rather than the words uttered by Margaret, on whose "sland'rous tongue" he vainly tries to lay the blame (*R3* 1.2.99-102). Richard does not deny however the belief in the harmonious correspondence between each sin and the parts of his body, between sin and its ordered narration. His breast opens up, unloosening the mouth and the flow of sweet words of self-accusation: "My tongue could never learn sweet smoothing word; / But now thy beauty is propos'd my fee, / My proud heart sues, and prompts my tongue to speak" (172-4). Penance implies a materialization of its mechanisms, whereby the sinner's body offers a mnemonic device for remembering the sins and the medicine applied to them. Richard offers his breast as in a confession—a complying repentant, he knows his way through the tripartite posture he is mimicking: he offers Anne a sword, "Which if thou please to hide in this true breast, / And let the soul forth that adoreth thee, / I lay it naked to the deadly stroke" (179-81).[32] Shedding repentant tears, Richard claims that his heart is faithfully translated in his words, "figur'd" in his tongue (197). For Richard, confession tracks down the words and their journey through the mind. Once repentance over sins turns into narration, into a literary artifice, even the unspeakable interiority can be safely conveyed as just a sequence of words. In Richard's toppled theory of penance, the heart constantly precedes the tongue; the mouth, far from healing the sins it has committed, invokes for further crimes to be avenged.

Confession should be final and complete. Richard's words adduce other words of excuse, further away from his heart, whereas the requisite mechanisms of confession were assumed to vent, once and for all, the secrets of his heart. For confession, duly preceded by contrition and crying, was the refined moment where the sinner was granted an absolute knowledge of his past and an intimation of his redoubtable status in the next life.

This book revolves around episodes of suspension. Barabas's lot ultimately evokes the dissolution of matter, whereas Donne's "The Extasie" hinges on the more rewarding type of consummation effected by sexual ecstasy: what do lovers see while peacefully sleeping after the amorous combat? Likewise, tearful confession by the mouth and from the heart brings the sinner to a place of vision—what does the sinner see in those moments of suspended self-analysis?

Richard's confessional mode tucks up his conscience in further words of excuse. In spite of his deferral of the last reckoning, the power of confession as a last moment before consumption is evident in other passages from the play. I will momentarily move away from both the *materia propinqua* of the acts performed by the hardly unrepentant Richard in his mock confessions and the *materia remota* of his sins, which in his confession multiply themselves into sophistic pleas. To these will I return at the end, ideally suspending the sinner while he is venting out his burden through copious tears and words.

One of the most lovingly detailed sections of the *summae* concerned the problem of the confession *in articulo mortis*. Alan of Lille (1965, 3.13-5, 17) maintained that *in extremis* no sinner who is to abandon his body (*si egrediantur a corpore*) could be denied the last viaticum. But here is a nice problem: can the terror of death be legitimately enough for renouncing the necessary works of satisfaction? This possibility is to be granted only to the sinner who is about to relinquish the body for good (*quis de corpore exiens*). If he is in despair of life, and yet is saved at the eleventh hour, he will not be allowed to take the sacrament before having fulfilled the time of penance stated. But casuistry can always think of even better cases for prodding the reader into further admiration. What about those suspended on the gallows (*in patibulo suspenduntur*) after their confession? Are their corpses entitled to regular rites? Alan's way out of the mire is wondrously neat. If they offered complete, general confession of all their sins and received the communion, the answer is yes, for it is written that God (and American juries, as loads of Hollywood movies have shown us) never judges twice (*non judicabit Deus bis in idipsum*, Na 1.9, 12). The Good Thief was redeemed by his last-minute confession, *in ultima confessionis hora*.

In fact, the Good Thief offered a thorny test for the debate about the immediate judgment and the last judgment each individual soul has to pass. This outstanding exception aside, confession continuously takes place as if in point of death. The manuals on confession posited a mental place, an internal representation of the act of premeditated memory and tearful report that precedes the actual cleansing of sins. For confession *in articulo mortis* offered a last, absolute chance of salvation, and as such it was adduced as one of the few examples where it might be delivered even to laymen. The amount of grace and knowledge these last moments could grant can be seen in the Dantean episode of Buonconte da Montefeltro: his final words spell out the name of the Virgin ("la parola / Nel nome di Maria finì") and cause the devil's complaint about the theft of a soul snatched by a minute tear— "per una lacrimetta che 'l mi toglie" (*Purgatorio* 5.100-1, 107). An analogue, albeit bordering on the bathetic, is the epitaph of a rider that found salvation in the very nick of time: "Betwixt the stirrup and the ground / Mercy I asked, mercy I found" (Deyermond 1984, 132-3).

All kinds of confession, however, virtually forebode each instant as if it were the last. The recalcitrant sinner has to ponder in his own heart the pains of hell (*gehennam in corde considera*) that will befall him if only he means to postpone repentance (Tertullian, *De Poenitentia* 12, *PL* 1:1247). As a prop to spur his memory, he is warned that it is better to be ashamed in the private resort of confession than in the choral scene of Judgment's Day—"for he who will not in this world confess his sins with true repentance shall be put to shame before God Almighty, and before his hosts of angels, and before all men, and before all devils" (McNeill 1938, 410). If the confessor has the impression that the sinner is morose in denouncing his sins, he may conjure up the abode of Hell, a fictional place side by side with the actual place of confession (*penas inferni terribiliter ei preponat*, De Butrio 1477, A3r).

Richard III offers illuminating examples of the confessional gaze cast upon the infinite on the very last moment before being plunged into the chasm. Buckingham, Richard's acolyte, salutes his death on All Soul's Day as his doomsday (*R3* 5.1.12). In another occurrence of that festivity, he had performed acts of villainy towards King Edward. Now he is only granted a perfunctory confession *in articulo mortis*, a "feigned prayer" (20). In his subsequent re-entry as a Ghost visiting Richard, he wishes his boss a similar lot as an unaccomplished repentant. Richard will peruse the herd of his unspeakable sins, unable to confess them: "Dream on, dream on of bloody deeds and death; / Fainting, despair: despairing, yield thy breath" (5.3.172-3).[33]

The breath that, being made up of words, could bring salvation to the sinner leads us back to Clarence's dream, one of the most intriguing "confessional" scenes in the play.[34] As the Keeper asks Clarence, this dream garnered a last-moment perusing into what lies ahead: "Had you such leisure in the time of death / To gaze upon these secrets of the deep?" (*R3* 1.4.34-5). Confession in the last nick of time might acquire eternal salvation in the other life, yet Clarence declares that he would not spend "another such a night / Though 'twere to buy a world of happy days" (5-6). Clarence's senses are filled to the point of spasm with despair, yet the revealing snippet concerns the mouth. The dream ends with the impossibility for the sinner to stop the inward flow of jarring images and signs of damnation encircling him, an image of unfathomable conveyance which Clarence translates along the confessional internalization of words: "Often did I strive / To yield the ghost, but still the envious flood / Stopp'd in my soul, and would not let it forth" (36-9). This is the moment of final reckoning, when Clarence realizes he has committed those crimes that now give "evidence" against him (67). And yet God's impending wrath cannot be dispelled by prayers, for he will be "aveng'd on my misdeeds" (70). The *vindicta peccati* entails the complete report of sins, interrupted in its delivery by the opposing flood of damnation. Conscience moves a final *échec* to speech and stops the sinner's mouth—unless it be Richard's, all but adept at performing the tripartite workings of the repentant breast and acquiescing his conscience with words.

For Perkins (1966, 7), conscience enables continuous narration, since it "observes, & takes notice of all things that we do" and "doth inwardly & secretly within the heart, tell us of them all." In *Richard III* this incessant tale turns into a fractious sequel of interrupted morsels of confessional ejaculations, a place of suspension where Richard masterminds the confessional mode into an *intermittence du coeur*. In the conversation scene, Richard almost stages a lay version of a *sacra conversazione* by his sanctimonious rebuttal of the mundane hopes proffered by Buckingham on behalf of the people. Richard might have been relieved to read in a *summa* how to cope with any diversion from internal conversation with God. In his relatively abridged treatise of one hundred cases (a most commendable saving effort when we are reminded of the existence of ten-thousand-case handbooks), Razzi (1585, 68-9) pondered whether it might be lawful to say one's prayers while physically engaged in manual work. Here is how the casuist mind proceeds. Razzi distinguishes between private and public prayers. The private prayers can be delivered while performing any kind of manual operations, like spinning the bloom, gathering flowers and crowns, watering the garden and so forth. Just as lay people find recreation in mundane songs about love and fun, no consideration should bar churchmen from similarly accompanying their manual work with serious chanting. Razzi also excuses the priest who, while reciting the service, devotes small attention to some minor activities like putting on his boots or some comparatively menial chores like dressing for Mass. On the other hand, public prayers must not be said while working manually, for this would prove outrageous to the people as well as disrespectful to God. Manual labor hinders the full attention that the priest is supposed to devote to God's service. Most importantly, devoting one's attention to diverse things together diverts strength from the meaning and the intention that each of them requires (*a più cose intento, meno può il senso*).

Diversion, in its unlawful variety, informs the episode of Richard's holy conversation. Accompanied by reverend fathers and well-learned bishops, Richard has retired within, "Divinely bent to meditation; / And in no worldly suits would he be mov'd / To draw him from his holy exercise" (*R3* 3.7.61-3). Buckingham and the others vainly try to have conference with him, for when "holy and devout religious men / Are at their beads, 'tis much to draw them thence" (91-2). Yet Richard suffers the "interruption" of his devotion (101). More (1963, 2:78) quipped that Richard "could not fynde in his hearte in this pointe to enclyne to theyr desyre." Shakespeare's Richard has "fynde in his hearte" how to stage not only the mocking version of a holy conversation, but also the malicious interruption of conscience.

Richard's dreams are other places of interruption in the flow of conscience and its confessional ejaculation.[35] For once, the authors of handbooks and *summae* seemed strangely silent on the subject of dreams. According to the true conduct of penance, as stated by Ambrose (*De Poenitentia* 2.16.96, *PL* 16:520), renouncing to the world also entails less time devoted to sleep than would be nature's due. One may also quote the analogue of the *nocturnae illusiones*—wet dreams—which represented a sin only if before sleeping one had voluntarily indulged in lustful thoughts, entertaining morose thinking (*morosa cogitatio*), which is in itself an assent to mortal sin. Such a sinful occupation might be a mortal sin if preceded by repeated overeating or lustful premeditation (Peter of Poitiers 1980, 13.5-10).

The tale of conscience takes its toll in Richard's *nocturna illusio*. In his mock confession to Anne, he traces back the cause of all his crimes to her beauty (*R3* 1.2.126-7).[36] In dreams, words cannot be uttered, nor can the contrite heart mediate the past sins through the mouth. More (1963, 2:87) reported that, after the abominable deed of the princes' murder, Richard took on all the signs of a soul troubled past the point of confession: "He toke ill rest a nightes . . . troubled wyth fearful dreames, . . . so was his restles herte continually tossed & tumbled wᵗ the tedious impression & stormy remembrance of his abhominable dede." Touching upon the night before the battle, Holinshed (1966, 3.755/I745) observed that Richard had "a dreadfull and terrible dreame: for it seemed to him being asleepe, that he did see diuerse images like terrible diuels, which pulled and haled him, not suffering him to take anie quiet or rest." The ghosts that visit Richard before the final battle harness the unrepresentable burden, the cluster of visions that "sit heavily" on his soul: "Let us be lead within thy bosom, Richard, / And weigh thee down to ruin, shame, and death" (*R3* 5.3.153-4).[37] Drawing on Rom 2.15.16, Perkins (1966, 7) compared conscience to "a Notarie, or a Register that hath alwaies the penne in his hand, to note & record whatsoever is said or done." Richard's half-voiced confession evokes both the posthumous accusation that our conscience will petition against us and the several circumstances of mortal sins duly listed by Catholics, yet delivered in a fragmented confession by word of mouth: "My conscience hath a thousand several tongues, / And every tongue brings in a several tale, / And every tale condemns me for a villain" (*R3* 5.3.194-6). In this unrelenting process of immersion and expulsion, the *nocturna illusio* ransacks Richard's speechlessness and plunges his sins back into the hothouse whence they originated. What does Richard see in this moment of suspension, where both the armies of Catholic confession and Protestant conscience seem to be launching a joint attack? There is no promise of forgiveness: "I myself / Find in myself no pity to myself" (203-4). Richard's conscience is a place of solitude, where there is no hope, no god:

> What do I fear? Myself? There's no one else by;
> Richard loves Richard, that is, I and I.
> Is there a murderer here? No. Yes, I am!
> Then fly. What, from myself? Great reason why,
> Lest I revenge? What, myself upon myself?
>
> (183-7)

In confession "there's no one else by." It is only a talk to the solitude of the self. For the play had been kicked off by the overturning of confession as the tripartite expulsion of sins. In his first lines, Richard's mouth gushed out plots, inductions dangerous, drunken prophecies, libels, dreams and deadly hate, only to hold them back and ingest them into his depths—"dive, thoughts, down to my soul" (1.1.41).

In this mundane interpretation, evil repeatedly ingests thoughts and deeds. While confession intended to respond to sins by analogically expelling them, *Richard III* iterates the structure until making it revertible: words and sins freely leave and return to the heart. The confessional thoughts of salvation have become thoughts, simply, which can be retrieved and stored back at will.

Richard's confession envisions the words he would have to say: the sinner sees himself in this dream and ponders the echoes of his perplexed speech. For the writers of *summae*, sincere conversion did not rest on the humility of confession, but rather in renewing the inward man (*homo interior*), as he, amended by divine inspiration, begins to hate what he formerly loved and to love what he used to hate. Richard has truly become an inward man: he has seen what lies in his heart, and there he has found himself—no forgiveness, no God, nothing but his own words and dreams, maliciously keyed on a confession that will never abandon his heart.

In the Middle Ages and the Renaissance, the tenet of confessional self-accusation spawned stories of demons that rejoiced in barring the final confession of unrepentant sinners. One such story concerned a Peruvian slave-girl who refused to confess her mortal sins on her death-bed, obstructed by a black dwarf frolicking by her side and apparently unaided by the presence of Mary Magdalene on the other side of the bed. One hermit was explicitly revealed in a vision the existence of three demons, "one named *Claudens corda*, who closes the heart of those listening to pious homilies; one named *Claudens crumena*, who leads penitents to evade making restitution; and one named *Claudens ora*, who induces them to make imperfect confessions" (Lea 1896, 348 n. 1). A lady who had omitted to confess a mortal sin she had committed in the bloom of her youth, was encircled by demons on her death-bed; as they stopped her mouth whenever she tried to confess, she managed to deliver her confession only "cum maximo dolore et contricione et continuo profluvio lacrimarum" (*Liber exemplorum* 57).

An overarching sense of interruption informs the texture of *Richard III*. In his dream, Clarence is occluded from his final confession by a similar pack of demons: "A legion of foul fiends / Environ'd me, and howled in mine ears / Such hideous cries" (*R3* 1.4.58-60). As one might expect, Richard frequently interrupts such confessional actions. When he appears at the maimed rites of Henry VI, he is saluted by Lady Anne as a fiend coming "to stop" those pious deeds (1.2.35). Should this not be enough, Richard is saluted as an intelligencer from hell (4.4.71) and a *cacodemon* (1.3.144). Richard himself escaped a fatal interruption at birth, for his mother "might have intercepted thee—/ By strangling thee in her accursed womb—/ From all the slaughters, wretch, that thou hast done" (4.4.137-9). Perplexity was the confessional term for interruption. Quite a damning point for all *summae*: it could render a confession void, for instance if the priest was unable to release a sinner from some formal obligations, or if the priest was to be found at fault under any hierarchical or bureaucratic respect. Take the case of a priest who, at the very moment of the consecration of the Holy Host, while he is about to say the words *hoc est corpus meus*, suddenly remembers a past mortal sin he has not yet confessed and satisfied with penance. What shall he do? In the few moments he is conceded, the priest will repent, offer his contrition and propose to confess as soon as possible (De Butrio 1477, C2r).

Richard is granted the knowledge of his heart through interruption and perplexity. By counterfeiting the requirements of confession, both in the Catholic and Protestant traditions, Richard ultimately alights on the source of contrition, tears and univocal report of sins—a man, alone, able at dialectical tricks, who has no other delight to pass away the time than to spy his shadow in the sun (*R3* 1.1.26). Perhaps Richard could have told us what stopped the confession of the young American woman unable to explain what phone sex might ever be like, all but stuck into the tearful confession by word of mouth only one moment before the commercials, our veritable "fatal bowels of the deep."

2
What the Matter Is With Barabas

A vendre ce que les Juifs n'ont pas vendu
—Rimbaud, *Illuminations*

Duke Valentino's treacherous butchering of his arch-enemies Vitellozzo Vitelli and Oliverotto da Fermo, admiringly reported by Machiavelli (1550) in a concise work, was one of the most violent feats to endure permanently in Renaissance memory.[1] Vitellozzo and Oliverotto had risen to the status of redoubtable enemies for Valentino's policy of expansion in Central Italy. Biding his time for the best occasion, Valentino negotiated a rendezvous with the two and their victorious followers. By a breach of the diplomatic truce, he had them killed and their soldiers taken prisoners.

The fact took place in Senigallia, a coastal town on the Adriatic Sea halfway between Ancona and Urbino. Host to an important Renaissance Fair that attracted numerous traders from the Near East, the city was a natural extension of the rule wielded by the Rovere in Urbino. Francesco Maria della Rovere, whose poisoning at his barber's hand in 1538 was the likely seedbed of the Gonzago story in *Hamlet*, was born and baptized there. And there Michel de Montaigne received a pleasant overnight accommodation while returning from his pilgrimage to the near sanctuary of Loreto. Montaigne attested the beauty of the nice small city, taking time to mention the tiny, efficient harbor that, much like the canals of seventeenth-century Amsterdam, enabled the immediate clearing of customs and the efficient delivery of goods. Another relic from the Renaissance is the beautifully preserved Rocca Roveresca, a four-towered moated fortress founded on the original sea-line as a stronghold against the Turks.

As Senigallia is my hometown, I have an idea of the mongrelized version even such an exemplary Renaissance story might suffer among schoolkids. In a spurious mixture of the staple ingredients of Italian Renaissance plots and conspiracies, my older brother told me that Valentino had enticed Vitellozzo and Oliverotto into a room of the Rocca (an edifice with whose name I was often associated by the kids around my block, much to my annoyance). As Valentino pulled the ropes and magically set in motion some clanging machinery, the floor collapsed and let open a pit bedecked with a carpet of barbed pikes, on which the two guests fell past any recovery. During one of my earliest visits to the Rocca, my brother even signaled to me the dark room where the fact had allegedly occurred. Lest this not be enough, the two victims had also carved their names in a desperate moment of awareness on the marble ledge of a window in the adjoining cell.

In fact, the event occurred in an edifice near the Rocca, now disappeared alongside much of the cult of local reminiscences and renascences. The scribbled signatures had been left by the prisoners of the Pontifical State. There was no clanging machinery employed, even though Machiavelli reports the siege of the fortress of San Leo. As to Vitellozzo and Oliverotto, they were treated to unsavory entertainment. Valentino had them led into his quarters in Senigallia and there made prisoners in a secluded room (*in una stanza segreta*, 97). Senigallia was ransacked. After the tumults had abated, the Duke saw it fit, as Machiavelli wonderfully puts it (*al duca parue*), to have Vitellozzo and Oliverotto brought into another room and there strangled. Machiavelli reports that their confessions *in articulo mortis* contained no words that could befit their past lives: "Non fu usato d'alcuno di loro parole degne della loro passata vita." Vitellozzo implored Valentino that the Pope, the Duke's father, grant him plenary indulgence for his sins, while Oliverotto, discombobulated by his copious crying, bestowed on Vitellozzo's head all the guilt of the enterprises conducted against the Duke.

To readers of Marlowe, the false image of Valentino as the busy arch-fiend who directly sets in motion his machinery while violating diplomacy and takes uncouth pleasure in personally polishing off his enemies should not seem completely unprecedented. In the last scenes from *The Jew of Malta*, Barabas appears "*with a hammer above, very busy*" and then asks: "How stand the cords? How hang these hinges? Fast? / Are all the cranes and pulleys sure?" (*JM* 5.5.1-2). Even the final coup de théatre ("*the cable cut by Ferneze; the floor of the upper stage giving way, Barabas falls into a cauldron, discovered below*," 62) uncannily recalls the trap that had allegedly welcomed Vitellozzo and Oliverotto.

This chapter also treads on unstable ground. I will analyze Barabas through the framework of the Christian theory of the perfect merchant who incessantly transforms the matter he daily handles. Barabas ultimately extends this cyclical undoing to himself, a passage to be juxtaposed with the classical and Renaissance theories of *mercatura* and the philosophical tradition on the generation and corruption of matter. I will present four different pieces that, each theoretically standing on its own feet as an independent comment on *The Jew of Malta* and its incessant peroration for change, unanimously rehearse the transformation of matter and its related narratives like the Senigallia hoax.

According to Aquinas (1954, 50.2.3:279), one of the reasons for discouraging the presence of foreign merchants in a city is that they are naturally bent on their own lucre, rather than on the general interest. Since their negotiations tend *ad lucrum*, the practice of covetousness is instilled by such examples into the hearts of citizens: "per negotiationis usum cupiditatis in cordibus civium traducitur." The city will be open to fraud and lie-mongering: each citizen will pursue his own interest, and civil commerce (*civilem conversationem*) will become corrupt.

Alongside its blatant anti-Semitic tone, the hatred fomented by the Maltese against Barabas harks back to this tradition of distrust of the accumulation of riches as a means in itself. For trade should not constitute profit as its ultimate aim, but as the means through which the merchant operates the commutation of the goods necessary for the existence of the city. Aristotle praised the Attic system of the preservation of wealth and care of property, where they sell their products and buy what they want, instead of unordered accumulation in storehouses (*Oeconomica* 1344b30-4). In another passage, he directly reprimanded the trader's constrained kind of life for its being directed toward what should be a means to something else, not a conduct of life (*Nicomachean Ethics* 1.5.8.1096a6-10).[2] One looks for happiness as a good that is not sought for something beyond itself. This dogma was still alive in the Renaissance. In an English translation of Cicero's *De Officiis* (1.42.150), trade necessarily implied vulgarity on the part of those "that bye of marchants, that oute of hand they retaile again. For, nothing they profit, onlesse they lie apace: and trulie dishonester thing is ther none, than a vaine tonge" (Cicero 1556, H3r).

The aversion against mercantile greed did not, however, bar consideration for the good trader, who was supposed to be a benign agency of incessant change and permutation, steered only by the force of communal good. Cicero praised the human creativity displayed by the good merchant, who puts into contact the most distant parts of the world. While immediate retailing borders on sordid vulgarity, trade on a large scale (*mercatura*), "if it be greate, and well stored, conveyeng many commodities rounde aboute [*magna & copiosa, multa undique apportans*]: and disparsing those same into many mennes handes, withoute vaine wordes: it is not much to be dispraised"; Cicero also noted that rich merchants, satisfied with the usage of the riches conveyed through the seas, set sail for a more liberal voyage to secluded life: "If being satisfied with gaine, or contended rather, as it hathe often comme from the sea to the heauen: so it chaunge from the hauen into landes, and possessions" (*De Officiis* 1.42.151). For traders bestow the privileges of wealth on the cities they live in by means of enriching the means necessary to survival. The incessant transportation of goods is the chief argument for the salvation of the trader. Merchant ships supply abundance of goods from all parts of the world. Indeed, Cicero says in *De natura deorum* (2.40.151-2), trade transforms present reality, creating through manual work almost a second nature (*quasi alteram naturam*).

For the trader to be perfect in the whirlwind of commutation, fairness was of the essence. Scholastic economy reprised the Aristotelian distinction between commutative justice, resting on reciprocity between citizens, goods and services, and distributive justice, concerning the distribution of property and salaries. The canonists stressed the element of the expenditure of time and labor and money the trader has to go through. If no expenditure is involved, the gain is the *turpe lucrum* unflinchingly condemned by theological tradition. As most commercial enterprises involve the investment of labor and capital, however, they produce the *honestus questus*, the fair recompense for the trader's investment (Gilchrist 1969, 56).[3]

Aquinas trenchantly clarified the point of fair recompense (Gilby 1958, Spicciani 1977, 156-8). As Aristotle had implied, the augmentation of money as an end in itself is unnatural, and so is the branch of *mercatura* that pursues this goal. Discussing the legitimacy of trade, Aquinas repeated the Aristotelian distinction between two kinds of *commutatio rerum*, for commutation is the trader's own. The former is a natural, necessary thing, consisting of those negotiations that satisfy the needs of life (*propter necessitatem vitae*). As such, this form befits the housekeepers or civil servants, rather than the actual merchants. The latter kind of exchange concerns instead the commutation made not to serve basic needs, but for profit, and this is the type naturally vindicated by the *negotiatores*. The first type is commendable as it responds to natural needs, and the second is reprehensible as it fosters the greed for profit, which has no limit in itself, but rather tends to infinity (*in infinitum tendit*). How does one get there from here—from the boundless drive toward the enhancement of profit to the virtuous usage of the same? Even if profit, the end of any negotiation, does not entail anything either honest or necessary in itself, nevertheless it does not connote anything inherently vicious or opposite to virtue if directed to some necessary, virtuous end. And thus is negotiation made lawful: if a trader obtains a *lucrum moderatum* that might expedite things for the upkeep of his household or for the assistance of the needy, as well as for the public good, preventing the shortage of things necessary to the city, and while so doing requires profit not as an end in itself, but as a payment for his labor (*non quasi finem, sed quasi stipendium laboris*), his transaction will be lawful (*ST* 2-2.77.4).

The act of exchanging things and money is not sinful in itself. Trade naturally requires the transfer of goods. The pious Venetian traders who stole St. Mark's body and brought it to the Serenissima performed a lawful translation, and condemnation was only reserved for he who would have wanted to sell the martyr's corpse (*martyrem distrahat*) for his own gain (Tucci 1993).

How about England? The Ciceronian praise of the great merchant, united with the Aristotelian theory of just commutation of goods and money, can be detected in English tracts on commerce as well. Trade is made for "the maintenance of Humane Societie"; human beings "bestow and employe not onely the quickenes and industrie of their spirites, but also the labour and travaile of their handes, and sides": it is "from hence, as from a root or fountaine first proceedeth the estate of Merchandise, and then consequentlie in a rowe, so manie, diverse, and sundrie Artes . . . all the world choppeth and chaungeth, runneth and raveth after Martes, Markettes, and Marchandising, so that all things come into Commerce, and passe into Traficque (in a maner) in all times, and in all places" (Weeler 1931, B1v-B2r). Yet the praise of traffic rarely surpassed the status of an introduction to more practical descriptions of every part and parcel of foreign business that occupies England. A peroration for continuing trade with East Indies, a line of business that stood accused of depriving England of precious riches, thus evokes Cicero: "The trade of Merchandize, is not onely that laudable practise whereby the entercourse of Nations is so worthily performed, but also . . . the very Touchstone of a kingdomes prosperity." Yet certain rules are to be respected, and the proportion and quantity of foreign wares is to be carefully observed; the most necessary goods for life are also to be preferred. Thus "the kingdome of England, is endowed with such abundance of rich commodities, that it hath long enioied, not onely great plenty of the thing before named, but also, through a superfluity, hath beene much inriched with treasure brought in from forraine parts" (Mun 1954, 5-6). Another tract praises "the abundance of all things" with which the countries grow potent, drawing power from "their never dryed fountaines of wealth"; the consideration is, however, capped by the analysis of the power force in herring fishery (Raleigh 1966, 5). One learns that "the abundance, plenty, and riches of an estate or nation, may be said, principally to consist in three things," that is "naturall commodities or wares," "artificiall commodities or wares," and "the profitable use and distribution, of both by Commerce and Traffike." The natural goods are those that "either the earth doth naturally & originally afford, or such as by the labor of the land is brought forth," while the "artificiall," quite simply, consist in "the manufactories of all commodities" (Lewes 1954, 60, 63). Little is offered in the way of the theoretical analysis of how wealth is processed and produced by the merchant.

When it comes to theory, Italians do it slightly better. For a closer portrait of the theory of Renaissance trade as practised by merchants like Barabas, one may conveniently turn to the perfect Christian merchant portrayed in Cotrugli's *Della mercatura e del mercante perfetto,* originally written in 1458 and published in Venice in 1573. In this paean, the perfect merchant enjoys good, lively nature, bears a natural attitude to learning, prudently administers his body, and even defers eating and drinking when pressed by the circumstances. For trade requires *arbitrium,* and hence prudence and wisdom: the perfect merchant musters the discernment of good and evil, and as a virtuous man remembers the past, ponders the present and provides for the future (Cotrugli 1990, 7v-10r, 51r-v). He must display confidence and yet be daring, commending the success of his enterprise into the hands of God and fortune. He must be astute as well, provided that he does not offend others, nor lets others offend him (55r, 56v, 57v).

Mercatura, Cotrugli contends, is a liberal art—a point utterly denied by Cicero—that intervenes between legitimate persons for the conservation of the human species and nonetheless the hope of profit, "per conservatione dell'humana generation, con isperanza niente meno di guadagno" (6r). Its origin was due to the fact that a nation might lack a type of good that is in excess in another country, hence the commutation and bartering that preceded the invention of currency (6v). Bartering, the simplest form of *conmutatione,* was invented because of its evident expediency for both parties (11v).

Then traders began to practice this art with the hope of profit. The second form of commercial negotiation implies the adding of money from one of the two sides. It can be done with cash, which is devoid of any danger or doubt: the merchant will be more advantaged, as the counterpart is easily convinced when he can lay his hands on real money—"si lascia correre per tocchare danari" (13r). This type of selling is always lawful when the good is not sold a price higher than what is fair.

Vendere al termine is the most common type of selling: the merchant makes a contract in which he promises he will be able to pay by a fixed date. Without this agreement, it would be impossible to make voyages to the heathen nations, such as the Turks or the Moors. No profit would be raised, with the result that all arts, especially the general disciplines that factually support the nations, would fall in abeyance; all cities and households would decay: "ne sequirebbe il disfacimento delle ciptà et delle case particulari" (13v). Currency would not be enough even for the negotiations that take place among Christians, let alone for taking home the goods from the heathens (*supplimento delle cose aliene*, 14r). Lacking enough cash, merchants carry goods with them, then buy other goods in the lands where there are plenty of them and bring them to the sites where they are short. Now, as the shipping costs, added to the passing of time, would curtail not only the trader's profit but also his capital, it is a requisite that merchants should not waste their labors on piecemeal retailing, but rather sell their goods on a large scale. If he is not to forsake profit and capital, the good merchant has to buy the goods needed by the country where he brings them. By doing so, the merchant will favor the abundance of money and goods, fostering the local arts and trades: "Fanno abundare arti di diversi mestieri, inde le ciptà et patrie" (49v).

Yet a word of caution has to be said on the effects of the incessant commutation of things. Cotrugli advises the perfect merchant not to trust priests, monks, clerks, scholars and soldiers: having no habit of handling money (*fuori d'ogni consuetudine di maneggiare danari*), once they have it, they will grow so fond of it they will not be able to pay up their debts. Even merchants would behave likewise, were it not for the fact that they continuously give and receive money, and the commutation is converted into usage *sanza alcuna passione*, with no passion (16v-17r).

Barabas masterfully practices the art of *vendere al termine*, embracing into his entrepreneurial gaze all the ships that bring him profit from all parts of the world, and advocating the free commutation of goods and money. His shrewd commercial skills echo the Ciceronian praise of the good merchant who transforms his city into the hub of the world: "So that of thus much that return was made: / And of the third part of the Persian ships, / There was the venture summ'd and satisfied" (*JM* 1.1.1-3). Greenblatt (1980, 218) argued that Barabas is paradoxically the true representative of the Christian society that despises him, the scapegoat who, through his self-consuming desire for wealth, voices the "suspicion that all objects of desire are fictions, theatrical illusions shaped by human subjects." I would like to add that Barabas's commercial practice explicitly espouses the portrait of the virtuous Christian merchant. Like the courageous merchant envisaged by Cotrugli, Barabas trusted "such a crazed vessel, and so far" (*JM* 1.1.79). Barabas is awaiting the return of one of his argosies (a type of merchant ship named after Cotrugli's Ragusa, by the way) from Egypt, a vessel crammed with the goods he intends to sell in Malta (44-7). As a canny merchant, Barabas is entitled to hope for profit. He also distrusts the handling of money, the same that will eventually induce the local herd of monks, governors and soldiers to confiscate his wealth.

Barabas's penchant for the abundance of gold conveys however the supererogatory nature of profit,[4] the virtual encompassing of all that it could redeem and purchase, in clear excess of any legitimate *stipendium laboris*:

Fie! What a trouble 'tis to count this trash.
Well fare the Arabians, who so richly pay
The things they traffic for with wedge of gold,
Whereof a man may easily in a day
Tell that which may maintain him all his life.

(7-11)

For truly Barabas is an *alienus* in Malta. The description of his nation's lot, in his short-lived sense of affiliation with his brethren, adapts to Israel the Ciceronian praise of the merchant as an agency of incessant change for the general profit of his nation:

What more may heaven do for earthly man
Than thus to pour out plenty in their laps,
Ripping the bowels of the earth for them,
Making the sea their servants, and the winds
To drive their substance with successful blasts?

(105-9)

Indeed heaven cannot do much more than this, nor can even nature do anything but pay service to the *alteram naturam* effected by Barabas and similarly-minded traders, who rip the bowels of the earth and enslave the sea.

Barabas's praise of the supererogatory value of gold misconstrues the necessary commutation between goods and money into a poetics of transformation. A far cry from both capitalistic pride and egoistic covetousness, Barabas's fascination lies with incessant change. For him, the surplus can transform the matter. Israel may well be a scattered nation, but "we have scambled up / More wealth by far than those that brag of faith" (120-1). All this abundance of wealth does not concur to the general (and Barabas's) good: it exceeds counting, much as the gold used by Arabs in their dealings can allow a man to see in a day what may buy up all his life. Barabas's excess extols what the good Christian merchant was supposed to use only in limited forms: the commutation and transformation of matter.

In the aforementioned discussion on the legitimacy of *mercatura*, Aquinas maintains that the trader who sells a thing unchanged (*rem immutatam*) will receive a just wage for his labors. In the Italian Renaissance tradition, the question whether the form of the good being sold had been altered by the merchant argued the question of legitimacy.

In *De mercatura* (1553), the Anconitan Benvenuto Stracca parsed the requirements for the good Christian merchant by laying an emphasis on the transformation and commutation of matter. The merchant is he who buys a good to gain a profit from selling it whole and unchanged (*integram & immutatam*). Goods are frequently permutated by him, yet he sells them neither piecemeal nor having changed their form (*non minutatim, nec mutata per se forma distrahat*). Thus, the general definition of the *mercator* is he who buys goods on one occasion in order to sell them later (*qui semel merces emit ut venderet*, 4v-5r).

Stracca insists on the quasi-contemporaneity between buying and selling the good. Is it lawful then to call merchants those who buy things and then sell them after having reduced them into another form by way of their own work (*sua opera in aliam formam redactas*)? Stracca gainsays the point: they ought to be dubbed *artifices* instead. Anybody who buys a good not to sell it unchanged, but for it to be matter of transformation (*ut materia sibi fit aliquid operandi*), is as damnable as the merchants whom Christ threw out of the temple. Then Stracca recalls Aquinas's interpretation of the lawfulness of trade: the merchant to be dispelled is he who constitutes his ultimate end in profit itself, rather than in the just reward for his labor and in the means of sustenance for himself and his household (8v, 9v). Nor is Stracca thinking only of the usurers who explicitly handle money. For usury threatens even those who buy a good and sell it back the same day at a higher price without having changed its form, as well as to those who take into account external factors like the harvest time, and do so not for necessity but for their own profit. All such merchants are to be ejected, exterminated or at least eradicated from the commonwealth, for they stampede immediate commutation and, by dint of selling goods at a higher price or conversely at a poorer quality than expected, vitiate both sides to the contract (10r-11r).

Yet good merchants must thrive. Stracca thus qualifies his argument. He has often seen his fellow citizens buy goods and then have them transformed before being conveyed to foreign countries.

Merchants they still are: their office does not convert into artifice, as the form is not changed in itself (*non mutata per se forma*). Stracca seems to imply a salvific nature in mobility. Immunity is thus to be granted only to the merchant who owns the majority of his wealth in goods. There are merchants who undertake commerce with countries beyond the sea and simultaneously exercise local commerce in their hometown: merchants they will still remain, provided that the largest part of their capital and commercial enterprise is devoted to the first type of trade. For the *proprium* of *mercatura* consists in the commutation, permutation and selling of things mobile in nature. To repeat, *mercatura* is the *officium* that takes place by exchanging and frequently selling goods neither changing their form nor retailing them (8v, 12r, 14v, 21v-22r). The good merchant praises and practices mobility, and the majority of his wealth must reside in what is currently being acquired or sold in other countries. Furthermore, the transformation of the matter he handles daily is allowed only inasmuch as he does not fall upon retailing. His trade surplus must comply with just price and profit for himself and his household, without affecting the very nature and form of the goods he handles.

Briefly touching upon the question of Jews (Ancona was home to one of the most flourishing Jewish communities in Italy), Stracca observes that, since they lost their kingdom, they are to be considered as slaves (41r). Barabas's praise of surplus equates with the act of outbuying all characters and ultimately enslaving them. The play takes place in the temporal frame of Malta's overdue tribute to the Turks, a sum that "all the wealth of Malta cannot pay" (*JM* 1.1.181). The one-month respite granted by the Turks further delays the exacting of the impending tribute. The play ends, however, with the recognition of an opposite bond between Malta and Turkey, for Calymath will not be released before his father "hath made good / The ruins done to Malta and to us" (5.5.110-1). Malta wields an extraordinary fate, a tightrope walking on a logical paradox, as its rulers can only theoretically gauge the amount of the tribute: "That we have cast, but cannot compass it" (1.2.47).

Stuck on the bankrupt island of Malta, a privileged hub of commerce with the Mediterranean countries, Barabas cannot but practice mobility. He lists a series of goods that are to be found without any need to change their form, for they are liberally lavished by the earth on the fortunate natives, such as the "wealthy Moor, that in the eastern rocks / Without control can pick his riches up," heaping pearls and diamonds whose tiniest portion "may serve in peril of calamity / To ransom great kings from captivity," as Calymath will learn (1.1.21-2, 31-2).

Barabas's heaps of gold encompass all such unchanged goods and buy them out, much as pearls might ransom lives. Good merchants, says Barabas, should detach their commerce from "the vulgar trade" and rather, "as their wealth increaseth, so enclose / Infinite riches in a little room" (1.1.35-7).[5] Seen in the context of the debate over the legitimacy of trade, Barabas proposes a *reductio ad absurdum* of the postulate of absolute mobility that forces the merchant to convert his wealth into goods and incessantly distribute them. Surplus is a cause for change, a virtual possibility to transform matter into different forms.

Barabas's wealth can buy up the whole city and change the form of all goods. "Half of my substance is a city's wealth" (1.2.85), claims the proud merchant, and Ferneze, his Catholic counterpart, happily confiscates his goods and wares, which exceed all the wealth in Malta (132-4). The surplus also includes the prospective wealth that has just approached Malta, another swathe of virtual riches modulated on Job's wealth and his long list of camels, oxen and she-asses: "I had at home, and in mine argosy / And other ships . . . , As much as would have bought his beasts and him, / And yet have kept enough to live upon" (1.2.187-90).

Barabas translates the mobility that the good merchant should perform into the transformation of matter. Contained by the island he can easily buy out, he thought well to hide a coffer of pearls and jewels that will acquire back his wealth and even buy the town (2.3.201). Barabas applies the surplus to all the characters he subsequently deletes from the scene: by promising her daughter to two local Catholics, as Ithamore notes, he purchases both their lives (365). He promises to donate all his commodities to the religious house that will redeem him (4.1.62-9, 74-5). Luring Calymath into deceit, Barabas promises him a pearl that will entertain the Turks for a month (5.3.27-31).

Yet Barabas's supererogatory wealth exceeds the Machiavellian display of villainy or the capitalistic pride of the predatory merchant. Surplus implies the use of more volatile goods, such as his own cunning: "Why, is not this / A kingly kind of trade, to purchase towns / By treachery, and sell 'em by deceit?" (5.5.46-8). For the good merchant, mobility and permutation constantly transform the matter he handles daily. The incredible amount of wealth conveys mobility, an infinite desire not just for lucre but also for the incessant flux of all things that can be conveyed and permutated through the Mediterranean—Barabas included.

Aristotle is conspicuously silent on the discussion of flux as either the property of sensitive becoming or a metaphysical principle (Caizzi

1988).[6] In the *Physics*, he considers the antithesis between subject and form. For one sees both the concrete individual being, a thing that can be counted, and the form, which for instance includes order, culture or other such predicable qualifications. Therefore, one could argue that the principles of changing are just two: the actual change occurs between the terms of an antithesis, cultivated or uncultivated, hot or cold. But how many are the principles of things in nature? Is there something that underlies all opposites, and does opposition involve two terms, as previous authors had maintained (1.7.190b-191a5)? In other words, how does one reconcile a physical continuity principle, where no gaps are possible, and the substratum principle, where there must be something changing (Scaltsas 1994, 8-10)?

Aristotle proposes two solutions to fix this glitch. First, he recognizes the existence of "form" and of "lack of form" (shortage, or *steresis*) as factors in becoming. It is true that nothing can come to be in the absolute sense out of the non-existent. Nonetheless, all things that come into being derive from shortage, from the incidental non-existence of something (*Physics* 1.7.191b13-28). Then he reprises the distinction between existence in *potentia* and in *acto*. Aristotle's theory rests on the triad of matter, form and shortage (or absence of form). Matter is eternal, representing the incidental non-existence of attributes, something that desires and yearns towards the actually existent (1.9.192a17-9). As such, it is not a seat of shortage, but a potentiality of receiving forms that cannot perish. Matter is the ultimate underlying subject that survives the destruction of a thing (1.8.191b30, 1.9.192a5-35).

The second Aristotelian analysis of the problem I am considering here is drawn from *De generatione et de corruptione*, translated by the Loeb curator as "coming-to-be" and "passing-away." Is the process of change so unceasing because the passing away of one thing is the coming to be of another, and vice versa? (*Of Coming-to-Be* 1.3.318a24-6) Aristotle considers the differences as to what something changes into. The material cause for the continuous process of coming-to-be is the *substratum*. Things constantly change into one another: as all elements are characterized and distinguished by their contrarieties, it is a process "into contraries and out of contraries" (2.4.331a14). Some elements change into others only by the passing-away of one quality, and others come-to-be from the transformation of two into one by the passing-away of more than one quality (331b35-332a1). In conclusion, nature always strives for the better, and matter strives towards the existent, for being is better than not-being. Yet being cannot be present in all things, granted their distance from the original source:

God, therefore, following the course which still remained open, perfected the universe by making coming-to-be a perpetual process; for in this way "being" would acquire the greatest possible coherence, because the continual coming-to-be of coming-to-be is the nearest approach to eternal being. (2.10.336b33-337a1)

Lucretius and Ovid also offered two antagonistic models on the generation and corruption of substances like souls. In *De rerum natura*, Lucretius commences his praise of Epicurus by wondering whether the soul grows together with the body: "Vis animi pariter crescit cum corpore toto" (3.747). The concept of the immortality of the soul is false, much like the contention that the immortal soul can be altered by the change of body (*mutato corpore*, 755). What is changed, is dissolved and thus destined to perish—"Quod mutatur enim dissolvitur, interit ergo" (756). Dissolved in its parts, the body comes to extinction, and so does the soul: "Traiciuntur enim partes, atque ordine migrant" (757). Nature decreed that the soul could neither originate without the body, nor survive once removed from the spirits (788-9). Thus, the soul is mortal; changed by such a dramatic undoing, the soul relinquishes life and its pristine senses; when the body perishes, the soul is torn to pieces (*distractam*, 799).[7]

Ovid's Pythagoras proposes a different "distraction" of the souls through the doctrine of metempsychosis.[8] Nothing perishes, for the souls of animals are conveyed into humans and vice versa. Humankind needs not be frightened by the cold terror of death, by the false dangers sung by the poets. Our bodies will experience no pain, either if they will be consummated by the fire or by an inveterate disease (*mala posse pati non ulla putetis*, *Metamorphoses* 15.157). Souls cannot experience death, for they constantly vacate their former mansion and take up new homes (*novis domibus vivunt*, 159). All things change, nothing perishes—"omnia mutantur, nihil interit"—the soul roams about until it occupies a new body: "Errat, et illinc / Huc venit, huc illuc, et quoslibet occupat artus / Spiritus" (165-7).[9] *Cuncta fluunt*—all things flow (178). Likewise, the human being is never constant, as bodies are commutated unceasingly. The very elements are unstable, swapping places in the universe. Two elements are more burdensome (earth and water), and the other two, air and fire, naturally tend to the top (*alta petunt*, 243). Even fire is subject to incessant change. Thickened, it transcends into the air: "Ignis enim densum spissatus in aera transit" (250). Because of this incessant permutation of places and elements, the world will not perish, but rather change and renew its appearance, leaving the final outcome unchanged: "Summa tamen omnia constant" (258).[10]

The last source on destruction comes from a neighbor of Marlowe's.[11] In *De la causa, principio et uno*, a dialogue first printed in London, Giordano Bruno (1973) has his spokesman, Teofilo, spell out the theory of the incessant transformation of matter. Two are the kinds of substance in nature, form and matter.[12] Much as art requires matter for its operations, matter in nature has no particular form, yet it can receive all the forms through the operation of the active natural principle. In art, the variation of forms is endless, and yet the underlying matter always remains the same (63.22-67.31). Likewise, nature implies the presence of a sole type of matter under all its forms, "una sola materia sotto tutte le formazioni della natura" (69.20). Only the mind can apperceive this matter. Nothing is annihilated, except the exterior, accidental, material form (71.12-4). Now the first principle is all that it can be, where act and potency are the same thing. Therefore, the first principle, the one and only, is all that it can be, containing all being in its being, whereas for all other things the potency does not correspond to the act. The man is instead that which he can be, but not all that he can be (82.22-8). Death is not a question of act and potency, but rather defect and impotence, which are proper of those things that are not all that they could be, and are accordingly compelled to be what they can be. As they cannot be many things at once and simultaneously, they lose their own being in exchange, often suffering from reduction, imperfection and mutilation in the process (*diminuite, manche, e stroppiate*, 84.5-11).[13]

Barabas's boundless yearning for infinite riches contrasts the incessant undoing he suffers from his enemies. Often seen as an almost farcical figure, bound to a crude form of infantile acquisitiveness,[14] Barabas is in fact the protagonist of a tale of destruction. "To undo a Jew is charity, and not sin," says the infidel Ithamore (*JM* 4.4.76). Ferneze's policy towards the Jewish merchants he means to dispossess for obviating bankruptcy reveals an incessant drive towards the material undoing of the counterparts. Initially, each merchant has to pay one half of his estate; if he denies to do so, he will forfeit his identity and become a Christian; if he denies this as well, he shall lose all (1.2.76). When Barabas retorts that half his wealth equates with all Malta, he is threatened with the loss of all his material riches (88-9). For Barabas has been handpicked to deter complete annihilation, "the ruin of a multitude," as Ferneze inverts Caiphas's argument for the sacrifice of Christ instead of all the Jews: "And better one want for a common good, / Than many perish for a private man" (97, 98-9).[15]

The incessant transformation of matter that, as a good merchant, Barabas has unflaggingly achieved so far, is reversed on his head. He will be allowed to stay in Malta, "where thou gott'st thy wealth, / Live still; and, if thou canst, get more" (101-2). And then follows the transformation of matter in the hands of Barabas, whose wealth has been conflagrated into undifferentiated substance: "[W]hat, or how can I multiply? / Of naught is nothing made" (103-4). Yet Barabas creates new matter out of the void, pushing the limit of commutation and change to the further end of consumption, until being created anew. The moment of complete nothingness (or so it seems to gullible Christians) coincides with Barabas's selling of the last good he has been left with, his own life—"And having all, you can request no more" (140). Barabas advocates the complete transformation of matter: "For so I live, perish may all the world" (5.5.10). In the process, he is transformed and reduced into matter, a nameless residual ("the Jew's body") to be thrown over the walls for vultures and wild beasts (5.1.58-9).

Barabas's transformation into undifferentiated substance heads for the cauldron. The play had already obliquely referred to fire as the consuming agency that undoes all. Barabas professes he is perusing the nuns out of a burning zeal, adding in an aside that he hopes to see their house ablaze (2.3.89-90). Fire is the punishment for the priest who breaks the seal of confession (3.6.34-6). And Ferneze achieves his triumph over Calymath after destroying the Turkish headquarters in a well-timed coincidence with Barabas's destruction in the cauldron (5.5.103-4).

The cauldron has always represented a veritable crux for Marlowe's critics as well. A contemporary source (William Harrison) maintained that in London "such as kill by poyson are eyther skalded to death in lead or seething mater" (Cole 1970, 128). Yet Hunter (1964, 233-5) traced its imagery to the traditional image of the hell-mouth, which spells out the Antichrist figure of Barabas and conversely exposes the hypocrisy of the Christians, all but ready to undo the evil represented by Barabas while perfectly replicating his policy. Levin (1952, 98) recalled an emblem by Whitney (1584, D4v), meant as an exposition of the evangelic precept against self-exaltation (Lk 18.14) and rendered through the image of the smoldering cauldron—"The boylinge brothe, aboute the brinke dothe swell, / and comes to naughte, with falling in the fire."

Truly, Barabas the overreacher constantly "comes to naughte," the same nothing from which he incessantly rises up again. For the cauldron is redolent with much of the philosophical investigation of matter I have briefly surveyed. Barabas replies to the undoing performed by his enemies with a further dip into substance, through a pattern of recurrent resurrections and destructions. His adversaries vainly think him "a senseless lump of clay" (*JM* 1.2.216). He is a much finer concoction of elements, "born to better chance, / And fram'd of finer mold than common men" (218-9). And he will not disappear into the void, reduced to an airy nothing, nor will "vanish o'er the earth in air, / And leave no memory that e'er I was" (262-3).

Barabas protests to resist total annihilation—yet there lies his last policy for further profit, his last experimentation in the transformation of matter, and as such is rendered in his dying words. As in a last alchemic experiment, where fire, as the most noble element that inherently tends to the high spheres, refines all concoctions and abstracts their quintessence—"quello altro che si fa chimicamente, che abstrae le quinte essenze, e per opera del fuoco" (Bruno 1973, 105)— Barabas advocates change in the throat of death. His final blasphemy uncannily evokes the advice given by Job's wife to blaspheme against God and then die (Jb 2.9), in a further reversion of Biblical lore: "Die, life! Fly, soul! tongue, curse thy fill and die!" (*JM* 5.5.88).[16] In his comment on the Pythagoric denial of *inferi* expounded by Ovid (601C), Pontano thus glosses the hypothetical syllogism hereby implied. If the *inferi* exist, then either the body or the soul will suffer. Now, the body does not feel any pain, for we see it to be reduced either into ashes after the burning or into consummation by putrefaction. Nor do the souls experience any pain: well conversant with death, they immediately migrate to other bodies. Thus, there is nothing that can be affected by pain: "Ergo quod ibi torqueatur nihil est." The *inferi* would be a useless existence—QED. Pontano observes, however, that there is a false assumption, namely, that the souls do not descend to subterranean places and rather stay on the earth after death like the new lodgers of other bodies. The end is in the beginning—at odds with Pythagoras's theory of the soul, Barabas will not "vanish o'er the earth in air" until flying to a new mansion. In his confession *in articulo mortis*, the matter according to Barabas is the undifferentiated substance where words are still possible. Barabas has descended to the subterranean place, his mind, where all the matter has always been flowing from form to form, where something can be still made out "of naught."

A classical enunciation of the cyclical destructions that underpin the fabric of the world occurs in Plato's *Timaeus*. An Egyptian priest reveals to Solon that many have been the destructions suffered by humankind, especially by fire and water (22B-C). The result of these cyclical interventions is the regeneration couched in ignorance, for they leave only the uncultured behind them—"so that you become young as ever, with no knowledge of all that happened in old times in this land or in your own" (23B).

A similar destruction of cities occupies the background of Marlowe's play. Rather than giving up Malta to the Turks, says Ferneze, "[f]irst will we raze the city walls ourselves, / Lay waste the island, hew the temples down" and "[o]pen an entrance for the wasteful sea" (*JM* 3.5.13-4, 16). Barabas rampantly harps on this mood of complete destruction of cities, a symbol of human ignorance in Plato. After having been thrown out of the city, he portends its destruction at the hands of Calymath, offering to help him fire the churches and pull the houses down (5.1.64-5). Yet Barabas's theory of destruction is elegantly diplomatic. It is a game of opposing policies, where the undoing of the city occurs through its conduits being let open, in a reversion of the navigation through the sea which lies at the basis of the merchant's wealth: "The rock is hollow, and of purpose digg'd, / To make a passage" (87-8).[17] For Barabas egregiously dives through the underworld of Malta as well, setting up a "dainty gallery" whose floor is ready to sink into "a deep pit past recovery" (5.5.33, 36).

In the whirlwind of impending destruction, the annihilation of Malta is yet another element of Barabas's overarching theory of transformation, attuned to a political note. For this is all policy, seen in its most extreme term as the incessant undoing of the existing conditions. To Barabas, the cyclical destruction of cities, much like his own annihilation, occupies yet another step in the transformation of matter by loosening all bonds. Policy, as the art of dismantling alliances, cities and truces, requires such swift changes. The transformation of matter is a masked metempsychosis, as we are told at the very outset by the strangest of lecturers, Machiavelli: "Yet was his soul but flown beyond the Alps, [. . .] To view this land, and frolic with his friends" (*Prologue* 2, 4).

"It is a precious powder that I bought / Of an Italian in Ancona once" (3.4.64-5), says Barabas of the poison he will send to the nuns. Near Ancona, Valentino had staged one of those exemplary stories, the assassination of Vitellozzo and Oliverotto. Seen now through the anachronistic perspective of Barabas's absolute alchemy, the Senigallia hoax requires the subtlest experiment in transformation.[18] After his military defeat, Valentino tried to find out whether he could hold in check the new mood of the winners with the pretext of a pact: "'l Duca si volse tutto a vedere se posseva fermare questo umore con le prattiche d'accordo" (Machiavelli 1550, 93). A most apt dissimulator, he spared no labor to make them believe they had moved war to him who, content with the title of prince, only wanted them to be the owners of what he had conquered. With all his cunning, he persuaded his enemies to wait for him in Senigallia. The three enemies paid their courteous homage to the Duke, who reciprocated with a sociable face: "salutatolo umanamente, furno da quello riceuuti con buono volto" (96)—the end of the story is already known.

The Jew of Malta rests on the quickness of motion that the shrewd merchant or politician wields in his daily transformation of matter. It is tempting to conjecture that Plato might have offered two spurs for this commingling of commercial and philosophical tradition into the praise of motion. In the *Sophist*, Socrates entrusts his primacy in disparaging the practice of the Sophists to the Stranger. One of the dialectical definitions of the sophist here offered is the comparison with a merchant. Sophistry is an art of acquisition by exchange (*metabletike*). Whereas Socrates goes to no other city and has no doctrine to sell or present, the sophist sells the goods of others, having neither produced nor acquired any knowledge of his own (223C1-224D3). In Ficino's commentary on the *Sophist*, the sophist is compared to a merchant who heaps on arguments and teachings with the aim of selling them for a reward—"qui disputationes disciplinasque morum eo consilio passim accumulat, ut mercede quadam commutet atque vendat" (Allen 1989, 2.6:222-3). For Heidegger (1987, 47.207), this dialectical division of the sophist fittingly describes the process of continuous exchange between the sophist and the other people, despite the negative criticism implied by the fact that the sophist markets something he has not produced: "The sophist does not merely draw people to himself and let himself be paid by them, but he also gives something in exchange for this wage."

Barabas, a stranger and merchant who constantly processes and retails all kinds of knowledge, also bears resemblance to another passage from Plato. Apparently representing the theory of the natural correctness of names upheld by his opponents, in *Cratylus* Socrates produces a longwinded, dizzily poetical theory of etymologies.[19] Names are given by voluntary imposition, rather than by the natural relation between things and names. Socrates' hilarious sketch of the genesis of ethical terms mimics the incessant description of flux and change. His axiom is that the earliest thinkers transmitted the whirling nature of their search and the intimate nature of things to the very formation of words, much as most philosophers dizzy themselves in their search for the nature of things. Therefore, even the names of the most current philosophical concepts testify to the belief in incessant motion and flux. Thus, wisdom (*phronesis*) is either a perception (*noesis*) of motion (*phoras*) and flowing (*rhou*), or else is benefit (*onesis*) of motion; intelligence (*noesis*) is the desire (*hesis*) of the new (*tou neou*), and things are new just because they are always being generated, for all things are in motion (411D-E).

Socrates then considers the term "profitable" (*lusiteloun*), related to the good and the beautiful. His explanation invokes the trader's transformation of matter, in a summary that ideally crowns the peripety of Barabas, the merchant who handles destruction:

[T]he name-giver gives the meaning to *lusiteloun* which it has in the language of tradesfolk, when profit sets free (*apoluei*) the sum invested, but he means that because it is the swiftest thing in the world it does not allow things to remain at rest and does not allow the motion to come to any end (*telos*) of movement or to stop or pause, but always, if any end of the motion is attempted, it sets it free, making it unceasing and immortal. It is in this sense, I think, that the good is dubbed *lusiteloun*, for it frees (*luei*) the end (*telos*) of the motion. (417C)

The end of the motion, the concept of quickness, the transformation of matter in the hands of the alchemic merchant, the annihilation of matter and substance—Barabas pursues himself and his own consumption. He is the *telos* in itself, directed not to the virtuous usage of the riches but rather to the motion and transformation of matter. Barabas is yet another experiment in suspension: while claiming, as a truly mechanicist philosopher, that "nothing violent . . . can be permanent" (*JM* 1.1.130-31), his own career on the redoubtable scene of Malta is an experiment in the permanence of destruction, a suspended pursuit for the end of the motion.

3
The Invention of Perdita

L'Azur! L'Azur! L'Azur! L'Azur!
—Mallarmé

In 1519, King Emanuel of Portugal signed the Treaty of Evora, formally renouncing Spain, the Canary Islands and *Insula Perdita*, the Lost Island. Far from having been technically lost, the last-mentioned domain had not yet been found. Nor was its resilience simply a vestige of late medieval superstitions: the last expedition set sail as late as 1721 (Graf 1964, 107-8). This loss did not, however, prevent a commodious flow of the riches from the lands beyond the sea—a Lisbon bank still bears the title *ultramarino* in its name.

Either as loss or wealth, the myth of the lost island and its discovery rested on the *admiratio* that prompts the soul into the recognition and interpretation of novelty (Platt 1992). Patrizi's non-Aristotelian theory of wonder resorted to a geographical image to render the Renaissance reaction to discovery. Aristotle saw wonder as something to be made credible in poetry, provided that the marvelous events occur "contrary to expectation yet on account of one another" (*Poetics* 9.1452a4-5). Patrizi, who defined novelty as one of the sources of wonder, instead perorated the case for the *potenza ammirativa*, the faculty that is shocked by the recognition of something unexpected. Our soul, says Patrizi (1970, 10:101v-102r), is entrapped in an inherently contradictory motion, which leads us to believe and not believe, "un movimento dell'anima, quasi contrario in sé medesimo, di credere e di non credere." The soul is moved toward belief by news, and yet is checked by ignorance until real knowledge is attained. Therefore wonder is a motion of the *facoltà ammirativa*, aroused by some new element (*per notizia nuova sorto*), and fomented by our previous ignorance before actual knowledge. To this movement between expectations and revelation, Patrizi attaches the imaginative term of *lontani*, the far-off things, the sources of wonder awaiting discovery and report.

Mindful of the twofold meaning of *inventio* as the act of discovering and of inventing, could the Renaissance fictional discoverer of Insula Perdita and other *lontani* be technically entitled to boast that he had found what had been lost? This apparently idle question did receive a nonplussing answer when America, the legitimate descendant of Insula Perdita under many respects, was discovered. Hardly a big break in the news, the wonderful newness of the lands beyond the Ocean was often toned down by rhetorical diminishment. In this sense, Johnson (1976, 623) underlined the constant use of "invention" (*Erfindung*) among the German geographers who divulged the discoveries of Columbus. Here one sees the archetype of the controversial Renaissance attitude towards the two extremes of geographical discovery, utter novelty and post-factum legitimization. In his 1493 letter, Columbus referred to the recently found islands (*nuper inventis*). This ambiguity also found scope in the Latin term *novus*, which uncannily resonates with intimations of both late discovery and utter newness. Reporting the relation of the anonymous pilot in Cabral's discovery of Brazil, Fracanzano da Montalboddo (1507) referred to the *Paesi nuovamente retrovati*; Grynaeus (1532) entitled his work *Novus Orbis*.

The Renaissance genre of the *navigatio*, a tradition of travelogues comprising geography and trade in its description of secular travels, copiously employed this twofold trope of the "invention" (O'Gorman 1961). It was not solely the thorny question of what Columbus initially believed to have found and the heuristic progression through which, on the occasion of his third voyage, he reached the conclusion that the Western Indies were the *otro mundo* (Colombo 1988, 45), utterly unknown to the entire world (Sale 1989). In fact, the potential for rhetorical *meiosis* remained rampant throughout the sixteenth century and nigh into the early decades of the seventeenth. An accompaniment to this post-factum invention of discovery was the natural nexus between the island theme and its potential for utopian ambience, the condition of its being beyond all the current bonds and limits that ultimately erased the historical data of the European country that had discovered it (Jameson 1977). Another component of the "invention" was the impetuous striving forward of Renaissance civilization, which subsumed any and every discovery under the label of relentless progress. Local variations were also possible: English-speaking readers could add their own sense of satisfaction over the safe distance separating their enterprises from the appalling reports of Spanish cruelty against the natives (Goldstein 1976).

In spite of post-factum invention, discovery was couched into loss. This interplay is also evident in the significant nuances between the Italian and the Latin text of Pancirolli's *Rerum Memorabilium*, a comparative list of the most remarkable things that had gone lost respectively on the moderns and on the ancients. Pancirolli singled out the new world (*novum illum orbem*) discovered by Columbus as the most glorious of modern inventions. This event is a veritable source of surprise and elation, which never fails to strike the author into further wonder—"magis me magisque cogitantem in admirationem saepius traxit" (1622, 1). Galvano similarly reported that Columbus and crew "found many Islands, which they called the *Princes* because they were the first that they had discouered" (1601, 26).

Pancirolli soon qualifies his argument, however, by saying that land was new (*antea nulla erat notitia*) provided that those islands were not the Fortunate Isles whose existence had long been attested and commemorated by sailors and mariners of all traditions. Even more ruthlessly, the Italian edition (Pancirolli 1612, 346) rebuffed the characteristic Colombian flourish emphasized by Todorov, the entrepreneurial account of potential gains.[1] Sure enough, the human desire for novelty that Aristotle underlined as our inherent legacy from nature, together with our covetous ambition to reign, nowhere shone more conspicuously than in the *inventione dell'Indie*. Yet this discovery ranked first not quite because of its sheer novelty, for the land was already known as the Fortunate Isles, but only because of the material, truly wonderful flow of valuable commodities (*diverse, e pretiose cose*) that had gushed out from there.

The diminishment of discoveries also gained momentum from the postulates of the equal distribution of lands and of their supposed habitability. According to the widely accepted "T in O" map, the emerged lands constitute a sort of giant island circumscribed by the Ocean. This model implied a counter-weight (*antichton*), also entailing the habitability of the antipodes (Broc 1980, 167-72). Pancirolli referred to the ancient theory of the *oikoumene* circumscribed by water, as new islands were incessantly sired by the all-encircling Ocean.

Yet this is no Atlantis. While reporting the similarly monstrous event of the disappearance of Atlantis, Pancirolli (1622, 26) jettisoned the fantastical opinion of some authors who argued that Phoenicians and Carthaginians had already gone beyond the Fortunate Islands and thus discovered America. Other scholars instead aggravated the mythical parentage of America with the lost continent. The German geographer Franck (1534, 200, 220-25) maintained that Columbus's discovery hardly went unprecedented, as the Atlantic explorations allegedly carried out by Phoenicians and Carthaginians substantiated Biblical wisdom: Solomon remains forever true—nothing new under the sun. To such a skeptical sect did Grynaeus belong. All prudent scholars—and he was obviously counting himself in—had been ready to discard the notion that such a huge mass of water had been merely relegated into the Ocean from the beginning of Creation without a contrary coacervated mass of land (1532, 79). Similarly, the commentator to Pancirolli (1622, 25) recalled the huge lack of land from both sides of the Equator that sailors had already observed in their pervagations, lured by their distaste for paucity of lands (*paupertatis odio*) opposed to Asia and Africa. In the unanimous opinion of geographers, America was necessarily the fourth and largest part of the world. A more material note could however be swiftly pressed, and the concept of rediscovery materially applied to grounding the Western possession of the New World in natural law. According to the *derecho de reversion*, Gonzalo Fernandez de Oviedo referred the New World to the Hesperides, thus called because of Hesperus, the legendary twelfth king of Spain, to which country God had providentially returned this domain after so many centuries (Greenblatt 1991, 62).

One constituent of the invention of discovery by backdating the news was the widely disseminated myth of *Insula Perdita*, the island floating in the Ocean that constantly eluded both the acts of possession and charting. The Greeks posited the existence of an unreachable island (*aprositos nesos*), identified by Ptolemy as one of the Canary Islands. The Arab compilers of medieval wonders reported the existence of a mobile island that is only visible from a distance; if accosted, it constantly receded from sight until fading away as in a sea-mirage; it only reappeared when the observer had regained his former viewpoint.[2] A similar mirage appeared to be perceived by the inhabitants of the Canary Islands somewhere between the sea and the sky. Las Casas reported that Columbus had personally heard many trustworthy Spaniards, living on the island of Hierro, swear they could see land to the west of the Canaries (Las Casas 1988, 2v).[3] The imagery was occasionally adapted to the Fortunate Isles, which could be found *casu et fortuna*, "by chance and luck," rather than proper investigation. Onorius of Autun spelled out the unchanged rule of engagement: the lost island is found by chance, and when sought after it is not to be found again—"quae aliquando casu inventa, postea quaesita non est inventa, et ideo dicitur Perdita" (Graf 1964, 109).

The myth is also attached to the quest for the Earthly Paradise reported in the *Navigatio Sancti Brandani*. The forbidden place is an island enshrined in the most brilliant light, cut through by a river which marks the off-limits ground even for those pious travelers, at least until it will be time to come there for good (*Brendan* 1928, 226b). An alternative version posits the existence of Seven Cities (*Sept Citez*), a haven for seven bishops who had escaped the Moors together with their believers and, as it happens, the treasures stored up in their cathedrals. Galvano (1601, 26) thus reports the chance "discovery" of the island in 1447:

> [I]t happened that ther came a Portugall ship through the streight of Gibraltar; and being taken with a great tempest, was forced to runne westwards more then willingly the men would, and at last they fell upon an Island which had seuen Cities, and the people spake the Portugall tong, and they demanded if the Moores did yet trouble Spain, whence

they had fled for the losse which they received by the death of the King of Spaine, Don Roderigo.

By no means a medieval wonder, the myth of the lost island surfaced in Renaissance travelogues. The island of St. Brendan, initially placed roughly at the same latitude as Ireland, descended south towards the Fortunate Isles in later maps. In the pre-Columbus 1492 map by Martin Behaim, the island went definitely west, near the Equatorial line. Peter of Medina deliberately interpreted the lost island as *Antilia*, the mythical island located somewhere before (*anti*) the Portuguese Coast, which was later to give its name to the newfound lands. For Galvano (1601, 26), the island of Seven Cities found in 1447 by the Portuguese sailors "were the Antiles, or Newe Spaine."

Not that this indeterminacy of location was unprecedented. In his effort to demonstrate how close the Indies could prove via a westward voyage, Paolo dal Pozzo Toscanelli bridged the distance between *Antilia* and *Cipango* by placing the former at a convenient distance from the Canary Islands as a sort of intermediate stop; then, he virtually elided it under the intersection between the Eastern and Western wings of the map he probably sent to Columbus (Crinò 1941, 16-7). Analogously, Grynaeus (1532, 79) reported that the new islands are *conterminae Indiae*. In Las Casas's report of Columbus's diary, one reads that he believed these Indies to be very near the Canary Islands, less than four-hundred leagues distant (1988, 57r).

The maps after Columbus's discovery testify to this flickering status. The lost islands alternatively disappeared, were identified with actual lands, or conveniently placed where their existence could be neither disproved nor confirmed. In the 1506 map of the world by Giovanni Matteo Contarini, the first known printed map to represent Colombo's discoveries, the Antilles were reported immediately west of the Canary Islands as the lands which Columbus had found (*invenit*, 1924, 3). The globe that appears in Holbein's *Ambassadors*, doubtfully attributed to Schoener (1525), reports the Hesperides, the Azores Madera, Espaniola and the *Antiglie Insule* (Heawood 1921). An analogous, albeit more simplified map appears in De Jode's *Speculus Orbis Terrarum* (1578), which simply situated the Antilles together with the Azores and Capo Verde. In other cases, the lost islands continued to part company with the new discoveries. Mercator (1961) situated the island (*sic*) of Brazil to the west of the southern tip of Ireland, Vlaenderen (Flanders) south of Brazil, St. Brendan west of Brazil, and Sept Citez between Newfoundland and Brazil. The islands of St. Brendan and of Sept Citez still feature in *Theatre of the Whole World*, the 1606 English edition of Ortelius's *Theatrum* (Ortelius 1968). In Van den Keere's map (1980) the isle of St. Brendan directly adjoins Newfoundland.

Even though the rudiments of Medieval and Renaissance geography
can be hardly severed from their symbolical meanings (Gillies 1994),
the fuzzy location of the lost island conveyed both presence and
absence: it is placed somewhere over there, before the likely discoverer,
and yet it agonizingly escapes observation—Perdita is always far
beyond. The first printed sea-atlases intuitively reported a constellation
of islands vaguely placed before the coast, owing to the prevalent type
of coastal navigation and consecutively of geographical charting that
represented only the islands opposite the coasts (Waghenaer 1964).
Reports contended for instance that Portugal had discovered "certain
islands that lie against Cape Verde"; an analogous situation beyond the
Azores had been used to rename the islands found in the famous 1431
expedition of the King of Portugal (Hakluyt 1985, 8:50). Pancirolli
reported that, after careful guesswork set out by mathematicians and
cosmographers, King Henry of Portugal had set sail on the spur of the
wild rumors being circulated by some Dutch sailors. Craving to repeat
Alexander the Great's eastward feat, the King found many countries
inhabited by barbarous and heathen nations: "trouò diuerse terre
habitate da gente barbare, e pagane" (1612, 347).

"Beyond" verily describes the uncharted seas that circumscribe the
lands. Mandeville (1968, 1) introduced his travels as a quest for the
land beyond the sea; also the "gravelly" sea testifies to this imagery:
"no man may pass that sea by navy nor by no manner of craft, and
therefore may no man know what land is beyond that sea" (30.210).
Mandeville performs an eastward periplus that constantly moves on
beyond each isle until the unreachable destination: "Of Paradise ne can
I not speak properly, for I was not there. It is far beyond, and that
forethinketh me, and also I was not worthy" (33.234).

For the myth of the lost island required contrition on the
discoverer's part. Perdita remains an unapproachable place that
nevertheless lures the discoverers into a moral quest as well. Galvano's
report of the discovery of Brazil (1601, 1-2) grounds the logical
possibility of the complete discovery of the world on moral terms:
"Some there be that say, that the world hath fully beene discouered: and
they alleage this reason, that it hath [beene] peopled and inhabited, so it
might be frequented, and navigable." Yet, even if the world is well
peopled and inhabited, it must still conceal some undiscovered
province: "There be others of a contrarie opinion to this, holding that all
the earth could not be knowne, nor the people conversant one with
another. For though it had beene so once, yet the same would have
beene againe by the malice of men, and the want of justice among the
inhabitants of the earth."

Perdita implied a moral lapse, an absence of justice. It required
repentance of the discoverer who plays with God's inscrutable justice.
Thus, it was not by chance that the ancients had lost Perdita as well.
Pancirolli (1622, 35) argued that the absconded New World had been

stored up as a secret of the divine mind, well preserved and reserved until AD 1492 (*veteribus incognitum in secreto divinae mentis latuisse*). As Bacon (1962, 1.129) concludes, "the introduction of famous discoveries appears to hold by far the first place among human actions; and this was the judgement of the former ages. For to the authors of inventions they awarded divine honours." While all other kinds of reformation entail violence and confusion, "discoveries carry blessings with them, and confer benefits without causing harm or sorrow to any." Yet, even if discoveries are "as it were new creations, and imitations of God's works," they must eventually be interpreted through the perspective enigmatically stated by Solomon: "The glory of God is to conceal a thing; the glory of the king to search it out" (Prv 25.2).

In *The Winter's Tale*, King Leontes searches out the past represented by Perdita, the daughter he has lost because of his sins, by morosely awaiting in Sicily, rather than charting the eponymous islands.[4] Not only laziness, though: the Mediterranean had a general reputation for benevolence, even though open-sea navigation was still a dangerous feat in the seventeenth century, when tramping along the coast represented the rule (Pryor 1988, 12; Braudel 1977, 35, 50). The archetypal test of the young child adrift at sea is staged on an ancient route that had been one major hub of navigation in the Mediterranean from the times of the ancient Corcyra (Corfu), which had established colonies in Syracuse and Illyria; the prestige of this route was made paramount by Virgil by deviating Aeneas's voyage from Crete to Illyria (Cordano 1992, 11-2, 20-7, 123).[5]

In *The Winter's Tale*, the sea represents the passage of time and its effects on the characters. The Renaissance idea of time had gradually abandoned the religious framework and approached a secular perspective: whereas divine providence used to ensure the sanctification of time, now time had to be redeemed and purchased just like a commodity (Waller 1971). In Shakespeare, this movement toward a representation of time as "'presiding' over characters and 'residing' in the mental landscape of individual characters" had already been practised in the mature comedies (Westerweel 1993, 55).[6] The romances structurally delineate time as an agency that entails the solution of the plot: the Renaissance notion of the triumph of time makes justice of all the apparent twists and turns of the plot, and time itself is promoted to the status of an absconded character that reconciles chance and Providence in the ending of the romance. Nor does this rosy landscape of redemption elude the practicalities of literary creation. Shakespeare first had to convincingly reshape what Muir (1977, 271) termed the "absurdities" of his source, Peele's *Pandosto*. Family continuity and the creating power of nature do inform the play, constructing it around the theme of the return of what once was lost (Quinones 1972, 433).

Yet the image of time as an actor that in its turn buys out the characters and their casual actions should not be taken too providentially. Much of the consolation lies stored in the final, casual twist in the plot, rather than in the means used by the characters to buy out time. I will offer a reading of the play through the vantage point of the myth of Perdita, and then will turn to what fails to tally with this happy ending, the consideration of chance.[7] The myth of Perdita underscores the element of chance involved in abridging this "wide gap of time," strenuously contained and legitimized by the Renaissance travelogue.

The immensity of the sea is immediately coextensive with time: as Lord Archidamus says to Camillo, "you shall see . . . great difference betwixt our Bohemia and your Sicilia" (*WT* 1.1. 3-4). The brotherly, timeless friendship between the two kings, a miracle enacted by their communal childhood and then preserved by spiritual communion, fills in the expanse: "They have seemed to be together, though absent; shook hands, as over a vast" (28-30). Before the separation, these kings were "two lads that thought there was no more behind, / But such a day to-morrow as to-day, / And to be boy eternal" (1.2.63-5).[8] The blessed ignorance of the "doctrine of ill-doing" also bars the future discovery of what may lie 'beyond', both in space and in time. To this potential unknown beyond the sea, intended not as the destination but as the lapse of time the voyage will encompass, Polixenes addresses his tentative counting of time, occasioned by the impending confrontation with the sea: "Time as long again / Would be fill'd up, my brother, with our thanks" (3-4). Leontes refuses the attempt to reconcile time. In his post-lapsarian perspective, his discovery of time as conveyed by the vastness of the sea is a loss: only when he loses what he has got, both his family and the childhood memories, does he become capable of grasping time and its effects. After having got wind of the aborted poisoning of Polixenes he had commissioned, Leontes seems to be a disgruntled king who has just renounced a dominion, "[a]s he had lost some province, and a region / Loved as he loves himself" (369-70).

No longer a heavenly promise, time demotes into the painful consideration of the similarity between King and son, a reminder of both the king's adolescence and the suspicion that has women be false as waters (132). The similarity between parents and children, which Perdita will eventually restore, achieves the creating faculty of nature by accomplishing the discovery of continuity and pattern (Quinones 1972, 435). Before the confrontation with the sea, however, similarity only fosters destruction. The somber sequence of the events in time elicits the sense of macabre annihilation that Mamilius eerily conjures up with his sad tale of spirits and goblins. All bodies and fictions alike stand in need of a metamorphosis, a transformation of post-lapsarian frailty that has to be repeated continuously through the agency of sin and chance (Bishop 1996, 160). Each generation has to actualize and repeat the loss of innocence and the discovery of time as a new form of the myth of the Fall (Peterson 1973; Grantley 1986).

The Winter's Tale colors this denial of repetition with chance. When Leontes denies the fair line of succession through similarity, refusing the idea that his daughter might be "the whole matter / And copy of the father" (*WT* 2.3.98-9), he rejects similarity in favor of chance. The decisive answer will come from beyond the sea, from the oracle of Delphi. The sea will also sanction the fate of the child, destined "[t]o some remote and desert place, quite out / Of our dominions" (175-6).

This is the first echelon in the romance's construction of myth: the child is invented as Perdita and entrusted to chance and hazardous navigation. Since she came to the King "by strange fortune," she will be commended "to some place / Where chance may nurse or end it" (2.3.178, 181-82). By expelling the fruit of time and making it become what is lost, Leontes entrusts the child to the realm of the sea ordeal and of the unlikely return. Once unsealed, the Oracle reflects the destiny of Perdita as the one who has to be invented: "The king shall live without an heir, if that which is lost be not found" (3.2.134-6). The lost child garners a prophetic promise: she encompasses both the past of her departure and the future lineage descending from the King. In a paradoxical result, Leontes is reconciled with his childhood memories: in his hyperbolic desire for repentance he imagines piling up penitent time while waiting for her return (211).

It is in this moment that the lost child, after being invented, is found and named. The action of the play moves over the sea to Bohemia. Characteristically, a sea dream heralds the naming of the lost child. Antigonus refers that Perdita's mother accosted him in his dreams in an aptly nautical garb: "I never saw a vessel of like sorrow, / So fill'd, and so becoming: in pure white robes" (3.3.21-2). She imparts her christening to the child, Perdita, "for the babe / Is counted lost for ever" (32-3). The almost farcical appearance of the bear that will feast on Antigonus's shoulder bone, as well as the shipwreck of his mates, sanctions the entrance into the remote land of Bohemia, where time is congealed into a pastoral setting. Instead of reiterating the imagery of the lost island as seen from this world, the second part of *The Winter's Tale* is the Paradise news coming from the land beyond sea and time. The Clown bestows the sea-mirage on Antigonus's sinking ship, described in words that smack of the dim recognition of the moving island as the storm blurs the picture: "I have seen two such sights, by sea and by land! But I am not to say it is a sea, for it is now the sky" (83-4). Indeterminacy also affects the shipwreckers—"sometimes to see 'em, and not to see 'em: now the ship boring the moon with her main-mast, and anon swallowed with yest and froth" (90-3). In this inversion of perspectives, Leontes' world becomes the lost island beyond the sea where repentance is taking its toll on the king. Perdita dispenses grace and remembrance under the symbols of rosemary and rue (4.4.74), epitomizing the chasm that his penitent father is exploring in the other land beyond the sea.

The paradigm of loss edges its way out in Bohemia as well. In fact, the apparent idyll of the pastoral festivity in Bohemia offers a ruse for the disguised Polixenes to botch the test of his son's love for Perdita. Much as the timeless childhood of the two kings, his Arcadian court precipitates into the same fall of human malice, thwarting the succession from father to son that the pastorals were meant to celebrate. And it is the discovery of the missing island that dictates prince Florizel's putting to sea: reconciliation is achieved through the absence of the innocent, the specimen of similarity, both in the family lineage and in the repetition of the loss. In the Mediterranean, each land is a missing island that craves to be conquered after repentance has been achieved.

Meanwhile, in Sicily repentance has apparently filled in the gap of time separating the King from grace. Having perfected a "saint-like sorrow," Leontes only needs to forget his evil. But his failed succession, decreed by the loss of Perdita, entails the return of similarity: the other heir who will be found is the selfsame Perdita, and Leontes can theoretically marry another Hermione (5.1.74). Remembrance requires the formation of an artificial gap of time, encompassed by the sea. Polixenes reports to Leontes that Polixenes has constantly wished to regain former innocence by gauging the sea: "He had himself / The lands and waters 'twixt your throne and his / Measur'd, to look upon you" (142-4). Only the sea, by embodying the prodigious expanse and the changing of time, enables the solution of the Oracle, whereas Sicily and Bohemia are entrapped in fixity and repetition. The chain of endless repentance ends with the passing of time: Leontes concludes the play by inviting his queen to a mutual account of the parts played since they were first dissevered— apparently, time is a *pharmakos* to its own evils.

Despite the apotheosis of recognition, *The Winter's Tale* reveals an unfathomable anticlimax. The real content of the action is the return of the past, conveyed by Perdita and Hermione as the highest tokens of similarity. In this sense, similarity does invert and conquer death (Ketterer 1990). Thus, it is no surprise that the myth of the lost island informs the recognition scenes as well. The encounter between Leontes and his adviser Camillus reads like a discovery that in fact acknowledges the previous loss: "They looked as if they had heard of a world ransomed, or one destroyed" (*WT* 5.2.14-5).[9] The discovery of Perdita also unleashes a chain of discoveries, a series of further losses: "Our king, being ready to leap out of himself for joy of his fond daughter, as if that joy were now become a loss, cries 'O, thy mother, thy mother!'" (50-3).

In fact, the myth of the lost island retraces a less joyous than literally hazardous meaning beneath the final reconcilement. While positing immemorial heavenly innocence beyond the sea, the same story of human frailty occupies both sides of these domains: Leontes and Polixenes had already lost their own paradise island. Bacon may be adjourned: the King both conceals his own secret and then searches it out, for he is alone on both coasts of the sea. He has discovered the invention of the loss of Perdita, the loss of the providential pattern of sin and repentance.

Seen from the blithely providential perspective of the Renaissance discoverers that set sail for Perdita, *The Winter's Tale* also alters the relevance of chance to the plot of the discovery.

For chance was already there on the pious traveler's side. Apollonius of Tyre was providentially tossed about on the sea (*per diversa discrimina maris iactatur*) until, steered by God (*gubernante Deo*), he found the daughter, whose mother had been committed to the sea (*Apollonius of Tyre* 1991, 39.1-2, 44.11). *Pericles,* a close adaptation of the Apollonius story, iterates the elements of chance in the voyage. As we are told in crude, probably non-Shakespearean verse,

> [H]e, good prince, having all lost,
> By waves from coast to coast is toss'd
> . . . Till fortune, tir'd with doing bad,
> Threw him ashore, to give him glad.
>
> (*PER* 2.Chorus 33-4, 37-8)

Having become the ball for the vast tennis-court where waters and wind rule (2.1.59-61), Pericles, as he who has lost all, faces "the god of this great vast" (3.1.1). Yet "fortune's mood" pursues him, and there goes "sea-tost Pericles" (3. Chorus 46, 60), until the point where, apparently lost, he concludes his unwitting voyage: "We there him lost, / Whence, driven before the winds, he is arriv'd / Here where his daughter dwells" (5 Chorus 13-5). He has alighted on the site of god Neptune's annual feast.

Gods were truly instrumental to his erring. Reading the "passport" accompanying Marina, Cerimon summons inspiration from Apollo, the god of learning: "Perfect me in the characters" (3.2.68-9). Facing his daughter, at the outset Pericles makes to send her back to the enraged deity that is apparently persecuting him (5.1.143). The family reunion is capped by the final pilgrimage to the temple of Diana, whereto Pericles will be revealed how he lost his wife at first (5.1.242).

Incensed gods that divert ships and accord reunion after apparent loss did require perfection in reading the characters. For Apollo, the god speaking through his Mediterranean oracle, has obscurely sanctioned the fate of Perdita as well. Among the plethora of epithets,

Apollo was celebrated as the archer-god striking from afar. The ancients referred the epithets of Apollo *hekebolos* not only to his symbolical dexterity in the long-distance shot, but also to his ability of hitting the mark at will (*Cratylus* 405C-E).[10] Thus, the *Homeric Hymn to Apollo* concludes with the legend of Apollo Delphinius, the god leading the ships of merchant adventurers.[11] Under the guise of a monstrous dolphin, the archer god diverts a ship to the island where his most famous Oracle will be founded.[12] When the impetuous winds have subsided, he asks the unwilling prisoners if they have traveled so far just to barter or to wander idly over the sea like pirates (*Hymn to Apollo* 1976, 452-5). The merchants have sailed there against their will, steered by some immortal (471-3). Apollo promises a gratifying reward for this change of destination. What seemed utter chance, the malicious outcome of a storm that stultifies men's will over the wide gulf of the vast sea (*hyper mega laitma talasses*, 481), portends in fact the knowledge of the recondite secrets of the gods, the wish of the immortals (*boulas t'athanaton eidesete*, 484).

In *The Winter's Tale*, the element of chance that providentially canvasses the sea between Sicily and Bohemia turns into an act of stoical will. Despite the return of both lost baby and Queen, the secret wish of the immortals demands the daring worship of chance. The lost island was found by chance: when sought, it receded from sight. The lost islands of the New World were also found by a venturesome *volta do mar* that first stopped at the Fortunate Islands and then sailed on into the unploughed seas. Apollonius entrusted himself to the open sea (*tradidit se alto pelago*) both to save his own life and to find his daughter (1991, 6.17, 38.15-6). Columbus traveled to those islands that had no knowledge of religion (*quibus nulla est religio*), where *anarchia*, a favorite byword in all the accounts reported by Grynaeus, ruled. Columbus set sail to the unploughed seas, and subdued himself to the atrocious Herculean labors that beset the violator of these *maria incomperta* (Grynaeus 1532, 79).

Less providentially, the voyage in *The Winter's Tale* not only implies that Perdita is restored by chance, but that chance itself is discovered and found. The play "invents" chance as the ultimate destination of the voyage, the element that will cover the gaps of time and sea. One always has to go westward—*versum occasum semper*. Florizel renounces "all the sun sees, or / The close earth wombs, or the profound sea hides / In unknown fathoms" (*WT* 4.4.490-2), ready to obey his wild dedication to "unpath'd waters, undream'd shores" (568)—here lies the true *pharmakos*, the contrapuntal discovery of solitude and hazard that can be opposed to our condition as "the slaves of chance" (541).

4
Inducting Pocahontas

Since I was a mere pragmatic English novelist,
he would get a better interview out of me
if he perhaps approached such larger matters
by way of smaller, lighter ones.
—Julian Barnes, *Cross Channel*

Cannibalism may be considered one of most consuming models of intercultural negotiation. Not only does it visually subsume the other by bringing it closer to oneself: it can also be used to ingest one's satirical butt. Pondering the acts of savagery witnessed by European warfare, where living bodies had been tortured, roasted and even bitten to death by dogs and pigs, Montaigne deemed actual cannibalism less barbarous (Marchi 1993). After all, only dead bodies were subjected to roasting and eating: the logical comparison between abstract terms poignantly claims that "il y a plus de barbarie à manger un homme vivant qu'à le manger mort" (Montaigne 1587, 257). By the same token of rationality, Montaigne argued that American natives might be considered barbarous only when judged by the universal *regles de la raison* (258). A similarly decentralized observation of European barbarity was expressed by three Brazilian natives who visited the French Court and found the local spectacle of social injustice "en premier lieu fort estrange" (265).

Montaigne's passage seems to actualize what Hamlin (1994, 426, 416) defined as "the European characterization of the non-European interpretation of the foreigners' status," accompanied by the "linguistic apotheosis" of the divine attribution bestowed on the Europeans.[1] Apart from discourse, was there also a logical apotheosis, an attempt to interpret the American natives with respect to the *regles de la raison*? The inductive assimilation of Pocahontas seems indeed to prove the existence of such logical cannibalism as a debased form of Aristotelian dialectic, in turn overset by the parody of discovery that Ben Jonson staged in the two masques witnessed by Pocahontas in London.

The commonplace evidence of this simplified dialectic emerges from the beatification of the new islands and the humanization of the natives. Both helped to make the natives more familiar, thus reducing the menace that stemmed from the undeniable similarity between Europeans and Americans. The beatification literally consisted in translating America into the Blessed Islands by adapting the Biblical overtones of the Earthly Paradise.[2] But it also implied a European-styled humanization, carefully encapsulating the natives into a recognizable pattern of human similarity. One of the results was envisaging a possible identification with the Indians, which was otherwise forbidden with the Africans (Orgel 1987, 49).

The sense of similarity was ultimately interwoven with religious proselytism. Febvre (1968, 423) detected the most striking emotional response caused by the discovery in "une étonnante ferveur de prosélytisme," the absence of any serious objection against the universality of the Revelation. Consequently, paganism became a central organizing category, launching a process of domestication to which the New World inhabitants were subjected before being assimilated (Ryan 1981, 525).

All these economic, social and religious arguments posit the underlying philosophical question of subsuming the unknown under some recognizable logical categories. And the most common philosophical source was the Aristotelian theory of dialectic, wherein similarity and difference were thoroughly tested either by way of induction or deduction. For Aristotle had indicated dialectic as a helpful tool not only for intellectual training, but also for conversations and casual encounters (*Topica* 1.2.101a27-37).

Aristotelian dialectic aims to discuss the foundations of all arts and sciences.[3] These principles would remain otherwise impregnable, for they "are primary in relation to everything else, and is to necessary to deal with them through the generally accepted opinions on each point" (*Topica* 1.2.101a37-101b1). In fact, any form of doctrine and learning that is based on discursive thought develops from antecedent knowledge.[4] If such an upward progression to previous knowledge were denied, the individual would either learn nothing or learn what he already knows (*Posterior Analytics* 1.1.71a29-30). The solution given by Aristotle to this potential impasse lies in the distinction between the "prior" and the "more knowable" in nature and in relation to us: "By 'prior' or 'more knowable' in relation to us I mean that which is nearer to our perception, and by 'prior' or 'more knowable' in the absolute sense I mean that which is further from it. The most universal concepts are furthest from our perception, and particulars are nearest to it" (1.2.71b35-72a5).

The distinction offers a way out of the dual role Plato had assigned to dialectic. Aristotle rephrases these upward and downward paths, respectively corresponding to induction and deduction, as two different types of intelligibility.[5] The absolutely intelligible ultimately leads to deduction, whereas that which is more intelligible to us intimately calls for induction. This insight is embodied in everyday dialectical activity.[6] Syllogism, being based on deduction, is more powerful, although it is based on objects that are more removed from sense. Induction, being the progress from particulars to universals, can instead infer the universal through the consideration of similarity (*Topica* 1.18.108b10-12), a dialectic task often called upon by most casual encounters with the New World.

On a more mundane level, deduction offers a powerful way of restating the obvious, whereas induction conducts from sense to new knowledge. From a dialectical point of view, making the New World a messianic fulfillment of the Old World in fact transformed an interpretative problem—the missing knowledge represented by the natives—into a truth that can be deduced from the messianic principles of Christianity. The Saturnalian setting is evident in Hariot's comparison (1888, 14-5) between Virginia and his native country: "The grounde they neuer fatten with mucke, dounge or any other thing: neither plow or digge it as we in England." In a strictly utilitarian inference from the Golden Age to the age of gold, Rolfe (1951, 34) declares that "triall be made, what lieth hidden in the womb of the Land: the Land might yerely abound with corne and other provisions for mans sustenaunce." This argument implied a more general logical consequence. Whitaker (1613, B1r) extolled the new land as "a place beautified by God, with all the ornaments of nature, and enriched with its earthly treasures." Much of the hermeneutic shock released by the discovery was attenuated by those elements that, albeit relegated into a messianic realm, were already known to Europeans.

Within this deductive framework, the natives raised a crucial problem for the religious cannibalism of conversion—another logical term—whose solution was tagging them with the European label of imperfect reasoners. Echoing what Aristotle had said concerning the foundations of arts and sciences, Hariot (1888, 25) partially endows the natives with some kind of ingenuity deriving from their autonomous rules of reason, although they make a poor performance when compared with our principles: "In respect of vs they are a people poore, and for want of skill and iudgement in the knowledge and vse of our thinges, doe esteeme our trifles before thinges of greater value: Notwithstanding, in their proper manner considering the want of such meanes as we haue, they seeme very ingenious." The quest for knowledge, which arises from a striking sensorial experience, also emerges from the famously metonymical anecdote verging on the materiality of the Bible whose contents Hariot was trying to divulge. By mistaking the symbol for reality, the natives ineptly followed the inductive way to knowledge: "Many [were] glad to touch it, to embrace it, to kisse it, to hold it to their breasts and heades, and stroke ouer all their bodie with it: to shewe their hungrie desire of that knowledge which was spoken of" (27). Not simply equipping the natives as potential Christians, Hariot also transformed them into faulty searchers of inductive knowledge.

Indeed, the potential for knowledge was yet another Christian requisite along with natural piety. Describing "the ignorant inhabitants of Virginia," Whitaker (1613, 23-4, 25) detected a motive for dialectical hope even in these "naked slaues of the diuell": they are "a very understanding generation, quicke of apprehension, suddaine in their dispatches, subtile in their dealings, exquisite in their inuentions, and industrious in their labour." Much of the argument for possible conversion, in fact, was based on the contrast between the opposed models of European and American reasoning. Let us logically reconstruct the passage that Rolfe (1951, 40) devotes to denying the likeliness of general conversion. The European observers of natives are bound to be struck by their similarity, as they cannot look at their faces "without Sorrow, pittie and commyseracion: seeing they beare the Image of our heavenly Creator, & wee and they come from one and the same moulde." Yet any potential for induction is short-lived: the principles of "piety, clemency, courtysie and civill demeanor (by which meanes som are wonn to vs already)" will eventually fail "to convert and bring [the multitude] to the knowledge and true worshipp of [J]esus Christ." Rolfe's despair is heightened by the fact that the natives apply the wrong principles for their deductions. Their damnation is willingly accepted not only because of their "ignorance of God and Christ," but also from the constant applications of "their old supersticions and idolatries, wherein they haue bene nursed and trayned from their infancies."

Conversion, then, was also to be made to Western principles of thinking. Johnson (1612, E4r) advises the English to "take their children and traine them up with gentlenesse, teach them our English tongue, and the principles of religion." Inevitably, this claim needed a philosophical proof, achieved through the extensive usage of induction that had already been imposed upon the natives. If such a glutinous group of imperfect dialecticians can be fractured into a wondrous individual, boasting both extreme similarity with the Europeans and a potential for dialectical training, then conversion could be proved.

Aristotelian induction was a natural candidate for informing the European, cannibalistic appropriation of strangeness. In a truly Montaignesque mood, cannibals made a passing appearance in Jonson's *Staple of Newes*: a cook designs his grotesque plan for their conversion into "good, eating *Christians*" (*BJ* 6:3.2.158) by the same culinary art that

> Would make our *Caniball-Christians*,
> Forbeare the mutuall eating one another,
> Which they doe doe, more cunningly, then the wilde
> *Anthropophagi*; that snatch onely strangers [.]
>
> (176-9)

Alongside this shortened form of deductive reasoning, the play also drops one the earliest literary references to Pocahontas, recalling the prosaic anecdote of the visit she paid to the Devil Tavern. Also Pocahontas, then, "hath bin in womb of a tauerne" (2.5.124).[7] On a more symbolic level, the embedding of Pocahontas reflects the quest for assimilating her into Jacobean London.[8] The singular strangeness of Pocahontas sparked an inductive reasoning from the species to the genus of American natives that left its marks on the congeries of pseudo-anthropological disquisition and religious and commercial proselytizing, as well as on the literary rendition of strangeness and discovery as offered by the Court masque.

Similarity and singularity in fact turn into the sense of "firstness"— the particular that proves the argument by induction—which is conveyed when Pocahontas enters this picture.[9] From a dialectical point of view, her "firstness" fills in the logical gap within the proof of the possible conversion of the native. In her first, anonymous mention she is singled out as the most talented reasoner who "not only for feature, countenance, and proportion, much exceedeth any of the rest of his people, but for wit, and spirit, [is] the only Nonpareil of this Country" (*True Relation* E3v). She is the first Indian that can be discerned away from the barbarous crowd because of her intellectual and, consequently, religious virtues. Smith (1986, 121) reiterates both his own "firstness" ("I being the first Christian this proud King and his grim attendants ever saw") and Pocahontas's historical primacy as "the first Christian ever of that Nation, the first Virginian ever [to speak] English, or [to have] a childe in mariage by an Englishman." From this respect, the proselytizing job proves the general assertion by means of a special case. Inviting his readers to the Sisyphean task of converting the barbarous Indians "to the sauing knowledge, and true worship of God in Christ Jesus," Hamor (1615, 48, 24) points to the special case of Rolfe, who married Pocahontas "merely for the good and honour of the Plantation."

Accordingly, all references to Pocahontas's barbarous birth and nature were prudently blotted out.[10] In a letter to a London minister, Thomas Dale praised her civil behavior: after having been "carefully instructed in Christian Religion," she "renonced publickly her countrey Idolatry" and "openly confessed her Christian faith," inspiring constant hopes of increasing "in goodnesse, as the knowledge of God increaseth in her" (Hamor 1615, 55-6). Before her visit to London, Smith (1986, 121) informs Queen Anne that Pocahontas "was taught to speak such English as might well bee understood, well instructed in Christianitie, and was become very formall and ciuill after our English manner." Pocahontas seems to have been instructed in the proper art of thinking as well, together with true religion and civility. At least, that had been the task of her pious husband, who frequently woke up in a cold sweat at the thought of being "in loue with one whose education hath bin rude, her manners barbarous, her generation accursed, and so discrepant in all nurtriture from my selfe" (Hamor 1615, 64).

Much as the Brazilian natives reported by Montaigne, Pocahontas had the chance to point her half-estranged, half-anglicized look at a European Court during her fated visit in 1616, marking the full success of the inductive argument. Judging from the general benevolence that accompanied her tour, it seems that Pocahontas's Christian piety and reasoning skills prevailed upon the display of exoticism.[11] As usual, the American native generated disparaging comments about the barbarity of the Europeans, namely the courtiers maligned by Smith (1986, 123): "They did thinke God had a great hand in her conversion, and they have seene many English Ladies worse fauoured, proportioned and behavioured." By conforming to these canons of civility, Pocahontas was reintegrated by Purchas (1625, 1774) into her former princely status: she "did not onely accustome herselfe to ciuilitie, but still carried her selfe as the Daughter of a King, and was accordingly respected . . . in [the] hopefull zeale by her to aduance Christianitie." She was also posthumously hailed as "the first fruits of Virginian conuersion, leauing here a godly memory, and the hopes of her resurrection." At the end of the inductive process—and of Pocahontas's life as well—her most wonderful quality was caught in yet another facet of her firstness. The "first fruits" of the civilizing encounter with the Old World perform a blatantly colonialist triumph of dialectic. A previous source of the unknown, she could only be subsumed under the loose category of heathen and then inductively shaped by proper instruction into a refined Christian princess. The preachers literally brought the point home, first by setting up Pocahontas's primacy as an inductive example for instructing the Indians into European thought and religion and then by presenting the living proof that attaining the knowledge of God, to use a recurrent expression, is by no means different from reaching any kind of knowledge.

In this ethnographic cannibalism, the indistinct multitude of Indians was reduced into a wonderful singularity. Yet the circularity of the underlying argument, proving by way of induction that the singularity of Pocahontas could be assimilated into the more general category of the Christian converts, was hardly limited to employing her as a logical proof. In an uncanny reflection, the visit of Pocahontas realized what many court shows had depicted as a conventional homage to the

English Court. For she was entertained at Lambeth "with festival state and pompe" (Purchas 1625, 1774); the monarchs were pleased "honourably to esteeme her . . . both publikely at the maskes and otherwise, to her great satisfaction and content"; this satisfied his request to amaze Pocahontas into wonderment, to "ravish her with content" at the spectacle of the royal honors (Smith 1986, 122-3). Pocahontas even made part of the audience of Ben Jonson's 1616 masques. A serendipitous singularity already processed as a logical commodity thus faced the Court Masque, in its turn a fictionalized encounter between the two worlds that probably inspired the European descriptions of the New World.

Prefiguring Pocahontas's visit to London, the Indians discovered the Old World in fiction as well. A formal coming of Indians to England had been staged in Chapman's *Masque of the Middle Temple and Lincoln's Inn*, performed at Whitehall in 1613. Strangeness celebrated the moderation ideals of the English Court. On top of two triumphal chariots, a set of musicians reproduced the prototype of the strange Indians against whom Pocahontas's pious performance was later to be gauged. Attired like the Virginian priests who adore the Sun (Phoebades), they displayed "strange hoods of feathers, and scallops about their necks, and on their heads turbans, stuck with several coloured feathers, spotted with wings of flies, of extraordinary bigness, like those of their country." The chief masquers paraded in a literally outlandish garb, "the ground-cloth of silver, richly embroidered, with golden suns, and about every sun run a trail of gold, imitating Indian work." This introductory procession was "altogether estrangeful and Indian-like." In fact, the golden imagery was instrumental to the moral meaning of the masque, advocating the liberal use of riches. One can, however, envisage an inductive reasoning beneath the estranged pageantry. Imitating a mock-discovery, the central rock of the scene opens up to offer a rich mine of gold, wherein "the Phoebades (showing the custom of the Indians to adore the sun setting) begin their observance with the song" (Chapman 1874, 342-4).

Although acting as garish, silent pieces of decoration, the Indians also lay out the basis for a possible conversion: if the actual adorers of the Sun-gold can be converted, then also our misers can. Domesticated by their reduction to the cult of the riches, the Indians are subjected to the reciprocating discovery of the Old World. A troop of them, worshipping Plutus, triumphantly sit in a goldmine set in a moving island approaching Britain. Not only indebted with the continental tradition of the Court shows, the impressing scenic action also seems to mirror the process of inductive cannibalism by the very act of bringing the Indians closer to European thought, representing the sense of strangeness that accompanied the European tour of Montaigne's natives through the amazement in the face of the splendor of the English Court.

Yet a successful form of inductive reasoning is required: their conversion is to be achieved by means of abandoning their superstitious beliefs and modulating their cult of gold into the worship of the Golden Age. The Indians are graciously invited to redirect their cult to the King, "our clear Phoebus." The process of inductive discovery assimilates them as discoverers to be tamed in their turn by proper reasoning. "Firstness," the striking singularity of the New World, is now given over to Europe. The conversion of the Phoebades foresees Pocahontas's conversion to the Golden Age, where Christian piety ensures the redemption from the errors of misdirected thought, the "superstitious worship of these suns, / Subiect to cloudy darkenings and descents," and the devotion due to "this our Briton Phoebus, whose bright sky / (Enlighten'd with a Christian piety) / Is never subject to black Error's night" (Chapman 1874, 348-9). Chapman's masque and Pocahontas's conversion live off the same inductive process of domestication.

Once Pocahontas becomes the tamed Indian Princess, she can be the proper spectator to the Court masque, where all scenic codes are employed to bring the audience closer to the glory of the Sun-King. Her apparent honor in being fêted by the Monarchs is the final result of assimilation to the poetics of faked discovery constantly enacted by the Court Masque. From this point of view, Jonson's masques also resorted to strangeness and magnificence in order to convey the fruitful discovery of the Kingly order. Jonson posits a double movement of the eye within the structure of most of his masques: the audience's attention alternates between the spectacle of strangeness that is being staged and the solemnity of the spectacle played by the Royals.[12] Both shows were called to comment upon each other, in a strictly inductive progression from the ludicrous, almost heathenish homage of the antimasque to the convenient celebration of the King's powers.

This interplay of expectations is, however, blurred by the denial of induction and, hence, of discovery, that marks the last part of Pocahontas's travel in London. Jonson's 1616 masques, *Christmas His Masque* and *The Vision of Delight*, betray no direct echo of her presence in their audiences.[13] Contrariwise, both masques look decidedly intended for Londoners in their reflection of contemporary life. Yet it is the very power of induction, embodied by the logical catechism undergone by Pocahontas, that Jonson brings to a halt in his estranging parody of discovery.

Christmas His Masque, the first of the two shows, draws on the close knowledge of the London whereabouts, as well as of its carnivalesque rituals.[14] But it is not simply a masque "from little little little little London" (*BJ* 7:76). Under the pretence of adapting this elementary show to a higher place, Christmas brings an antimasque of singularity closer to the audience: "I ha' brought a Masque here, out o' the Citie, o' my owne making, and doe present it by a sett of my Sonnes, that come out of the Lanes of *London*" (18-20). While Chapman's Indians evoked a convertible type of strangeness, Christmas's sons display the outlandish strangeness of these waning popular customs, for instance in the attire of New-Yeares-Gift, parading "in a blew Coat, serving-man like, with an Orange, and a sprig of Rosemarie guilt on his head, his Hat full of Broaches, with a coller of Gingerbread" (52-4). Strangeness serves as a carnivalesque homage to the King, presenting "with all the appurtenances / A right Christmas, as of old it was" (173-4). This mock denial of carnival underscores different levels of symbolic activities, such as the difference of status, the London map of symbolic places, the gap between popular showmanship and Court pageantry, and so forth. Yet this evocation of an older London world, made almost incomprehensible by the change of theatrical and courtly fashion, emanates a kind of strangeness that cannot be converted into proper worship of the Sun-King.

The making of old carnival into a different world from the Court enacts the Jonsonian parody of discovery. Differing from the usual inductive pattern, these strange spectacles are the first fruits to be virtually assimilated in the masque, yet resisting their conversion into more general terms. In *Christmas His Masque*, the convention of describing the characters to the King reads now like a category of newly-found, yet hardly recognizable wonders. Obviously, it is another way of poking fun at the actors who are defectively enacting those mythological or popular characters. Apart from the conventional evocation of misrule before the triumph of the King's order, Jonson is in fact endowing such familiar spectacles with unnecessary strangeness in order to imply that this autonomous realm resists any assimilation or conversion. He exacerbates the inductive pattern, transforming even the most trivial scenic actions into an amazing discovery of the unknown. One cannot escape the impression that the concomitant presence of Pocahontas, the living champion of successful induction, in the audience could provide a counter-interpretation of the viability of that discovery. By representing the Londoners of old as domestic Indians and placing them into a separate world, Jonson denies the possibility of domestication and, hence, of induction. The audience can get nowhere starting from these single cases.

The Vision of Delight, Jonson's second masque of 1616, also rules out any potential for discovery by inductive reasoning. The rhythm of the scene is marked by the exaltation of change: "Let your shewes be new, as strange, / Let them oft and sweetly varie; / Let them haste so to their change, / as the Seers may not tarrie"(*BJ* 7:15-8).[15] Delight derives from appreciating the swift pace of the theatrical inventions. Initially, the comic element is borrowed from the old world of carnival, as the first Antimasque stages "a she Monster delivered of sixe Burratines, that dance with sixe Pantalones." As in the mummery of the previous masque, however, this show does not provide a formal contrast to the main spectacle. Detached from any real implication with the world of the Court, it cannot be converted to its ideals either. Nor can it constitute a singularity in itself. For Jonson reduces strangeness into sheer illogicality. Breaking forth from the Chariot of the Night, Phantasie inaugurates the realm of incongruous figures ("Now all thy figures are allow'd, / and various shape of things; / Create of ayrie formes, a streame," 46-8), and piles up a list of inexplicable contradictions: "Your Ostritch, beleeve it, 's no faithfull translator / Of perfect Utopian; And then 'twere an od-piece / To see the conclusion peepe forth at a cod-piece" (72-4). Jonson adapts utopian imagery not to the language of wonder or exoticism but, rather, to the logical incongruous or the figurative type of grotesque, such as the dream "with a Windmill on his head, and bells at his beard" (80). Phantasie merely indulges in accumulating images of chaos that no induction could ever interpret. Her assertion that "no proportion is boasted / 'Twixt an egge, and an Oxe, though both have been rosted" (91-2), could be expanded into denying any proportion between unconverted strangeness and the rules of reason. Phantasie concludes this illogical portion of the masque with a dissolving passage to the utopian wonder embodied by the Court: "But vanish away, I have change to present you" (120). Most simply, this realm of alogicality is *not* discovered at all. It exists before any inductive process, artificially conducting the audience to the second term of comparison: the Court.

The second part of the masque, usually heralding the discovery of the Court, performs a disguised return to deductive demonstration. The passage from the quick changes of Phantasie to the changelessness of the Bower of Zephyrus is in fact a deduction from prior principles, the sort of conventional knowledge the Court is always associated with. Wonder, a character, spells out the utopian peace of the Court, rhetorically asking if this spectacle grows out from "the wealth of Nature here, or Art" (142). The existence of this verdant paradise of mythological deities points to a syllogistic structure, equating Britain with the Blessed Islands where Zephyrus continuously blows: "I have not seene the place could more surprize, / It looks (me thinkes) like one of natures eyes, / Or her whole bodie set in art? Behold!" (159-61).

Europe has turned into the New World, prompting the beholder to experience wonder as the deduction of the identity between this Court and the Utopian paradise. As wonder is experienced because of this identity, rather than of the successful conversion of strangeness, one also understands why the verbal grotesque of Phantasie is defeated by the apparition of this courtly paradise. Deduction does not need any first fruits, but rather eternal fruits, which find their earthly embodiment in the Court of England. Nor is Nature investigated at all. Within this context of messianic regeneration ("the ayre so sudden cleares, /And all things in a moment turne so milde," 174-5), related to both the Golden

Age and its adaptations in the travel narratives, does reside the main actor/spectator of the masque, the King, "whose presence maketh this perpetuall *Spring*" (202).

In a hermeneutic twist from induction to deduction, Jonson transforms the ritual of discovery of the Old World into a parody of the European version of the dialectic travel engaged by the Indians, with the result of estranging the King. Whereas Pocahontas had been reinstated in her princely status at the end of her conversion to European dialectic and religion, this new version of the English Sun-King has made him almost a savage. Divine attribution it might well be, but in a dangerous similarity with the heathenish worship enacted by Indians.

Apart from estranging the American natives into the receding depths of paganism, a complementary attitude characterized them as potential European dialecticians, whose reasoning was susceptible of improvement. Conversion could be both religious and philosophical. For the American native did imply a double dialectic argument: induction, both a powerful means the explorer uses to give meaning to the unknown, and a synonym for discovery, also informed the way Europeans represented real and fictional Indians, whose paganism was decoded as incorrect reasoning. Yet this utilitarian survival of induction could also transform the European audience of the Jonson masques into a Pocahontas figure, an inductive thinker who is patronizingly led to recognize the splendor of the Court and thus the triumph of didactic deduction, hailing the European King's rule over knowledge. The Aristotelian "cannibalizing" of the natives reversed the same idea of barbarity which Montaigne had given over to Europe and expanded instead upon the logical failure that Purchas (1625, 1774) detected in Tomocomo, an inconvertible Indian: a "blasphemer of what he knew not," Tomocomo "is said also to haue set up with notches on a stick the numbers of men bein sent to see and signifie the truth of the multitudes reported to his Master. But his arithmetique soon failed."

5
The Likes of Viola

Never met a wise man
If so it's a woman
—Nirvana, "Territorial Pissings"

In the *Histoires Tragicques*, Belleforest (1578, 4:61, 211, 219-20) reports a close analogue to the main plot of *Twelfth Night*. Lactance envoys Romule, his page, to Catelle, the object of his love. Should it be some surprise that Catelle falls in love with the messenger instead? She rather bends her eye on the speaker and his *naïfue beauté* than lend her ear to his words. But the most interesting part is the origin of the disguise. For Romule is in fact a girl, Nicole, who chanced to hear that Lactance, her love, was bemoaning the loss of his page, to whom she uncannily bears similarity. Since Lactance is looking for somebody else like him (*vn semblable*), Nicole promptly changes dress. Belleforest's generalizing comment puts paid to all these misapprehensions as the logical fallacies of lovers: the more violent and sudden they are, the more volatile they prove, ready to be erased from memory as soon as the first object disappears from sight—"est effacee leur trace en la memoire dès que lon en perd le premier obiet." These fallacies proceed from a great imperfection in the judgment of the choice of what is truly profitable for us, as well as from the great inconstancy that often accompanies lovers.

To the inherent fallacy of lovers, the simultaneous presence of twins on the stage offers an iconic foil: the intricacies of love resemble those mistakes in the effort to exercise one's skills in judgment. One cannot but raise questions about the first object. In Plautus's *Menaechmuses*, interrogation dots the reconstruction of the past.[1] Not even the twins' mother could distinguish the *forma simili pueri* (19). Both brothers and their fellows are compelled to proceed by the dialectic habit of interrogation. The most poignant questions overlap with the dénouement of the two twins. Messenio ponders all the signs lavished by their mirrorlike similarity (*speculum tuum*, 1062), eventually concluding for the coincidence of all the indicia (*optime usque adhuc conveniunt signa*, 1110). The encounter between one twin and his alleged wife provides an equally revealing instance. Interrogation evokes the construction of identity as a progression between different personal selves (652-3):

Menaechmus. . . . Quis is Menaechumst?	
Matrona.	Tu istic, inquam.
Menaechmus.	Egone?
Matrona.	Tu.
Menaechmus.	Quis arguit?

Quis arguit? The mood of constant interrogation also resonates in *The Comedy of Errors,* Shakespeare's closest adaptation of Plautus. The logical faculty of arguing identity by interrogation extends, however, not only to the two couples of twins, but also to almost any character.[2] A soundly theatrical reason is that stichomythia cracks jokes like the one on monstrous Nell. What is she? "A very reverend body; ay, such a one as a man may not speak of, without he say "sir-reverence" (*ERR* 3.2.88-9). In fact, the separation of the two twins sparks off the quest for the pristine unity, which is to be negotiated through similar appearances. Relying on the general classes, characters have to reach the individual—their former husband, brother, or servant. The similarity between the two couples of twins describes every character by quibbles. An apparently innocuous volley of questions and answers immediately before the Nell passage unveils a deeper philosophical nuance:

Syr. Dro.	Do you know me sir? Am I Dromio? Am I your man? Am I myself?
Syr. Ant.	Thou art Dromio, thou art my man, thou art thyself.
Syr. Dro.	I am an ass, I am a woman's man, and besides himself.
	(3.2.72-7)

The passage recalls Agricola's definition of *genus* in his treatise on dialectic (1539, 1.5). Genus is the general predicate of all the species for instance referring to "animal": "Genus est quod de pluribus specie differentibus in quid est praedicatur." The good reasoner will therefore ask for instance: What is man? What is the ass? What is the bull? And the answer is: animal (the genus).[3]

The lovers' fallacies entail a similar game of contraries, a problem that could be solved by small-time logic. Lever (1573) defined the "disagreeable wordes" as those "which cannot be coupled and ioyned together in a true & perfect yeasay"; they are either "differing wordes, or gainsettes." The former are "those whereof one differeth from many, in lyke manner and sort," whereas the latter "are two disagreeable words whereof the one so setteth foote against the other, as against no other thyng in like sort: in so much that neither the one can be affirmed of the other: neither they both of any third thing, at one time, and in one respecte." Considering the concomitance of these pairs, Lever claims: "those things are most properly sayd to bee at once, which are doone, or haue their beeing, bothe at one tyme." Lever continues that in nature "those things are sayd to be at once, which are suche as the beeing of the one, followeth upon the being of the other, and yet neyther of them cause of others beeing." Viola and Sebastian would have been a case in point, for "twinnes are bothe at once" (53, 58).

Impossibly transported into the audience of *Twelfth Night* some forty-five years after, Lever would have probably braced up his dialectical skills to sort out the questions prompted by the fallacies happening in Illyria. For *Twelfth Night* raises a dialectic problem: how does one get from similarity to identity and thus ascertain the identities of all individuals?

In the midst of his disquisitions on the fabric of the universe and its incessant change, Giordano Bruno (1973, 62:11) takes Ramus to task as "un francese arcipedante." Ramus also makes a dramatically different appearance in Marlowe's *Massacre of Paris* as one of the martyrs of St. Bartholomew Night. Arguably, Aristotelian and Ramist rhetoric would have offered nice leverage for any dialectical task.[4] I will focus on the dialectical implications of similarity in *Twelfth Night*, arguing the interpretation of sexual ambiguity in the wider class of the *genus* as an ampler means of allotting and thus construing individual identity.

Plato defined the sophist through a series of further divisions (*dieresis*), one of which verged on the comparison with the merchant we met earlier on.[5] For Plato distinguishes between "true nature" (*ti estin*), and the *eidos* through a method of dieresis, where "the definition of an *eidos* must consist of correctly assigned other *eide* and correctly chosen *differentiae specificae*" (Solmsen 1968, 51).

In his critique of Plato, Aristotle defined dialectic as the art of reaching a conclusion by means of sorting out the elements offered by opinion.[6] It consists of making questions about alternatives, whereas scientific propositions argue one position only (*Prior Analytics* 1.1.24a23-7). And it is a means used both to discuss the general principles of all sciences and to validate common opinion (*Topica* 1.2.101a31-4).[7] Aristotle thus introduces a distinction between formal and dialectic syllogism. Whereas the former deduces its necessary conclusion from the given elements, the latter is drawn from elements based on those generally accepted opinions that the majority or the wise recognize as such (*Topica* 1.1.100b21-3). A dialectic proposition is a question based on such elements, as they are proper of each art (*Topica* 1.10.104a8-10).

Although differing from demonstrative science, dialectic must ultimately judge the external objects, assess their mutual relations and hence argue their identities and similarity according to their genus, species, and difference. Thus a particular man is included in the species called "man," and the species in the genus called "animal" (*Categories* 5.2a6-8). Now, all dialectical inquiry indicates a genus, a peculiarity or an accident (*Topica* 1.4.101b16-7). All objects can be ultimately brought to the division into these elements (Thompson 1975, 21-3). Definition indicates the objective individual essence, whereas "peculiarity" (property) is what belongs only to that subject. Genus is defined as

> [T]hat which is predicated in the category of essence of several things which differ in kind. Predicates in the category of essence may be described as such things as are fittingly contained in the reply of one who has been asked "What is the object before you?" For example, in the case of man, if someone is asked what the object before him is, it is fitting for him to say "An animal." The question whether one thing is in the same genus as another thing or in a different one, is also a "generic" question. (*Topica* 1.5.102a32-8)

Any time we consider a given object, we have first to ponder all the homogeneous objects and then check if that genus can be predicated of some of them. Genus can in fact be predicated of all the objects belonging to the same species, as Aristotle notes in complying with the "whole/part" structure that will surge flamboyantly in Ramus: the species partake of the genera, while the opposite is not true, since the species admit the definition of the genus (4.1.121a12-4).[8]

Genus must in fact separate the object from those belonging to other genera, whereas difference must separate it from the objects within the same genus. The nature of what is to be defined is mainly indicated by the genus, for Aristotle uses "partake" (*metechein*) to describe the relation of species to genus but not that of species to difference; it follows that questions about the nature of the subject will be more suitably answered by offering the genus, rather than the difference (Evans 1977, 109, 112-3). Therefore, genus is prominent in each definition.[9]

Similarity (*homoiotes*) is one of the means of assessing genus and species. Alongside considering the several meanings of an object and discovering the differences, Aristotle indicates the investigation of similarities as a means of forming dialectical syllogisms (*Topica* 1.13.105a24-5). Checking the differences between two objects will show that they are not the same object, and that a syllogism on identity and alterity can be allowed. Aristotle is thinking of general, founding terms insofar as they can be argued starting from single, real objects. These observations are useful for inductive discourses: it is easier to get to universality by means of induction based on single cases that are alike. Similarity contributes to creating syllogisms based on a hypothesis, since what is applied to one object can be applied also to those that are alike. Thus a syllogism will be correct when its three terms are drawn from the same genus (Thompson 1975, 19). Similarity also enables defining expressions, thereby implying the definition of genus: provided that we can see, in each case, what is still identical, we will be able to identify the genus in which to place the subject we are discussing (*Topica* 1.18.108b20-3). Similarity helps define genus. The second practical step is considering objects that may be argued to belong to the same genus or to different genera by dint of checking their similarity in terms of opposites. Aristotle identifies four forms of opposites (*Categories* 10.11b15-20): (1) correlatives (father/son); (2) contraries (black/white); (3) privatives/positives (sight/blindness); (4) affirmatives/negatives.

Let us now consider the causes for similarity in external objects. One first reason for similarity is that many senses can be predicated of an object. On a sensory level, moreover, objects that have the same species produce the same type of sensation. But then many opposites can allow for a middle term that is not identical to either: between a clear and an obscure voice, one has for instance "harsh." Aristotle's dialectical inquiry sorts out the possible predicates for the opposites, their possible middle terms, and thereupon argues their genus and species. One meaning can thus have many middle terms, whereas the opposite may have only one; the genera of the objects that are indicated by the same name may be different, and not reciprocally subordinated; their relationship may be comparison, synonymy or similarity (*Topica* 1.15.107a18-20).

Even though dialectic is a means both of constructing the other arts and of always having one's say in the field of opinion, this kind of inquiry requires a factual comparison between real (albeit not necessarily material) objects: "The discovery of differences is useful both for reasonings about sameness and difference, and also for the recognition of what some particular thing is. . . . For when we have discovered a difference of some kind or other between the subjects under discussion, we shall have shown that they are not the same" (1.18.108a38-108b1, 108b2-4). Far from being solely a theoretical task, dialectic based on similarity implies the close scrutiny of the objects: if something is (or is *not*) true of one of the like things, it will be true (or it will *not* be true) also for the others (2.10.114b29-33). Another stress on practical observation comes from the injunction to consider the consequences especially when two objects, very similar to one another, do not admit any superiority in the one over the other (3.2.117a5-8). As is made clear by the example of colors, which admit many nuances between black and white, Aristotle is adamant that the notion of contraries does not necessarily imply a strict dichotomy. The degrees of similarity, preferably judged by means of the predicates that can be made of the objects, introduce the many-tiered assessment of similarity, focused on the essence within the genus rather than on quantitative differences or relations of reciprocal inclusion—the very factors that informed Ramus's indictment of Aristotelian dialectic.

Ramus (1555, 1) attacked Aristotle's bisection of dialectic into one discipline for science and another for opinion. For him, dialectic is one and only discipline for the apprehension of all things, "vne & mesme doctrine pour aperceuoir toutes choses."[10] Stressing the independence from the ancients, Ramus envisages philosophy as a universal instrument of invention (*tous les moyens d'inventer toutes choses*, 4).[11] He also defines dialectic as the art of good discussion and reasoning on any subject, "art de bien disputer & raisoner de quelque chose que ce soit," which was in fact the traditional definition of logic.[12]

Ramus's most famous innovation was his dichotomizing habit. He has dialectic consist of *inventio* and *dispositio*, the first two parts of rhetoric: "la premiere declaire les parties separées, dont toute sentence est composée: la deuziesme monstre les manieres & especes de les disposer" (5). Subsequently, any part of dialectic is split up into two other parts, each of which can be subdivided into two other parts, and so forth. Argument, for instance, is artificial or inartificial (authorities and witnesses): artificial is what makes faith (the rhetorical *fides*) of itself and its nature; it can be "premier ou issu du premier"; the *premier* can be "simple & non issu d'ailleurs," and so on. One possible division concerns the first arguments, which can have four species (5-6): (1) *Causes & effectz*; (2) *Subiectz & adioinctz*; (3) *Opposez* (*contraires* [*affirmez, relatifz, adverses, niez, priuans, contredisantz*] / *repugnantz*); (4) *Comparez* (*quantité* [*pareilz, impareil, moins,* plus] / *qualité* [*semblables/dissemblables*]. *Effect* is everything that descends from the causes—quite so (6-22). As to the second type (*subject/adjunct*), the former *est à qui quelque chose est adioincte*, and the latter is *la chose adioincte* (22-7).[13]

The third and four types are more relevant to my inquiry. The main difference consists in whether we can oppose them by a two-only ratio or by a more-than-two ratio. The third type (*opposez*) includes those that cannot be predicated of one and the same thing in the same time and manner. They are equally notorious by their nature, and yet their juxtaposition makes each one of them more clearly perceivable (27-8). Ramus underscores the monodic, reciprocal relation between contraries, for they are opposed one to one, and can receive only one negation (32). On the other hand, the *opposez* can be *repugnantz*, which greatly differ one against all the others (*vn à plusieurs*), as is the case with the colors green and red in the black/white spectrum (27-33).

The fourth type (*comparez*) offers Ramus's treatment of similarity (*similitudo*) and genus. They are defined as things mutually compared, "choses conferées l'vne auec l'autre." This one-to-many comparison can be performed according to two species, respectively focusing on quantity and on quality. As to the former, in Ramus's distinctive usage quantity is chiefly examined through literary similes, rather than numerical notions. Thus, the *pareilz* stand for a same quantity, as in literary similes, whereas the *impareilz* can be either *moins*, when the less difficult object is explained by the more difficult one, or *plus,* when the more difficult object is explained by the less difficult one (33-40).

The *comparez* by reason of quality are to be gauged by similarity and dissimilarity (*similitude & dissimilitude*, 40-1). *Semblables* are those objects that have the same quality (*desquelz est vne mesme qualité*). This *marque de similitude* can be more or less evident, and the similitude (or simile, in Ramus's usage) can be more or less amply explained on both parts of the figure. Analogously, the *dissemblables* are those objects that have a different quality: for instance, philosophy is different from the other arts, and Ulysses was not handsome, but persuasive (44-5). Ramus's general practice of instancing his dialectical points with passages taken from orators and poets directly informs his concept of dialectic: all the examples he offers for the *semblables* are *similitudes feinctes,* that is, parables, fables and other literary figures (41-4). Similarity is not grasped in the predicates that can be attributed to the objects, or in the close scrutiny of their behavior, essences, effects and so on, as in Aristotle, but rather as a rhetorical representation and description of things.

Ramus's concept of similarity is explicitly adamant in his quantitative, whole/part conception of genus and species. After having described the first arguments, he proceeds to the concatenation of phrases and sentences that derive from them in discourse. Here one has *raison du nom* (when some reason derives from the name itself), *distribution* (the distinction of the whole in its parts), and *definition* (*raison, qui declaire proprement le propos ce qu'il est,* 46-50, 58-60).

Genus and species are discussed in the section devoted to the *distribution par les effectz.* To Ramus, genus is the plurality of things with similar essence, or the similar essence of diverse things, while the species is a part of the genus: "Genre est pluralité de choses semblables en essence, ou essence semblable de plusieurs choses: Espece est partie du genre" (50). Thus the genus "animal" boasts a plurality of objects that are alike in nature and in essence. Ramus also argues that one can go directly from the genus to the individual, the species that has no further subdivisions—"espece specialissime, qui n'a nulles especes inferieures: ce qui est appellé en l'eschole indiuidu, comme n'ayant especes esquelles puisse estre diuisé." Genus and species are the symbols of causes and effects. Briefly, genus contains the common causes of its species, whereas the species contain the effects of their genus (51-2).[14] From the qualitative approach, the study of the *essence semblable de plusieurs choses* veers towards a quantitative, inclusive nature. The genus-species apparatus substantiates any intellectual movement, and all dialectical relationships are reduced to genus and species, which are conceived in quantitative terms: genus refers to what is universal, and species to singulars.

The quantitative scope of Ramus's dialectic also informs his famous method, a disposition where several things are placed according to a descending or ascending order of notoriety. When it is arranged as a *methode de nature*, all that is more absolutely evident and notorious is placed up front, such as cause and effects, or genus and species, in a movement from the very general to the very special. This method pertains to arts and sciences: one proceeds from the antecedent, clear things towards illustrating the most obscure, unknown ones. All true doctrines and sciences have to proceed "par les choses generalles, & descendre degrez à degrez aux specialles," as in a golden chain. Quoting Plato, Ramus notes that although the arts were found and invented by the induction of particular things into the general things (*l'induction des choses specialles en montant aux choses generalles*), nonetheless they have to be deduced contrariwise by descending from the sovereign genus to the multitude of infinite species (119-22).[15]

To sum up, similarity, for Ramus, is first of all an inductive return to the most general genus. As such, it is only a part of the genus/species inclusive, quantitative relation, which dovetails with the constant inclusion of individuals into more general categories of which they are the simplest species. This method jars with the Aristotelian search for predicates and middle term, where similarity is a relation to be gauged in terms of difference and essence along a continuum that does not necessarily argue strict dichotomy. Aristotle posits in fact the recognition of differences and essence as prior to any construction of species and genera.

The two hermeneutic paths hereby implied allow for a different consideration of similarity between objects. The Aristotelian dialectician will try to assess the presence of an essence, quality, difference that marks different genera or, alternatively, different species within the same genus. Ramus's method, on the other hand, will preferably posit a *genre souuerain*, whose filiations are the real objects one has to decode through graduations of notoriety and evidence and the apt distribution of causes and effects.

Two images convey the hiatus between the two types of dialectic. For Aristotle, the ultimate aim of his dialectic was the assessment of identity, which can be referred either to number, species or genus. Now the "generic sameness" exists among the objects that fall under the same genus. Aristotle illustrates it with an example close to the image of the two similar drops in the *Comedy of Errors*:

> For all such things seem to be akin and similar to one another; for any water is said to be specifically the same as any other water because it has a certain similarity to it, and water from the same fountain differs in

no other respect than in its more striking degree of similarity; and so we do not distinguish it from the things called in any sense the same as belonging to one species. (*Topica* 1.7.103a18-23)

On the other hand, Ramus (1555, 136) reprised the problem of general knowledge, which is granted to humankind, and particular knowledge, where humankind can err. In his reply to Aristotle's dilemma, Ramus argues that, even if humankind completely ignored how to call things, this does not imply that it cannot carry out research and achieve the related invention, for it has been naturally imbued with the power of general knowledge. The task of recognizing the individual species and inventing them will be facilitated when the proper dialectician will have before his eyes the art of inventing by universal genera, as in a mirror which represents all universal images of all things, "quand il aura deuant les yeux l'art d'inuenter par ces genres vniverselz, comme quelque mirouër, luy representant les images vniuerselles & generalles de toutes choses" (69).

The characters of *Twelfth Night* echo these two dialectical methods while trying to interpret similarity and its ensuing fallacies. Similarity and its errors can be decoded either through Aristotle's image of the source or through Ramus's image of the mirror. To this inquiry, Viola and all the other characters of *Twelfth Night* add the equivocating essence of sexual identity.

Having defined as "simultaneous" those objects whose generation takes place in the same time, Aristotle applies the expression "simultaneous in nature" to those things where, while the existence of either implies that of the other, neither is the cause of the other—for instance, double and half (*Categories* 13.14b28-30). Yet also the objects that derive from the same genus can be called simultaneous in nature. The first mark of the similarity between the Shakespearean twins is their simultaneous generation, further complicated by the cleavage of the pair.

A similar fate awaits Viola, stranded on Illyria after the splitting of the ship. The comedy begins in the prevailing interrogatory mood of dialectical contentions, directed towards the identification of the objects. A Ramist love for description and definition rules Viola's first moves in Illyria:

Viola.	Who governs here?
Captain.	A noble duke, in nature as in name.

(*TN* 1.2.24-5)

Despite the eclipse of the twin pair, Viola still practices the descent from the genus to the individual, implied by her usage of the description. Orsino is introduced through the mention of his genus ("in nature") and then the individuality as conveyed by his name. An analogous Ramist attitude surfaces in the lines introducing Olivia. What's she?, asks Viola—"A virtuous maid, the daughter of a count / That died some twelvemonth since," then left in the protection of her brother, "Who shortly also died; for whose dear love / (They say) she hath abjur'd the company / And sight of men" (36-7, 39-41).

At this point of the comedy, individuals are still decoded by means of their causes, effects and circumstances and construed as the species of different genera, as the melancholic, illuminated Duke and the mourning lady. The Ramist belief in genera is also apparent in Viola's ensuing decision to act as a page and commingle her visual attire with her musical skills; the suppression of her former sexual identity complies with the genus of the empty slot she is about to occupy, the eunuch, "for I can sing, / And speak to him in many sorts of music" (57-8).

The Ramist belief in the mirror of universal genera interprets even crossdressed. Mentioning her/his potential similarity to a woman, Orsino describes Viola by means of similes (Ramus's *similitudines*) that could be best applied to another genus/species, underscoring the belief in the genus-species descent: "Thy small pipe / Is as the maiden's organ, shrill and sound, / And all is semblative a woman's part" (1.4.32-4). The similarity refers to the cluster of all these attributes, which can be decoded *specie Ramista* as ambiguously referring to different genera. Orsino is not speaking in terms of difference, but of different genera: the concept of "semblative" recalls the similarity between causes and effects, duly explained by referring either to the genus of the effeminate page or to that of woman. The reflection between the two genders, resting on the potential middle term of the transvestite page, evokes rather the dialectic between individuals (the species of different genera) than between the two sexes. Following this pattern, Viola's uncertain status strikes a conciliatory note between two possible aggregations of elements, or middle terms, within the male genus, as is clear in the pun-ridden dialogue between Olivia and Malvolio:

Olivia.	What kind o' man is he?
Malvolio.	Why, of mankind.
Olivia.	What manner of man?
Malvolio.	Of very ill manner: he'll speak with you, will you or no.
Olivia.	Of what personage and years is he?
Malvolio.	Not yet old enough for a man, nor young enough for a boy[.]

(1.5.152-9)

To Olivia's soundly dialectical interrogation, Malvolio replies by manipulating different variations within the same genus and playing down sexual ambiguity to an effect of age, hence to a species.

All these passages cherish the interpretation of individuals as discrete allotments into particular terms of larger classes. The similarity implied refers to such allocated classes of genera, and any character is gauged in the degree of compliance to a prototype. The following dialectical interplay between Viola and Olivia, resounding with frequent questions and descriptive answers, is only apparently undermined by Viola's equivocating comment on her fictional status: Are you a comedian?, asks Olivia; Viola is not, yet she is not what she plays—Are you the lady of the house?, asks Viola; Olivia is, if she does not usurp herself (183-6). Alongside underlining the metatheatrical intention of Viola's words, the rest of the dialogue conjures up the framework of identity as the one-to-one correspondence with a genus. Olivia does not usurp herself because she boasts all the attributes of the lady of the house, just as Viola is usurping a different role by being vested with the attributes of another genus. It is an ambiguity between different individuals, rather than between the genera.

From this point onwards, the Aristotelian dialectic gains the control of all the inquiries on similarity between individuals and genera. Leaving the Ramist fondness for causes and effects detected in the descriptions of the First Act, Viola investigates the equally possible alternatives of male and female roles as the result of the observation of similar objects and their similar/dissimilar consequences. She discusses her actual self not from a quantitative, causative standpoint, but rather through the qualitative consideration of essence: "As I am man, / My state is desperate for my master's love: / As I am woman . . ., / What thriftless sighs shall poor Olivia breathe?" (2.2.35-8). Viola is not arguing in terms of concrete, singular individuals (the ultimate level of Ramist species), but of different substances that have to be discerned through the observation of similarity. The apparition of Sebastian inaugurates the consideration of apparently similar individuals to be tested on their appearances, behaviors and consequences. The result is the assessment of the actual identity of the similar objects, instead of the genus-species ratio implied by the Ramist method.

Twelfth Night presents characters that are more Ramist than others. Orsino professes to be such as "all true lovers are"; women, on the other hand, "are as roses, whose fair flower / Being once display'd, doth fall that very hour" (2.4.17, 38-9). Orsino's patronizing diminishment of women is opposed by Viola's adherence to the Aristotelian tenets on similarity in terms of predicates, rather than of attributes. Viola posits a non-existing woman who allegedly received her/his favor, having Orsino's age and complexion, in a series of possible middle terms between her and Orsino. Her new method is not to start from the most notorious elements, but rather to let her desire conjure up non-existing individuals that are similar to Orsino. The dialectical ruse is a conjunction of predicates: if she can be that woman, she will be his wife. The creation of another fictional individual is a parallel to the unknown existence of Sebastian, who will come to fit in the opposed place in relation to Olivia. Truth is gained by artificial similarity (Viola and the non-existing woman) and by the clearing of the actual similarity (the two twins). In this dialectical method, differences of gender are not as important as the distance between the individual Olivia and the projection of her desire. Much like Viola's fictional sister, this "blank" may be filled by the shrewd usage of similarity: "My father had a daughter lov'd a man, / As it might be perhaps, were I a woman, / I should your lordship" (108-10).

Viola masterfully guides the other characters along her dialectic syllogisms, removing them from the compliance to Ramist genera and its safely deduced inclusions and identities. Obviously, the following exchange belies the metatheatrical interplay on the actor playing self-encapsulated parts, but then it also tries to decode the similarity between proposed identities (what Olivia would have Cesario-Viola be and what Cesario-Viola actually is):

> *Viola.*   Then think you right; I am not what I am.
> *Olivia.*   I would you were as I would have you be.
> *Viola.*   Would it be better, madam, than I am?
>
> (3.1.143-5)

Viola is not what she is because she is not the right gender. But this is a difference that can be explored along the continuum of possible identities and their related middle terms, by no means reducible to the stark male/female dichotomy. Sexual difference argues the difference between actual and ideal individuals, resisting the Ramist temptation to see individuals as mouthpieces for different species. This type of Aristotelian dialectic implies more classes, to be considered through the similarity between the objects.

Before analyzing the conclusion of the play, let me now briefly refer back to the topic of identity in Aristotle and Ramus. For Aristotle, assessing the identity between two objects means seeing if they can be both identical to another object, if their accidents can be compared, or if they belong to a same category or to a same genus. One has to investigate if some impossibility derives not only from stating that two things are the same, but also from a supposition (*Topica* 7.156b14-8). In the Ramist scheme of things, similarity intervenes between the *comparez* and is recognizable by the presence of the same quality in the two objects. The rationale is ultimately deductive: from the *genre soouerain* we can descend to all the species and finally to the individuals sharing the same quality.

The conclusion of *Twelfth Night* recapitulates the overall contest between Aristotelian dialectic (Viola) and Ramist dialectic (all the other characters). The logical place Viola has been creating as a possible lover of Olivia is filled by her brother, the same who informed the potential for errors: "[E]ven such and so / In favour was my brother, and he went / Still in this fashion, colour, ornament" (*TN* 3.4.390-2). As in Plautus and in *The Comedy of Errors,* the reaction of the confused twin is a sense of infectious madness. Sebastian ponders the possible alternatives, not realizing that his fancy is a product of the similarity created by nature and by Viola's dialectical activity:

For though my soul disputes well with my sense
That this may be some error, but no madness,
Yet doth this accident and flood of fortune
So far exceed all instance, all discourse,
That I am ready to distrust mine eyes,
And wrangle with my reason[.]

(4.3.9-14)

The Ramist insistence on causes and effects (and ensuing fallacies) prevails in the last Act, when similarity presents its most ambiguous side. Antonio lists to Orsino all the favors he has made to Sebastian, trying to advocate an identity for himself (the generous friend) and for his ungrateful fellow (5.1.75). For the Ramist characters, similarity is not even suggested. Sebastian-Viola is one single unit that entertains some strange behavior and yet cannot differ from his previous attributes.

Only Viola advocates individuality. For her, Orsino is the subject that can fill the place created by her dialectical activity, transcending all relations (Ramus's genera). Where will Cesario go? —"After him I love / More than I love these eyes, more than my life, / More, by all mores, than e'er I shall love wife" (132-4). With the simultaneous apparition of Sebastian and Viola on the stage, the dialectic of similarity can be generally recognized and applied: "One face, one voice, one habit, and two persons!" (214). Rather than the presence of the same quality, the text ends with the Aristotelian consideration of the similar objects as belonging to the same genus: "Of charity, what kin are you to me? / What countryman? What name? What parentage?" (228-9). Viola will be recognized as herself only when "each circumstance / Of place, time, fortune, do cohere" (249-50).

Viola has in fact retrieved a wider conception of genus. Peter of Spain's *Summulae logicales,* the backbone of the logic curriculum in sixteenth-century Cambridge (Green-Pedersen 1984, 125-9), had distinguished three meanings of genus: while the last definition overlapped with the usual logical definition of genus as something to which a species is subordinated (*genus cui suppositur species*), the other two meanings of genus referred to a collection of several things, related both to each other and to a *principium*, a single source (for instance, a parentage descending from a single ancestor), and the very source of each generation (father and fatherland) (Peter of Spain 1990,

2.2). For a Renaissance logician like Lever, Viola's dialectical activity could well have implied these other meanings of genus. The interplay of sexual identities evokes possible identities and creates a potential for similarity. And it is by means of assessing or twisting similarity that the individual subject can be brought into being in its palpable uniqueness and distance from conventional genera.

The Protean flow between different states of mind and expressiveness was a trademark of good acting. The famous actress Isabella Andreini was eulogized by the staunch theatre-hater Garzoni (1587, 738) for her ability in making metamorphosis of herself on stage: "Fa metamorfosi di se stessa in scena." In *Twelfth Night*, Viola's usage of the genus conveys how the subject creates his/her identity and individuality on the stage by sorting out all possible tiers of similarity. Viola creates similarity. Her usage of potential doubles and similar objects discloses the possibility of theatrical action and ultimately the recognition of different subjects, whereas the Ramist attitude of the other characters merely perpetuates the stock-in-trade conventions of unrequited love. The Aristotelian dialectic, striving to give a positive or negative answer to a formulated question, prescribed in fact a careful investigation of the objects through all the continuum of possible similarity in the effort to attain the essence underlying the doubtful quality of the accidents. To assign the essence, one has to state the genus, rather than the differentia: a description of "man" as "animal" indicates the essence more appropriately than describing him as "pedestrian" (*Topica* 1.4.128a22-6). In this sense, Aristotle (4.5.126b13-6) reprobated the dialectical practice of the kind of reasoners who, "by a process of inversion, . . . sometimes assign genus as differentia and differentia as genus, calling, for example, 'amazement' an 'excess of astonishment,' and 'belief' an 'intensification of opinion'"—ample room, indeed, for imagining the Philosopher's posthumous astonishment at the current inversive usage of "gendered" differences.

6
A Poem On the Tube

You never give me your money
You only give me your funny paper
And in the middle of negotiations you break down
—The Beatles, "You Never Give Me Your Money"

In ways quite ecstatic, both *Titus Andronicus* and the Piccadilly Line share an attentive woman and a sleeping warrior. Enticing the Moor into the umbrage of adulterous love, Tamora describes the postcoital languor "after conflict" as the place of silent obtuseness where lovers surrender to sleep in the aftermath of their amorous fights: "Curtain'd with a counsel-keeping cave, / We may, each wreathed in the other's arms, / Our pastimes done, possess a golden slumber" (*TIT* 2.3.24-7). This pastoral prelude to procreation may be coupled with the scene of amorous exhaustion depicted by Sandro Botticelli in *Venus and Mars* (1483). Probably designed for a marriage chamber, the painting stages Mars sleeping under the attentive gaze of Venus, while satyrs are toying with his armor scattered on the ground.[1] *Venus and Mars* is on permanent display at the National Gallery in London, yet I was alerted to its theme of amorous exhaustion on a Piccadilly train calling in at Holborn Station, where I noticed Mars's sleeping face on the walls covered with the magnified replica of the painting. A case for perplexity: why was Mars depicted while sleeping?

"This Extasie doth unperplex," says John Donne. Both scenes of amorous exhaustion I have summed up portray a kind of ecstasy other than modern occurrences of the term. In the music of groups such as Happy Mondays, Prodigy or Chemical Brothers, ecstasy evokes a trance sequence, whose repetition induces an intimation of absence from present reality. Instead, the Renaissance interpreted the medical and philosophical nature of sexual ecstasy as a contrast between the sudden denial of reason and its allotment into procreation theory. It is my point that the two lovers of Donne's "Extasie" see and feel the procreation of poetry in their apotheosis of utter estrangement.

Like so many other stories, the theory of sexual ecstasy began with a match made in heaven. Adam and Eve did beget their offspring without any delight (*delectatio*), which might debunk any modern conceptions of heavenly bliss. For Augustine (*De civitate Dei* 14.26, *PL* 41:434), Edenic nuptials were consummated in the placid obedience of all limbs, which responded to man's perfectly formed reason without him experiencing the sinful heat and stimulation of lust (*sine ardoris inlecebroso stimulo*).[2] As to the issue (literally) of procreation in Eden, Adam would have continued to beget his progeny without sin if he had remained obedient. Just as the earth yields its fruits without any delight, the woman would have given birth without sin (Gregory the Great, *Exp. in Ps. Poen.* 5.19.27, *PL* 79:620). Edenic nuptials were honorable and chaste, devoid of the unrestful heat of covetousness (*sine ullo inquieto ardore libidinis*), and birth was accompanied by no labors or pains (Bede?, *Quaest. in Gen. PL* 93:271). Peter Lombard (*Sententiae* 2.20, *PL* 192:692) contended that if the first couple had not sinned, carnal copulation would have occurred without any concupiscence. The pertaining limbs would have remained obedient, without experiencing any unlawful movement; just as licitly as we move other limbs, for instance raising our hand to the mouth, without feeling any libidinous heat or bodily itch (*sine ardore libidinis . . . sine aliquo pruritu carnis*). Peter was bewildered by the almost incredible fact that, even after sin, the pudenda deserved to retain the physical movement (*motum*) that is ordained and administered by chaste nuptials, for our frail condition is bent on the ruin of lust.

Feeling pleasure marks in fact the inception of becoming, and movement the beginning of death. Adam's chaste movement took place much as other limbs are naturally moved without any disturbance (*sine ulla molestia*), by the same command and movement (*nutus*) that prompts the fetus to come out and move its feet. Whereas this movement was benign and almost ordained for the ritual of desire (*quasi pro ritu voluptatis*), the violation against God's precept evinced the beginning of the movement that, jarring with the law of reason, foisted death upon our limbs (*in membris conceptae mortis habere meruerunt*, Bede?, *Quaest. super Gen. PL* 93:271).

Much as laughter was championed as the property of humankind, as we will see, a similar attention was devoted to the question why sexual ecstasy, a transgression of our pristine edenic innocence, is still the most intense pleasure on earth. Since Hippocrates, the overwhelming pleasure of sexual ecstasy was attributed to the sudden discharge of the disturbance (*taraxis*) induced by the titillation of lust and by the subsequent consummation of the intercourse. Hippocrates noted that the emission of semen is contextual with pleasure, and that the latter can be inversely used as a proof that the former is occurring. The evacuation multiplies the sense of relief commonly experienced after the disposal of obnoxious itching and titillation caused by the presence of hot, dry humors.[3]

Aristotle's explanation of the intense pleasure (*hedone*) of sex rebuts the theory that semen is formed from a selection of humors coming from all parts of the body, whose simultaneous discharge would account for the intensity of the pleasure: the actual cause is the violent stimulation, which explains why those who often have intercourses receive less pleasure from it (*Generation of Animals* 1.18.723b35-724a3). Even though only a small quantity of semen is emitted, the great exhaustion that follows proves that semen is a residue, the final product of the nourishment received by the body (1.18.729a8-12). Aristotle also observes that man and some animals, to emit semen, must hold their breath (1.20.728a10-12).[4] This tallies with his distinction between the two genders. Man is responsible for the *dynamis* and the *kinesis*, providing the form and the principle of the movement, while woman provides the material. The pleasure accompanying copulation is due to the fact that man not only emits semen, but also *pneuma*, which contains the male form and the principle of movement proper to soul, a "hot" substance, or foam-like stuff, analogous to the element belonging to the stars (2.3.736b35-737a1).

Ecstasy procreates the future. The union between ecstasy and procreation is a veritable miracle of providential pleasure and physiological cogency. As the means chosen by Nature for the multiplication of the individuals, ecstasy pricks animals into procreation, titillating them with an extreme desire toward mating and the attendant greatness of pleasure: "Partant Nature a voulu que les animaux fussent aiguillonez d'une ardeur & enuie extreme de se coupler ensemble, & qu'à ce desir fust conioincte une grande & chatoüilleuse volupté." Even if the individuals were not endowed with reason, they would be goaded into procreation by the lure of sexual pleasure, "par l'aiguillon du plaisir." To this end, the genitalia are regaled with "un grand sentiment plus aigu & vif qu'à nulle autre partie." The pleasure is caused by the discharge of a serous humor (*une petite acrimonie piquante, & aiguillonante*), whose irritating quality, producing great disturbance, provokes the parts into the discharge of a great quantity of spirits, hence the copious pleasure associated with coitus, "accompagnee de grande quantité d'esprits qui s'eschaussent & desirent à sortir dehors" (Paré 1598, 911-2).[5]

The procreative aim of ecstasy surpasses the shamefulness of the coitus. The genitalia are imbued with the *principium generationis*, an inseparable libido that eggs animals into multiplying themselves (Bartholomeus Anglicus 1601, 5.48:205). Constantine the African argued that God created the procreative parts for the animal genera to exist; to this end He attributed them a natural virtue from which great delight might ensue (*virtutem indidit naturalem ex qua multum delectari posse*), and regaled coitus with inseparable delight; this pleasure deters the otherwise natural abomination of coitus to forestall the continuation of the species (Jacquert and Thomasset 1985, 111 n. 2). For Philo of Alexandria, pleasure recapitulates the beginning of creation: the species are made "sharers of eternal existence," as God "both led on the beginning speedily towards the end, and made the end to retrace its way back to the beginning" (Horton 1991, 65). Pleasure prefigures the future species and anticipates what is not there yet.

The salience of procreation bloomed up in Renaissance Neoplatonism and in its attendant theory of perfect love. According to Plato (*Phaedrus* 250E-251A), the non-initiated can fail to recognize the absolute beauty of the other world "when he sees its namesake here, and so he does not revere it when he looks upon it, but gives himself to pleasure and like a beast proceeds to lust and begetting."[6] The recognition of celestial beauty can erroneously identify the cause of the appetite for coitus in the loved body. For Pico (1994, 24:68), our senses see the genesis of beauty in the body, and brutes therefore recognize coitus as the end of love: "El fine dello Amore di tutti e' bruti è il coito." Reason, on the other hand, follows the inverse method and sees in the body the corrupted nature of true beauty: the separation from bodily beauty extols human dignity—"quanto più da quello corpo si separa, e in sé si considera, tanto più ha della tua natura e propria dignità e presentia." This consideration sets apart two Venuses, as described by Ficino (1973, 6.7-8, 11). The spiritual Venus prompts love to cogitate divine beauty (*a cogitare la divina Bellezza*), while the mundane Venus has love procreate beauty in the same matter of the world (*a generare la bellezza medesima nella materia del Mondo*). Thus, procreation is necessary and honest like the pursuit of truth, and in its status as a divine thing it also finds its accomplishment in beautiful subjects. It is divine, for it makes mortal things similar to divine ones by the act of continuing them: "Fa le cose mortali nel continuare simili alle divine."[7] Nature instilled in human beings the desire to procreate things similar to themselves, both corporal offspring like children and spiritual progeny like poems (Nobili 1895, 15v). The desire of procreation was given to animals as a hope of personal immortality, argues Patrizi (1963, 3:127). For Tullia d'Aragona (1975, 222), the man who simply pursues pleasure and procreation, as soon as he has reached satisfaction, will desist from his motion and will no longer love—"cessa dal moto e non ama più."

Even love is affected by generation. Leo the Jew (1929, 1:51) saw in perfect love a principle of mutual procreation. The momentum of love makes us desire the spiritual and corporeal union: while the first type of love is the son of desire, this second type is its own father and actual generator. When it attains the desired object and the amorous acts performed by the body have ended, love does not subside, unlike appetite or desire, which cease in their determined, local natures.

Perfect love ultimately transcends the inherent limit prescribed by Nature for those corporal acts, "il limite terminato che la natura ha posto in quelli tali atti."

"An albino—A mosquito—My libido—A denial." As in Kurt Cobain's lines, ecstasy is also a denial, an absence of consciousness and speech.

Ecstasy naturally recalls sleep and the loss of consciousness. Aristotle wondered why semen is more likely to be emitted in sleep by the tired and by the consumptive, surmising that, hot being the nature of semen, those who are hot and moist are more likely to produce the impulse from the inside needed by the body (*Problems* 5.31.884a). Conti (1567, 4.3:92v) reported that Genius, the benign god of generation and one of the two demons that continuously escort us (Starnes 1964), alternatively persuading and dissuading us as the moderator of our will, was sired by Jupiter in his union with Earth; yet that happened without any *amplexus*, for Jupiter's semen was shed on Earth in his sleep (*in terram per somnum profuso*).

The union between ecstasy and sleep also recurred in Aquinas's interpretation of the creation of woman. Why was Eve created from Adam's rib? The image signifies the social union of man and woman, for woman was assumed neither to use authority over man (as she was not formed from his head) or to be subject to his contempt (as she was not formed from his feet). The *socialis coniunctio* was also a sacrament, and thus it flowed from the side of Christ sleeping on the Cross (*ST* 1.92.3). In a more practical way, Joubert (1989, 113) maintained that one should not know one woman before going to sleep, since the loss of spirits caused by the coitus would badly conjoin with our tiredness. In fact, the most appropriate time is after the first sleep, when one has replenished the spirits dissipated by wakefulness, and the body has received its nourishment. We have to sleep if we want to prevent our bodies from decay. After the act, one is advised to sleep a little, in order not to suffer loss upon loss of spirits.

Another component of the theory of ecstasy, the question whether it is the man or the woman who experiences the most intense pleasure, also imports on the extreme wake of conscience caused by ecstasy. Who gains the upper hand in love? For Hippocrates (1981, 4.1, 7.472-6 Li.), the man feels a more poignant pleasure for his emission occurs more suddenly, as a result of a more violent disturbance than the woman's. Castro (1603, 61) thus reprised the question of man's primacy in sexual pleasure, a point denied both by Tiresia in Ovid and by Avicenna: man's pleasure is more intense, for his emission is more violent and he dwells less on the coitus—"in coitu moratur minus."

Ecstasy dislodges reason from its sway over human life. In his study on Erasmus's *Praise of Folly*, Screech (1980, 51) reconstructed the progression of *ekstasis* from the original sense of displacing or casting down a thing from its normal place or state to "a form of acute distraction, brought on by a strong emotion such as terror or astonishment." Is that permanent, yet? Augustine (*De civitate Dei* 14.16, *PL* 41:424) saw in the acme of post-lapsarian *libido* the temporary convulsion of the inhuman. Lust asserts its rule over all the body, also from within, producing a pleasure still unsurpassed. As a result, man experiences an almost total eclipse of acumen and, as it were, sentinel alertness—"extremum paene omnis acies et quasi vigilia cogitationis obruatur." Vives's comment on this passage recalled that Hippocrates had compared sexual ecstasy to a little epilepsy: man in the grips of pleasure is "voyd of all the functions of soule, and reason as long as delight lasted" (Smith 1985, 13).

Aquinas offered, as one might expect, a detailed interpretation of this point. In coitus man almost becomes like the beast because of the vehement delight (*propter vehementiam delectationis*). Now man was equated with beasts because of his sin: despite his position of honor, he failed to understand: therefore some argue that coitus was not present before the original sin. Aquinas's reply to this argument is that, as nothing can be void in God's creation, even if man had not sinned the intercourse would have occurred with the ordained distinction of the two genders (*ST* 1.98.2). As to the legitimacy of procreation, Aquinas contends that, even though procreation is a natural inclination, it is impossible to say whether the act is universally unlawful, as it does not admit of any virtuous moderation. An argument claims that even a lawful occupation about inferior things distracts our soul, so much so that it cannot achieve the union with God. And carnal occupation does distract man from God, as the mind is detained by intense delight. In his reply, Aquinas avers that the delectations coming from acts of reason (*actus rationis*) do not hinder reason. Neither do they corrupt prudence. But the extraneous (*extraneae*) pleasures, such as the pleasures of the body, do hinder the use of reason by their contrariety. Now sexual pleasure, while imbued with an amount of satisfaction that might be accommodated by virtuous reason, does in fact hinder the use of reason because of the attendant bodily change (*corporalem transmutationem*). While moral malice may be excluded, ecstasy is a fettering of reason (*ligamentum rationis*) whose malice derives from the original sin. Yet it is not morally evil per se, much as sleep, another fettering of reason, is not evil if used according to reason (*ST* 1-2.34.1 ad 1).

As a denial of reason, ecstasy also thwarts speech. We have seen that, for Aristotle, man has to hold his breath to eject his semen. Silence befits this scene. Another difference between man and brutes was that the former—allegedly—remains silent during the coitus. According to Augustine (*De civitate Dei* 14.18, *PL* 41:426), man is ashamed of these acts, and that is why he always commits them in secret. The sense of shame in sexual intercourse persists even in marital coitus: lawful it may well be, yet why should even a married couple want to seek a secret chamber with no witnesses? Albert the Great claimed that man arms himself in silence and secret as if he were going to war. Huarte (1594, 264) analogously reported the visual distaste for the genitalia evidenced by Aristotle, as well as its impediment of bare mention: "Nature hath framed these parts with such diligence and carefulnesse, and for an end of such importance, as the immortalising of mankind, and yet the wiser a man is, the more he groweth in dislike to behold or heare them spoken of." Yet Huarte rebutted Aristotle's opinion that "the lust of venerous acts, floweth from excesse, and is token of abundance"; in fact, "a man not only shameth to manifest the desire he carrieth to companie with a woman, but also to eat, to drinke, and to sleepe, and if a will take him to send foorth anie excrement, he dares not say it or do it, but with cumber & shame fastnesse, and so gets him to some secret place out of sight" (265).

Not only was this silence attributed to decency or to the attractiveness of the secret. Owing to the intense pleasure, the heart was thought to be constricted and man made silent, as if conquered by fear. Postcoital pusillanimity derives from this congealment of spirits (Jacquert and Thomasset 1985, 114 n. 3). This state corresponds to the *languor naturae*, an emotion similar to the loss of control experienced after the Fall (Baldwin 1994, 119). In this sense, Bembo (1991, 11v-12r) read a latent paronomasia in love (*amore*) and sourness (*amaro*) in his harsh attack upon mundane love: generated in our minds by lust and otium, love is nurtured by vain thoughts (*nelle nostre menti procreato*). And this imbalance had been occasioned by a surplus of words. *The Prose Salernitan Questions* defined coitus as the union of man and woman, accompanied by *operis multa comitante delectatione*. But why was sexual pleasure the greatest of all? Apart from the physiological notions of the release of humors through the most sensitive parts of the body and from the psychological pleasures deriving from the memory of the *delectatio,* it was maintained that as soon as Adam, who originally inhabited a temperate body, heard the serpent's words through Eve, he began to grow anxious in his soul and thus to chase immoderate things (Baldwin 1994, 127-8).

Discussing the topic of sexual fulfillment in the Troubadours, Paden (1979, 72) singled out a reference to *joy* that might denote sexual satisfaction, instead of the usual emotional state of the unrequited lover (Miraval 1971). In Renaissance literature, such a covert translation was hardly rare. The silence of ecstasy is contrasted by verbal abundance, by the display of words that might win out the loved one. A common ruse for effective procreation suggested by French writers was that the woman ought to be warmed up by cajoling words, for instance some pleasant love stories told by the nurse, as well as actual chafing: "Que la servante de l'espouse luy lise quelque plaisante histoire d'amour, . . . qu'elle luy frotte, le plus mignardement qu'il se pourra avec la main la matrice, jusques à temps qu'elle commence à sentir quelque petit feu et plaisir" (Liébault 1649, 251-2). The best moment for procreation obtains when the woman abandons verbal communication (*comme en bégayant*, Villeneuve 1512, 42; Laurent 1989, 19-20). Paré (1598, 914) explicitly invites the husband to perform verbal and physical foreplay: lying side by side with her spouse, he will caress and stroke her if she proves resistant to penetration. Just as the peasant does not plough the field of nature all of a sudden (*à l'estourdy*), the bridegroom will proceed by kissing his woman and mentioning the "ieu des Dames rabatües."[8] Even *salacitas* is a necessary requirement for the *appetitus ad venerem*, which mirrors the unspeakable appetite toward coitus, the *ineffabilem quendam concumbendi appetitum* instilled by Nature (Castro 1603, 60).

As a last instance of the Renaissance theory of ecstasy, the relation between ecstasy and poetry is adamant in Piccolomini's *History of Two Lovers*. The first amorous encounter between Eurialus and Lucretia sees the man swiftly conquer the lady. In the second encounter, love fosters new love and brings in new nourishment. But the mythopoietic quality of ecstasy is most evident in their last rendezvous. Ecstasy gives way to verbal excess, while the man ponders the nature of this joy and its relation with other altered states of the mind (Piccolomini 1973, 116, 128, 150): now it would be easier to die, now that this joy (*gaudium*) is recent; is he dreaming or actually embracing her? Is that ecstasy (*voluptas*) real or has he been led out of his mind (*extra mentem*)? Eurialus procreates mythological poetry thanks to the exalted state of amorous pleasure, as reports the English translation (Piccolomini 1996, G4r): "O round lymmes, o swete bodye, haue I thee in my armes? Nowe [w]ere d[e]the pleasante in the freshnesse of my ioye, that no displeasure myghte here after hurte it. Do I hold the or doo I dreme?"

Ecstasy is both a requirement for future procreation and a present denial of conscience, a sudden moment of speechlessness and a turn-on for poetry. It is also an exalted state of the *admiratio* that can be experienced by humankind when facing something utterly unknown and prodigious. For Fracastorio (1546, 23r-v), the lover's ecstasy transcends the spectacle of the loved one, inducing the mind to excess in admiration (*mentis phantasiaeque excessus quidem in admiratione*). This ecstasy requires a fantasy that is fleshed out in the lovers' eyes (*in phantasia perinde moveat, ac si in oculis esset*). As the body is the prison of the soul, the former visible and the latter invisible, like a room that stores the most perfect part, thus eyes first communicate with the corporeal forms, which then follow their path through the ears and the mind until they merge with intellectual love, those but the corporeal instruments (*strumenti corporali*) that help us participate in spiritual love through the knowledge they serve, "per la cognizione che da quelli ci è sporta" (Betussi 1975, 32).

Ecstasy thrives on perplexity, the bewildered contrast of mental states that is the natural ambience of the suspended setting of John Donne's "The Extasie." And the present survey on ecstasy, procreation and poetry might well resolve itself into the theory of Neoplatonic love exemplified by the poem, adducing its points of inversion, parody, burlesque or negotiation. Yet my interest lies in the chronology sanctioned by theory, where procreation followed the sudden occurrence of ecstasy. Where is Donne's ecstatic Mars?

In "The Extasie" Donne inverts the sequence reconstructed by the theory of ecstasy and procreation. The lovers are there, their bodies already led out of their usual mansions in ecstasy:

> Where, like a pillow on a bed
> A Pregnant banke swel'd up, to rest
> The violets reclining head,
> Sat we two, one anothers best.

> (*EXT* 1-4)

Ecstasy has brought the lovers to the realm of instantaneous, sudden rapture. All this is placed at the beginning of the poem, instead of flowing out of amorous exhaustion and lawful coitus, out of the place of "golden slumber" where only sleep and silence seem possible. Poetry gushes out of the ecstatic suspension of sense and reason:

> Our hands were firmely cimented
> With a fast balme, which thence did spring,
> Our eye-beames twisted, and did thred
> Our eyes, upon one double string [.]

> (5-8)

Procreation has already commenced. The two lovers see each other, their images reflected and introverted, and thus beget the propagation of themselves, if only by a visual multiplication:

> So to'entergraft our hands, as yet
> Was all the means to make us one,
> And pictures in our eyes to get
> Was all our propagation.

> (9-12)

The initial state of ecstasy is suspension.[9] Yet, whereas ecstasy should be an extraneous, external fettering of reason, here suspension enables the creation of poetry:

> As 'twixt two equall Armies, Fate
> Suspends uncertaine victorie,
> Our soules, (which to advance their state,

Were gone out,) hung 'twixt her, and mee.

(13-6)

Suspended out of their bodies, the two souls are caught in a negotiation dictated by sleep and rendered through silent images of death:

And whil'st our soules negotiate there,
  Wee like sepulchrall statues lay;
All day, the same our postures were,
  And wee said nothing, all the day.

(17-20)

Is Donne making a case for physical love through the knowledge granted to lovers in their ecstasy, as has been suggested (Novarr 1972, 219-44)? Or is he proposing a tender defense of sexual love, where sex would be used in its modern sense for the first time (Gransden 1969, 74-6), in a pervasive consciousness of the body (Sherwood 1984, 71-9)? It is my point that here ecstasy is hardly a denial of speech, a silent state of amazement whose description can only be negative, where Mars sleeps under the gaze of Venus. Instead, the poem delves back into the birth of poetry through the ecstasy naturally attached to procreation. Donne constitutes ecstasy as a scene where the spectator conversant with procreation theory can observe the creation of purer substances:

If any, so by love refin'd,
  That he soules language understood,
And by good love were growen all minde,
  Within convenient distance stood,
He (though he knew not which soul spake,
  Because both meant, both spake the same)
Might thence a new concoction take,
  And part farre purer than he came.

(*EXT* 21-8)

This backward progression annuls the containment of ecstasy into procreation. Donne's ecstasy deters any movement to explanation: the birth of poetry reaches back to the protracted ecstasy in the lovers' sleep.[10] The retreat probes deeper—as an instrument to understand the silence where poetry dawns, the perplexity of sexual pleasure is in fact a negation of puzzlement:

This Extasie doth unperplex
  (We said) and tell us what we love;
We see by this, it was not sexe,
  We see, we saw not what did move [.]

(29-32)

From this point on, the Neoplatonic theory of love and the formation of new souls take full center.[11] Be it a parody or a conceited version of orthodox Neoplatonic theory, the image of procreation harks back to the procreative propagation that had occurred at the beginning in the lovers' eyes:

> But as all several soules containe
> Mixture of things, they know not what,
> Love, these mixt soules, doth mixe againe,
> And makes both one, each this and that.

(33-6)

In the latter half of the poem, the bodies abandon their place of ecstasy:

> But O alas, so long, so farre
> Our bodies why doe wee forbeare?
> They are ours, though they are not wee, Wee are
> The intelligences, they the spheare.

(49-52)

While union and propagation are the two purposes of Neoplatonic love, here they seem to indicate the completeness of the lovers' passion, which suggests the inadequacy of the physical means they have used to achieve it (Guss 1966, 141-2). Yet the vision of the lovers' union has been granted by the ecstasy, the original displacing of the bodies occasioned by the eclipse of reason:

> We owe them thanks, because they thus,
> Did us, to us, at first convay,
> Yeelded their forces, sense, to us,
> Nor are drosse to us, but allay.

(*EXT* 53-6)

Now the bodies can produce movement by conveying the souls back to the lovers:

> So must pure lovers souls descend
> T'affections, and to faculties,
> Which sense may reach and apprehend,
> Else a great Prince in prison lies.

(65-8)

Donne's poem on ecstasy barely mentions pleasure—it is its aftermath.[12] The lovers are past pleasure. Love descends to the bodies as a principle of superior knowledge, the true offspring of sexual and poetic procreation:

> To'our bodies turne wee then, that so

> Weake men on love reveal'd may looke;
> Loves mysteries in soules doe grow,
>   But yet the body is his booke.
>
> (69-72)

The union with the bodies extols the value of corporal pleasure, those very acts that were supposed to annul the exercise of reason. Sexual ecstasy, not seen as a moment of rapture but as a protracted absence, procreates poetry while abstaining from the description of pleasure:

> And if some lover, such as wee,
>   Have heard this dialogue of one,
> Let him still marke us, he shall see
>   Small change, when we'are to bodies gone.
>
> (73-6)

The suspended incipit of the poem had introduced the expansion of ecstasy into an experience that, far from being chaotic and potentially unlawful, procreates poetry through the multiplication of the images. If the poem ends on a note of homecoming, both to the symbolical tenets of Neoplatonism and to the actual mansions of the lovers' bodies, the suspended inception brings the reader to the place occupied by sleeping Mars, where ecstasy is not only the acme of sexual pleasure, but the suspended hesitation that follows it.

One of the most famous, if brief descriptions of ecstasy was given by Paul: "For whether we be out of our wit, we are it to God: or whether we be in our right minde, we are it vnto you" (2Cor 5.13). Commenting on this passage from Paul, Donne the Court preacher (1995, 2:9.502-4) claims he is piously pursuing "a death of rapture, and of extasie," for the contemplation of God, and heaven, "is a kinde of buriall, and Sepulchre, and rest of the soule." At the beginning of the sermon, Donne compares in fact human beings to prisoners who are never allowed to leave their prison of death and sleep:

> Wee are all conceived in close Prison; in our Mothers wombes, we are close Prisoners all; when we are borne, we are borne but to the liberty of the house; Prisoners still, though within larger walls; and then all our life is but a going out to the place of Execution, to death. Now was there ever any man seen to sleep in the Cart, between New-gate, and Tyborne? Between the Prison, and the place of Execution, does any man sleep? And we sleep all the way[.] (14-21)

We are all asleep on the way to Tyburn—or to Holborn Station. In a less Augustinian mood, "The Extasie" describes ecstasy as a sleep where absence and the denial of reason procreate words, and poetry is the offspring of innocent rapture. Had Botticelli's Mars been translated into the male lover of this poem, he would have seen and tasted the "golden slumber" of ecstasy, the silent suspended sleep of reason where words are created.

7
Shakespeare in Laughter

here we are now
entertain us
—Kurt Cobain

A blank page would quite do now.

For laughter is never *here*. Blank pages, where laughter and its theory have egressed from the margins, would befit this report on the uncommunicative sound of laughter.

Yet pages (and comedies) must contain characters. The genesis of the present study was sparked off by a material absence I noticed away at a University of London Students' Union book mart a few years ago. The site is only a few yards from the venue where Nirvana's "Smells Like Teen Spirit" was performed in a much-acclaimed concert shortly before *Nevermind* jumped to the top slot in international charts and changed the rock-pop scenario of the 1990s.

Second-hand book shopping naturally triggers dejection. Usually one seeks an old classic, either narrative or non-fiction, that was missed at the time of its original forthcoming, rather than the new release or the latest market hype. On that occasion, I spotted an anthology of English satirical verse. Its parched cover, whose scant commercial appeal had been further diminished by the gooey remains of a chewing-gum, had oddly attracted me. I skipped ahead to the Elizabethan section, only to come across the striking absence of Shakespeare and his neighbors. That was not amusing.

With the benefit of hindsight, it was my own fault. Satire (or comic theory, for that matter) is not necessarily what one would liken to claptraps like TV shows featuring canned laughter. Nevertheless, that absence garnered such a spectacular anticlimax, coming as it did from the home of Monty Python. How could the tradition that begat the Ministry of Silly Walks fail to appreciate just how funny Shakespeare was? I skulked off on my own silly walk up to the unhappily abandoned old site of the British Library, eager to consult the catalogue on the subject of what would prove the tantalizing classical and Renaissance theory of laughter.

After devoting many a day to those texts and many others beside, a crippling intimation of absence still shuts the gate in the face of interpretation. For laughter keeps fading out in a bedeviling absence. Though placed at the very beginnings of Western literature—the *Odyssey* (1.579-81) mentions the *asbestos gelos*, the uncontrollable, enigmatic laughter of the gods at the spectacle of Vulcan's service as a cupbearer—and unanimously championed as one of our most universal features, if not *the* property of humankind, laughter escapes attempts at constraining it into theory. Like confession, laughter raises more questions for any theory to answer: is it proper of humankind only, or is it common to brutes as well? Do babies really smile? Why do women laugh more than men? Did Christ smile? Does laughter have any commerce with the devil? What do we laugh at? How do we laugh? What happens to our bodies when we laugh? How is laughter formed and emitted? Why do we laugh? And why, after all, do we need to explain laughter?

The best answer on the subject I have culled so far should be put down to Marx—Groucho Marx (1959, 87):

> Perhaps I'm not a comic. It's not worth arguing about . . . I'm a pretty wary fellow, and I have neither the desire nor the equipment to analyze what makes one man funny to another man. I have read many books by alleged experts, explaining the basis of humor and attempting to describe what is funny and what isn't. I doubt if any comedian can honestly say why he is funny and why his next-door neighbor is not.

Perhaps Groucho was right: it is not worth arguing about it. Much as one tends to agree with Groucho on this and many other subjects, his pessimism had been already preconized by Thomas Wilson in the sixteenth century, when the attempt to legitimate and describe laughter was raging on most sweepingly:

> Now to tell you in plaine words, what laughter is, how it stirreth and occupieth the whole body, how it altereth the countenance, & sodainly brasteth out that we cannot keepe it in: let some mery man on Gods name take this matter in hand: for it passeth my cunning, & I think euen thei that can best moue laughter, would rather laugh merily when such a question is put forth, then giue answere earnestly, what, & how laughter is in deed. (Wilson 1909, 135)

One is reminded of the words proffered by Luther to wave off the subject of hidden sins in confession—*extra meum captum est*. However, this avenue of negative thinking remained conspicuously barren during the Renaissance. Unlike most of the physical manifestations of human passion (perhaps with the only exception of tears, as we have seen in the first Chapter), laughter can boast a history. A growing flock of scholars, players, preachers, censors, philosophers and physicians have striven to give meaning to such a non-communicative, inarticulate phenomenon.

Yet tears were easier to understand as the vehicles of contrition and other passions like female piety or unmanly meekness. Instead, laughter has constantly scurried back to the margins of each and every comic theory purporting to circumscribe it. Differing from other structured, albeit violent manifestations of passion, the lack of a universally acceptable theory of the comic saps the foundations of the study of comedy (Bowen 1998, 6-7).[1] In a Roadrunner syndrome, the more laughter is pursued by the exquisite devices of critical theory of such volunteering analogues to Willy the Coyote, the more laughter seems to demand a theory, an explanation of its causes and its effects.

Nevertheless, had Groucho lived in the Renaissance (in which case he would have probably been a serious source of professional disquiet to Shakespeare), he would have been compelled to secede from his agnostic stance and envisage a comic theory that might include the amorous messenger from the Duke next door and his/her ludicrous double, the noisy mirth of drunken courtiers, the verbal wit of a corrupter of words and the ludicrousness of a Puritan steward fantastically cross-gartered. And these investigations are still vital now. Among the many efforts to outline a philosophy of laughter, modern authors have listed a superiority theory, modeled on Plato and Aristotle and directed at the risible object held in scorn; a relief theory, where laughter gives vent to an excess of nervous energy, as proposed by Freud (Szafran 1994); and an incongruity theory, which ultimately seems to inform most philosophical discussion on the subject. A scholar ventured, for instance, that laughter, resulting from a pleasant psychological shift, is the physical activity expressed by the feeling produced by that shift (Morreall 1987). Analogously, the sense of incongruity, which makes an object or a situation risible, is ultimately linked to a context, since a single object in nature could not be the only cause of laughter (Schaffer 1981, 5, 17). Another salient aspect is the suddenness of laughter, already intuited by Hobbes (1994, 9.13) in his celebrated remark on the "sudden glory" which springs from "a sudden conception of some ability in himself that laugheth". Laughter suddenly juxtaposes two universes, the familiar and the *unheimlich*; thanks to this sudden reversal, one grasps the relations of hidden patterns being made plain and manifest (Milner 1972, 27).

Yet, if one is to compare the theory (or theories) of laughter with a literary text, how does one proceed, by way of inclusion (Shakespeare may be explained through Renaissance comic theory, even as an exception to it) or by way of juxtaposition (both *Twelfth Night* and comic theory portray a baffling, inherently escapist phenomenon like the art of raising laughter, so much so that inevitable similarities will arise)?[2] Indeed, doubts about the direction of study abound. The critic should not quite define the nature of the comic as such, but rather show how literary works use comic structures of ideas (Farley-Hills 1981, 3). What is the proper study of comic theory, the analysis of the structure of the comic object or of the psychology of the perceiving subject, which respectively focus on the comic action itself or the audience's response to it (Kennedy 1984, 363)? An inversion of the pattern is also possible: one should rather study how laughter and representation etches out an idea of the comical, where the *vis comica* would rather reside within the laugher himself (Faure 1994, ii).

It is my contention that Renaissance comedies, and *Twelfth Night* chiefly among them, have often been studied through the lens of our modern notions of the risible: the comic plot of imbalance and excess resolves itself in the harmonious reconcilement between the expectations nurtured by the story and the surprise it reserves. And when some awareness of the historical scenario appears, it often leads to the exaltation of the transgressive usage of laughter. In this sense, the assessment of the essence of laughter in Elizabethan society has been likened to "a forbidding task of cultural archaeology"—an excavation preferably conducted with an eye bent on the array of transgressive practices miraculously cemented by the Bakhtinian concept of coral laughter (Mangan 1996, 24).

The Bakhtinian vision of the risible diverged from the Aristotelian tradition of laughter as a correction against deviations from the norm. It valued laughter as a Saturnalian order that resists containment (Pfister 1987). Endowed with an inversive force exemplified by fools, jesters and dramatists, "a current of radical, critical laughter . . . , instead of reinforcing accepted norms, sought to give the world a nudge in a new direction" (Thomas 1977, 78). Therefore, the good (Bakhtinian) reader will only have to "press his or her ear firmly to the page, attuned to a laughter that runs, like an underground river, just below the topography of the main historical events" (Sanders 1995, 198).

Perhaps out of distaste for such auscultative moods (which would have provoked enduring results with the sticky cover of the anthology I found in London), in his illuminating study on Renaissance laughter Bertrand (1995, 9-10) proposed to study "la mise en ordre du rire" by advocating a less trenchant division in time. The most prominent element of comic theory is its "relative inertie," or the *summa* principle in my own terms. In fact, a close reading of the texts undermines any neat division between popular and learned cultures.[3]

The difficulties in applying comic theory to a Renaissance play are manifest in *Twelfth Night*.[4] Yet the comedy generously retrieves the premises of Renaissance laughter. The holiday celebrations take place within the second world of Illyria, where Malvolio's self-delusion and

Feste's restorative role guide the action (Lewalski 1965).[5] The comedy is inscribed into the Saturnalian pattern of a debate between realism and romanticism, which translates the whole play into a festivity.[6] Alongside the punishment theme, the main plot of the comedy teems with images of musical recreation, as well as with the topic of the amorous interplay between lovers and messengers (Parker 1987). The insistence on the lost-found pattern, intimating a fascination with repeating loss, also underlines the presence of transition and transference in the comedy (Freedman 1991, 193).

Therefore, all these aspects could be parts of a full-fledged study of comic theory *in Twelfth Night*. That would be, however, "laughter *in* Shakespeare"—the prevalence of the excavation works in the opus, the reconstruction of the presences behind the text. I would like to quote a dialogue between Sir Toby and Sir Andrew, touching on the right way to approach Maria and have "better acquaintance" with her: "You mistake, knight. 'Accost' is front her, board her, woo her, assail her" (*TN* 1.3.55-6). In its original sense, "accost" means addressing with courtesy, as well as the nautical sense of going alongside the coast, the type of tramping navigation that offered a way out of the redoubtable depths of the ocean. The study of Renaissance comic theory likewise evinces the problem of how to accost girls, boys and texts. It demands a similar type of marginal thinking, an effort to represent an absence. To paraphrase an early Nirvana hit, one needs a difficult friend with an ear to lend, especially if one bangs such a taut drum as Derrida's "Tympan" (1982).

This quotation does not prelude to any critical affiliation or manifesto, an act of awareness that would imply a reasonable understanding of Derrida on my part. Having said that, Derrida's "margins" of philosophy can capaciously accommodate laughter as well. To paraphrase, comic theory has always meant to say its limit. In its tympan, a cloth has been stretched taut in order to take its beating, to amortize impressions, thus excluding the possibility of determining a non-comical place, a place of exteriority and alterity from which one might still treat of laughter. Derrida advocated an oblique approach to luxate the philosophical ear, to avoid frontal and symmetrical protest, opposition in all the forms of *anti*. I will try to invert the question: what if *Twelfth Night* envisages laughter as a scene of absence to be seen from the margins?

In this Chapter I will focus on what arguably constituted the quintessence of laughter for the Renaissance, its diverting nature. Nor did it go lost a very long time ago. The primary sense of laughter as an inmost diversion from our thoughts and cares, currently superseded by the exaltation of its inversive force, was still present in the eighteenth century, for instance when its cause was traced back to "une suite extérieure du désordre intime, & de la déroute secrète du principe intelligent" (De Sivry 1986, 57). Discussing how certain "insatiable sounds, especially when continued," can exert pleasant effects on the mind, Beattie (1779, 138) analogously argued that they "seem to withdraw the attention from the more tumultuous concerns of life and, without agitating the soul, to pour gradually upon it a train of softer ideas, that sometimes lull and soothe the faculties, and sometimes quicken sensibility, and stimulate the imagination."

Renaissance laughter constantly garnered an undercurrent of otherness, a sneering type of absence that observes the scene from its margins. Fregoso placed Democritus, the laughing philosopher who often featured in an antonymic dyad with Heraclitus, the weeping philosopher, in a setting that seems to predate extraterrestrial abduction tales. Guided by a divine youth clad in white clothes, whose visage radiates like a sun, the narrator is conducted to a pleasant hill off the vile hoard of plebeians). There Democritus wildly laughs at the madness of the people, so taken with scoffing that he simultaneously appears in his mad, albeit divine status. Democritus derides our common follies, almost carried away out of himself (*chio era fuora di me*, Fregoso 1511, A3v, B6r-v).

The classical and Renaissance comic theory involved all these elements of unexpectedness, surprise, incongruity and deformity. Laughter is subjected to definition (what is laughter?), partition (which is good and bad laughter?) and subsequent legitimization. The Pre-Socratic philosophers prescribed that the good-naturate jester never mock or ridicule the unfortunate (Grant 1924). Briefly touching upon laughter, Plato contended that the ridiculous derives from self-ignorance: by observing ugly, defective or weak persons, we are touched by their false conceits of wisdom (*Philebus* 48A-C).[7] The ridiculous always links with vice: the laugher should bilk only at human follies. Yet jesting must not be carried too far: laughter was one of the objects of explicit prohibitions for the Guardians in the *Republic* (*Laws* 7.816D-817D; *Republic* 1.388E; Gadamer 1980).

The cornerstone for Renaissance comic theory was Aristotle's brief remark on the ridiculous as the effect of something harmlessly disproportionate or inconvenient, which elicits no sense of pity in the beholder:

> Comedy . . . is mimesis of baser but not wholly vicious characters: rather, the laughable is one category of the shameful. For the laughable comprises any fault or mark of shame which involves no pain or destruction: most obviously, the laughable mask is something ugly and twisted, but not painfully. (*Poetics* 5.1449a31-35)

Aristotle listed laughter and amusement among the devices for relaxation and pleasure, seen as an intermission from general seriousness (*Nicomachean Ethics* 10.6.6.1176b30-36).[8] Wittiness, rather than foolery, is indeed a social virtue. Liberal jesting is marked by careful choice in frequency and language, also measuring the sustainable amount of pain inflicted on the victim (4.8.9.1128a30-3). Happiness differs from simple amusement: relaxation is not an end *per se*, but rather leads to the resumption of honest matters and habits (10.6.6.1177b.5-6). The jester must be tactful, since being laughed at causes anger (*Rhetorics* 2.4.13.1381a).

After Aristotle, laughter was mainly studied in its association with the carefully selected rhetorical wit that the ideal orator is to use with parsimony and liberality. Laughter helps to relax the audience (A*d C. Herennium* 1.6.10, 3.13.23). In the section from *De Oratore* about the origins of laughter, one of the most-quoted authorities in Renaissance comic theory, Cicero reports the Greek opinion that laughter scourges the type of turpitude confined to lesser faults: the field or province of the risible (*locus autem, et regio quasi ridiculi*) is limited to what may be described as unseemly or ugly in its turpitude and deformity. Accordingly, the risible is restricted to the actions or facts that do not represent outstanding wickedness and crime, provoking neither disgust nor sympathy. The ideal orator resorts to the liberal jests to relieve his audience, paying attention to propriety in expression and reverence for the authorities. Alongside the decorum toward the higher ranks, the jest must be in harmony with the author as well and refrain from obscenity and scurrility (*De oratore* 2.58.235-6, 238). Whereas mimes and trivial actors lavish jests as yet another means of eliciting unlawful laughter, the orator will avoid any such violations of decency (*Orator* 26.88). Quintilian, whose proviso was that the cause of laughter rests ultimately uncertain and ambiguous (*anceps*), demoted the usage of jokes and jests into short pieces with which the orator offers solace to the listeners in his *oratoria urbanitas rara* (*Institutio Oratoria* 6.3.36-110, 6.3.1, 8, 14). Discussing the salience of the elegance of expression, Demetrius (1979, 3.128) similarly argued that it "includes grace and geniality. Some pleasantries—those of the poets—are loftier and more dignified, while others are more commonplace and jocular, resembling banter."

A dent on this normative enclosure of prohibitions and restrictions was made by the set of positive nuances within the phenomenon of laughter. The orator's superior wit concurs to the affirmation of his *liberalitas*, the condition of being freeborn and thus adhering to the highest classes of society. His ingenuity is especially beckoned by the wittiness of sudden surprise, the *admiratio* that easily wins recognition among the audience. By way of unexpected twists and turns and, contrastively, assumed simplicity, the orator disappoints his audience's expectations and evinces lawful recreation by saying silly things and scourging foolery, "subabsurda dicendo et stulta reprehendendo" (*De oratore* 2.71.289).[9] For repetition, even of good jests, is hardly meted out with success (*De Oratore*, 2.60.246). Unexpectedness is the primal cause of the risible: we are naturally inclined to laugh when an expected conduit of thought is violently twisted by a witty joke— "noster error risum movet" (2.62.255).

To sum up the two arch-requirements of comic theory, laughter liberally upbraids painless deformity and thrives on ingenious unexpectedness. As a lawful entertainment, it momentarily suspends the flow of narration with a witty detour and offers further suspension in its concomitant surprise. "Good" laughter is an interlude between more momentous matters.

Renaissance comic theory insisted on the two aspects of the object (deformity) and the mechanism of laughter (unexpectedness). Much of its salience was enhanced by the notorious absence of the part of Aristotle's *Poetics* devoted to comedy, which let open a chasm to be filled up in theoretical discussion. Since the risible had been indicated as the hallmark of comedy, the Renaissance saw to it that every nook and cranny be clearly detected and systematized.

Thus comedy was explained as a correct entertainment in view of a superior virtue, offering an analogue to the purgation of passion performed by tragedy. Judging from the *Tractatus Coislinianus* (a tenth-century manuscript which, despite some quite likely mangled interpretations embedded into the text, seems to reflect substantially an Aristotelic tradition on comedy), one could venture that in Aristotle comedy was analyzed in the light of the specific pleasure it gives in view of the virtuous recreation it grants: "Comedy is an imitation of an action that is ludicrous and imperfect, of sufficient length, [in embellished language,] . . . through pleasure and laughter effecting the purgation of the like emotions. It has laughter for its mother" (1922, 224).[10] The first application of Aristotle's definition of comedy occurred in Pietro Valla's 1499 commentary on Plautus; a Latin translation of Averroes specified that the proper imitation of vices should not deride any brand of blemishes, but only those that are utterly ludicrous and do not solicit any sense of pity or pain (Herrick 1950, 38-9).

An example of the local applications of Aristotle to Renaissance comedy was Castelvetro's gloss of the definition of the risible as a list of the four kinds of objects that can elicit laughter, a set that can be easily matched up with the stock characters of comedy. Laughter can be aroused by meeting persons or things that have been lost on us for a long while or forever, as is the case with recognitions; by the deceptions suffered by others, for our nature, corrupted by our first parents in Eden, delights in the evil others suffer as if it should be some good for us; by the ill-doings of our soul or body, and by all things that pertain to carnal delight (Castelvetro 1971, 2.5.1449a.31-35).[11]

The burgeoning influence of Aristotle's precept on painless deformity informs the most influential Renaissance interpretations of laughter. Joubert's *Traitè du Ris*, a probable reference for Rabelais, ranked among the most harmonious treatises on the nature, causes and effects of laughter (DeRocher 1979). Joubert (1579, 17-8) grappled with the volatile nature of the risible by resorting to the two-pronged tradition originated by Aristotle and Cicero, respectively underlying deformity and unexpectedness. One laughs at all kinds of painless incongruity, which include obscenity, deformity, dishonesty, indecency, ungainliness or lack of decorum, provided that these ludicrous acts do not elicit any compassion on our side, "pour uet que nous n'an soyons meus à compassion." Joubert's choice examples seem to predate many of the experiments in public nudity and outrage which pinpointed the progress of youth protest in American Universities in the 1960s: the Renaissance antecedents of mooning and streaking (*sans aucune necessité ou contrainte decouurir les parties honteuses*), which would have aroused Cicero's condemnation, are benignly legitimized as examples of acts *difformes*. If they are devoid of any damage, they may be laughed at, as they mingle the two elements of laughter, deformity and absence of pity.

Nevertheless, laughter has to be aroused by something completely unexpected, says Joubert. Even in the most outrageous acts, deformity in itself is not enough to raise a laugh. Joubert postulates the existence of something unforeseen, different from what one had hoped for, as Cicero had argued in his theory of the *admiratio* (*De Oratore* 2.70.284). "Il faut, qu'il y ait quelque chose à l'improuiste & de nouueau, outre ce qu'on espere bien attantiuemant": laughter occurs in a moment of suspension, when the soul, left dangling in doubt, attentively considers the upcoming events—"l'esprit suspand & an doute, panse sogneusemant à ce qu'il an auiendra" (35). As ludicrous facts are usually capped with a conclusion that is other than the one we expected, we are made to laugh.

The pervasiveness of the joint Aristotelian-Ciceronian tradition was still indomitable in Renaissance writers. Puttenham's definition of the cause of laughter (1589, 3.24:243-4) offered a quasi-verbatim adaptation of Aristotle's brief precept: laughter derives from "a certaine absurditie and disproportion to nature, and the opinion of the hearer or beholder to make the thing ridiculous." Puttenham underlines the theme of decorum and decency that literally spoke volumes in the tradition of courteous laughter: "Most certainly all things that moue a man to laughter, as doe these scurrilities & other ridiculous behauiours, it is for some vndecencie that is found in them: which maketh it decent for euery man to laugh at them." As to the Ciceronian theory of *admiratio*, Wilson (1909, 139) referred that "we shall delite the hearers, when they looke for one answere, and we make them a cleane contrary, as though we would not seeme to vnderstand what they would haue." Maggi (1970, 305) extolled the importance of *admiratio* as the most prominent staple of good laughter: since jokes cannot deliver their precious gift if dissevered from surprise (*si non accedat admiratio*), it follows that even in the objects of real life laughter can never be detached from the union with *admiratio*.[12]

Why is this type of laughter "good"? The effect of deformity and unexpectedness offers a temporary diversion from the main course of the oration and, more generally, from the flow of incessant cares and concerns that beset our lives. Comic theory also prescribes the application of laughter as a means of temporary relief. The tradition of conduct books further expanded upon the task of framing the risible. One of the requisites of comely gravity is the "sildomnes of laughter" (*Rich Cabinet* 1616, 61v). Hence, the Renaissance cornucopia of texts on the right production and enjoyment of laughter, instanced by the genre of *facetiae*, a joyous summa that prescribed how a jest could offer virtuous recreation and solace.[13] Jests were accounted as an antidote for melancholy, since "a merry heart doeth good like a medicine, but a broken spirit drieth the bones" (Prv 17.22). They were suggested as yet another form of merry talk, especially "whan ye lorde is thynne, as of seruyce / Monght replenished with grete diuersite / Of mete y drinke" (*Book of Curtesye* B2v-B3r). Courtiers were generously encouraged to "make honest chere wyth softe speche" (*Fifteenth-Century Courtesy Book* 5b).[14]

The foundations for this belief in the regenerative virtues of "honest chere" resided in an inherently kinetic theory: movement is good. According to faculty psychology, the faculties are linked with an idea of constant movement (*kinesis*), changing from a passive to an active state. For Aristotle, we exist in activity (*Nicomachean Ethics* 9.7.1168a6-10); therefore, "a work of literature was regarded as capable of teaching and delighting because it was considered an object capable of causing the mental faculties to receive images and to abstract from them, activities which result in pleasure" (Salman 1979, 306-8).[15] Another element of this theory rested on the contrastive nature of the remedy given by laughter. Olson (1982, 31, 40-1, 48-9, 64) has shown the relevance of the medical concept of literary pleasure for the medieval theory of recreation. In the wake of Galen, Johannitius's *Isagoge* put forward the distinction between the *res naturales* (which constitute the body), the *res non naturales* (which affect the body, such as air, food, drink, exercise) and the *res contra naturam* (diseases, causes of disease, sequels of disease). Now, the nonnaturals represent a group of factors that, external to the body, yet do affect bodily health depending on their use; cheerfulness (*gaudium*), if produced by temperate exercises, such as reading a fiction, functions to preserve health. Drawing on this homeopathic theory of the preservation of health, Hugh of St.-Victor proposed the *theatrica*, a science of entertainments that contrasted the daily upsurge of disquiet and disturbance with the local application of the remedies oppositely intended. Frye (1965, 51) also remarked on the "kinetic stimulus" proper of comedy, which offers either a "response that produces gloom or cheer" or a "response of sympathy or indignation." And a similar kinetic, governing appetite would guide the theatrical action of *Twelfth*

Night (Hollander 1986, 134).[16] As Orsino proves only too well, in the topic of recreation the Renaissance reinvested the debate about the balance between *otium* and *negotium*: the Aristotelian concept of temperance, of moderate gaiety, led to the valorization of the *loisir*, to the establishment of the ideal of a well-ordered life whereby the prince might find solace and thus deflect his daily concerns (Blanchard 1995).

The art of causing recreation by laughter was therefore a choice requisite of the good courtier. For Castiglione, courtiers should have "a good understandynge with a certein sweetnesse to refresh the hearers mindes, and with meerie conceites and Jests to provoke them to solace and laughter" (Castiglione 1900, 152). Jests are acceptable inasmuch as they provide a prompt source of solace and recreation to the Prince, also signaling the courtier's promptness: "And althoughe all kinde of Jesters move a man to laugh, yet do they also in this laughter make diverse effectes. For some have in them a certein cleannesse and modest pleasantnesse. Other bite sometime privily, otherwhile openlye" (188).[17] Della Casa (1576, 64-5) analogously praised both the refreshing variety of jests ("Iestes do geue us some sporte, and make us merry, and so consequently refreash our spirits") and the decorous respect of circumstances: jests directed "to make a sport and pastime at his faulte, whome he doth loue and esteeme, and of whom he doth take more then a common account," must be amiable retorts that the victim can easily sustain, rather than plain wrongs.[18] Guazzo (1581, 26v-27r) added laughter to the set of polite accomplishments that can adorn civil conversation; only, jests must be graciously deprived of any slander and inspired to "a certaine wittie and readie pleasantnesse." This affability helps "to refreshe mindes ouercharged with melancholy and pensiue thoughtes." The Italian physician Parravicino (1615, 29-30) traced back the function of laughter to mirth (*allegrezza*), which concurs to the resolving of spirits piled up after meditations and labors of the soul, regardless of their copiousness and value.

The relief afforded by laughter was extended to the literary productions that naturally thrive on the production of humor. Puttenham (1589, 1.9:18) notes that poetry "in merry matters (not vnhonest) being vsed for mans solace and recreation it may be well allowed, for . . . Poesie is a pleasant maner of vtteraunce varying from the ordinarie of purpose to refresh the mynde by the eares delight." As for comedy, whose hallmark, as we have seen, is the risible, Speroni argues that our belabored soul finds a requisite, helpful rest in the laughter aroused by good plays (Weinberg 1961, 543). Our souls are to be purged of those passions that are occasioned by private and public activities: laughter was often indicated by Renaissance writers as one of the choicest ways of assuaging melancholy, together with music (Buonamici 1597, 34).

How about the very practitioners of the trade, the actors? On a theoretical level, laughter, as all false joys lavished by the world, equated with giving oneself up to death: "Vera verae mortis consignatio est" (Novarini 1637, 15). More concretely, the version of Catholic censorship on local productions of plays in Italy was that virtuous acting, deprived of buffoonery and obscenity, falls short of divine grace and is a florilegium of manifold graces (*un compendio di molte gratie*, Pandolfi 1957-8, 3.4.8:444).[19] Much in this vein, the actors of the Commedia dell'Arte portrayed the gracious actor as a virtuous Christian who elicits a moderate type of laughter among the audience. In their theoretical reflections, actors averred that the ridiculous derives from the ugliness of acts, words or chance, not from sheer vice (D'Oddo 1578, B1r). Their corporative defence of the trade was based on such a dignified, if sporadic use of laughter: the reader is continuously warned that actors use laughter as salt for their delightful, wonderful actions, while fools reduce all their acting to laughter. The famous Italian actor Pier Maria Cecchini (1622, 89.53) even proposed comedy as a pleasant moral reading, intended for those who do not have time for studying (*una dolce lettura morale, à gli otiosi*).

In the Renaissance application of this precept, laughter was explained away as the main effect of comedy, which purges the obnoxious passions and rivets the audience into upholding virtue. The theory of laughter also introduced a difference between legitimate and excessive forms of entertainment. Thus, for Fracastorio (1546, 42v), laughter is associated with *laetitia*, not mere *gaudium*, a quality naturally found in youth who have lots of good blood, though the old man may have it *per accidens* when he is tipsy among friends. On a more theoretical level, Demetrius's difference between *charis* and *geloton* surfaces in the oft-quoted passage from Sidney (1973, 1.200-1): "But our comedians think there is no delight without laughter; which is very wrong, for though laughter may come with delight, yet cometh it not of delight, as though delight should be the cause of laughter." Delight proceeds from things "that have a conveniency to ourselves or to our general nature," whereas "laughter almost ever cometh of things most disproportioned to ourselves and nature."

Championing the risible as its hallmark, comedy works on our passions much like tragedy. While the terror and pity unleashed by tragedy purge humankind, likewise the laughter of comedy calls out men to honest civic life: "Il riso, & le beffe nelle Comedie . . . chiama gli huomini alla honesta vita ciuile" (Giraldi 1961, 289). Not that delight (*diletto*) is good in itself. Comedy must be virtuous inasmuch as it purges the pleasure caused by ridiculous actions (Weinberg 1961, 538). As a wonderful union of profit and delight, laughter will eventually teach virtue by the imitation of base actions and characters (Trissino 1970, 30v). Such risible acts add beauty to the comedy and provide profit and delight through laughter, with no offence whatsoever to the audience (Da Cagli 1970, A10v).

At this point, one could venture that, by means of shifting the focus from the physical effects of laughter to its reduction within the stronghold of comedy, laughter has been purged away of all its negative connotations. In fact, the scenario is far hazier. Comic theory cannot be streamlined into a summa on laughter that could rule out those moments of suspension and perplexity that form the core of the next section.

In fact *admiratio*, as a suspension in the beholder's interpretative process of the ludicrous events taking place, implies the investigation of the most recondite proceedings of our soul. In his treatise on the sympathy and antipathy between things, Fracastorio (1546, 20r) raised the question of whether the cause of laughter, the ridiculous object, can really be something present. If one apprehends something in one's mind, *per phantasiam*, it means either that the object is not present or enjoyed, or that it not fully enjoyed, hence it is called desire: "Praesens autem non sit & non habetur aut non bene habetur." Fracastorio defined *admiratio* as this moment of suspension of our soul, an internal application and fixation (*suspensio animae seu fixio & applicatio intenta*). The appearance of something unexpected has the effect of producing laughter, whose end is to show our inner mirth in our faces (*laetitia interna in facie*). Laughter is a movement of mixed mirth and surprise. As such, it entails an inmost contrariety, a coincidence between opposites (*quaedam contranitentia*), for suspension implies stricture and mirth disclosure (*expansionem*). Fracastorio also noted that the opposite movements of suspension and expansion in the laugher's body entail great nuisance and disturbance (*non sine molestia fiat*, 23r-24r). To paraphrase Barabas, laughter, being a violent thing, cannot be permanent.

Another example of a diverging theory of laughter was Juan Luis Vives's emphasis on the perception of a possible good, the object of the *appetitus* in Fracastorio's terms, as the main object of the risible, rather than deformity. Mirth either derives from the soul's judgement that a good is already present or from the apprehension that this good can be reached for sure. On the other hand, *delectatio* is defined as an acquiescence of our will to a good that is recognized as congruous. Laughter is an outward action that stems from the inside, a movement that emanates from the heart to all the parts of the body. The heart is expanded by mirth or delight, and this movement is extended to the outward site (*exteriorem sedem*) of laughter, the face, especially the eyes and the part encircling the mouth (Vives 1555, 195).

Much as confession entailed a theory of the body, with its paraphernalia of contrition, tears and speech, comic theory implies the description of the laugher's body, where the most unaccountable elements of laughter eventually take the lead.

John Cleese famously illustrated the three major differences between the English and the Americans: "When we organize a world championship, we always invite teams over from other countries; we usually speak English, and you don't; when we meet our Head of State, we usually go down on one knee only." Any comic theory rests on the systematization of differences between expectations and the outcome. Also deriving from the perception of a difference, an element of unexpected incongruity in the object, the theory generates differences in the type and the usage of laughter.

Yet, apart from the mainly Anglo-Saxon community and the related stereotypes Cleese was lampooning, his joke bears on the universal tendency towards laughing in the face of such apparently offensive remarks. Laughter is by and large the most common reaction to the perception of these differences. The flurry of theoretical works that failed to convince Groucho probably seeped into this belief in the universality of laughter. In more recent times, even the conclusion of the missing girl's fake diary in *The Blair Witch Project* website is marked by the recapitulation of the most fundamental of human needs: "I want to laugh."

The Aristotelian tenet that laughter is the property of humankind (*Parts of Animals* 3.10.673a6-8) is present in all reflections on laughter. The second relation of Cartier's voyage to Canada illustrates one example of the universality of laughter. Jean de Léry, the author of a French-Indian lexicon, reported that, after having endeavored to no avail to make the Tupi natives pronounce personal names like Pierre, Guillaume or Jean, he decided to obviate by pronouncing things that were known to them in their mothertongue. Since Léry means "oyster" (*huître*) in the natives' language, the Frenchman introduced himself as "*Lery-oussou*," a big oyster. The reactions of the natives testify to the working of *admiratio*. Laughing, they replied they had never seen a Frenchman with such a name: "De quoy eux se tenans bien satisfaits, avec leur admiration Teh! se prenans à rire, dirent: 'Vraiment voilà un beau nom, et n'avions point encore vu de Mair (c'est-à-dire François) qui s'appelast ainsi" (De Léry 1994, 450).

The pervasiveness of the Aristotelian topos on laughter as our *proprium* did not, however, argue its general application. To the contrary: the tenet was alternatively extended and shrunk, either detaching humankind from beasts or sinking laughter into the common operation of beastly pleasure. Martianus Capella (1977, 4.348:113) listed *risibilitas*, the faculty of laughing, as one of the five predicables (genus, difference, accident, definition and property) that concur to the definition of man. Property (*proprium*) strictly defines a given species, marking it off from all the other things. So is laughter for man, since no one can laugh unless he is a man, and there is no man that cannot laugh when he means to, so far as his nature allows it. In the early Christian reflection on this property, it is prudently added, for instance by Peter the Chanter, that *risibilitas* is a proper predicate of human nature, yet the good Christian ought to pursue interior hilarity, the *mentis hilaritatem* (*Verbum Abbreviatum*, *PL* 68:205; cf. Resnick 1987, 98).

Being a property does not partake of the essence of the thing. For Aquinas, not everything that is proper of an object pertains to its essence, like laughter in man (*In Primum et Secundum Libros Posteriorum Analyticorum* 3B). One of the oft-quoted references in this domain of absolutes, where laughter may be interspersed with all manifestations of human nature and yet be demoted into an unnecessary, frequently disturbing commotion, was the example of Crassus, who only laughed once in his lifetime at the sight of a donkey eating thistles (Erasmus 1972b, 1.10.71). *Risibilitas* is our property because it is actually or potentially found in all of us, resisting all counterfeiting by wit or art (Isaac the Jew 1515, 7r). Lactantius instead claimed that a similar faculty could be seen in animals when they sport with men or their mates, a point reinstated by Erasmus, who in *De ratione concionandi* vindicated speech as our true property; Vives averred that animals do have cognate emotions; only, since they do not have a face that can betray any changes, they cannot strictly be said to laugh (Screech 1970, 219-20). Valeriano Bolzani (1587, 51) reported that the Egyptian hieroglyphic for laughter is a dog, observing that the melancholia associated with agelasts contrastively identifies the melancholy appearance, despite the present well-deserved popularity of apparently smiling puppies like Samoyeds and Golden Retrievers.

Laughter as one of the distinctive signs, if not the property of humankind, entailed the close description of its effects on the body. Apart from Bakhtin's concept of the joyous corporeality of laughter, breaking the sides with laughter was not just a trope. The Renaissance writers often reported the traditional cases of deaths occasioned by excessive joy, as in the case of the Roman mother who died upon seeing the son who had been falsely reported dead in the battle of Canne (Ravisius 1588, 117). Fatal epidemics of laughter raged in the Middle Ages; Thomas Urquhart was said to have died from laughter when he was told the news of Charles II's return to London (how proper for the first English translator of Rabelais), and a Danish physician suffered from a similar death after having seen *A Fish Called Wanda* (Quesnel 1991).

Laughter is so human, and yet it constantly defies explanation; it happens in our body because of the incongruity suddenly perceived without any attendant sense of pity, and yet it escapes our will. Much as good confession was located in the tripartite structure of the penitent breast, laughter was also studied as a physical phenomenon. Its volatile, elusive nature is thus unveiled by the observation of two facts: the disfeaturement of the harmonious composure of the human body in the laugher and the diversion of expectations and concerns that it fosters as our solace.

To describe how laughter often escapes our control, Aristotle resorted to an analogy with the turbulent movement of thunder, a physiological movement occasioned by derangement and deception (*Problems* 35.6.965a15-7).[20] Joubert similarly contended that laugher is a movement occasioned by the spirits commoved by the irregular, fitful agitation of the heart (*de l'esprit epandu, & inegale agitacion du coeur*), which alters mouth and lips, midriff and breast with its impetuous movement and interrupted sound, "auec impetuosité & son antrerompu" (1579, 167). Normal breathing is fractioned by the unnatural emission of spirits (*intercisa a spiritu*), so much so that it is emitted not continuously, but in partitioned moments, causing the varied emission of breath: "Divisim erumpit, & multiplicem infert expirationem" (Pesserl 1602, A4r). Goclenius explicitly compared this interrupted emission of breath to the more bathetic *crepitus ventris* in a Rabelaisian juxtaposition of the two orifices of the digestive canal. The *crepitus* derives from the screeching sound produced through certain intervals between sounds (*per certa sonorum discrimina crepat*), as if the concave were filled with rattles (1607, 1). Analogously, laughter sounds like interrupted sobbing emitted by the distorted mouth, "sono fere velut singultante, continuoque fracto & ore diducto" (Goclenius 1597, 21). A seventeenth-century collection of jests analyzed in like terms the mock debate on the corporeal or spiritual nature of farts: the proto-Swiftian remarks either on the corporeal nature of the *crepitus*, for everything that is composed by the four elements is organic (and farts can be *sicci, humidi, frigidi & calidi*) or on its spiritual essence, for everything that is invisible must be spiritual (*Nugae venales* 1648, 8-9), describes the token of singularity shared by farting and laughing, two comparatively irregular sequences of sounds.

Alongside the difference between laughter and speech, the Renaissance also mounted the case for the differences between the possible kinds of laughter, marked by diverging agglutinations of sounds, to the effect of itemizing dozens of different species. For the face faithfully reflects what is occurring inside the soul (*animi motum vultus indicat*), and so do all the physical movements that identify laughter (Puteanus 1644, 582). The Spanish physician Gabriel de Tarrega defined laughter as the sonorous movement of limbs (*motus sonorus membrorum*, 1524, 90r). Yet things soon became more inordinate, for instance in scholars like Politianus (1606, 19), who parsed the different natures and types of laughter. By way of subsequent partitions, which a Ramist reader would have no doubt appreciated, one learns that for the Renaissance laughter can be great or little; rare or frequent and dense, which might be elicited by indifferent things; late and morose, or quick; quick, in the sense that it is caused quickly and quickly subsides, and so forth.

The deformity caused by laughter jumps to view in the physiological events that shake up the body engulfed by sudden contrasting emotions. Let us consider three different treatments of the subject, respectively focused on the analysis of laughter as the effect of the passage of spirits from the heart to the face or from the brain to the face, and on the contrasting movements that bespeak laughter.

Musing on the fractious nature of laughter, Parravicino (1615, 17-8) remarked that laughter is one of those things, like sound or songs, that do not yield any permanence or stability, but are continuously in becoming, "continuamente sta in starsi." If we want to know what it is, we had better investigate it from its effects and thus opt for description, rather than definition. Parravicino describes laughter as a passion founded on the sensitive soul and derived by sudden elation (*subita allegrezza*). For the jest to cause laughter, argues Parravicino, it is required that it be sudden. At first, the soul receives the commotion, then the spirits abandon the heart, communicating the movement through all limbs, especially the face, which is greatly agitated in a sort of sanguineous erection.[21] The movement of spirits from the heart to the face is betrayed by the appearance of a reddish hue on the latter. Yet, pleasant things are not enough to make us laugh, if our souls do not move with the help of blood and its spirits almost to embrace the delightful object (*ad abbracciar l'oggetto grato*, 21). The image of this object, proposed to the soul by our senses, reaches the heart, which immediately craves to embrace it, and thus opens up and makes to reach for it: "esso come cosa grata volendola abbracciare, si slarga." As it is unable to move, the heart sends out its spirits: the effect is the inordinate movement of the parts of the visage we witness in the laugher (24).

Nancel adopted a different theory. The whole body reacts sympathetically to the agitation of the soul and the brain; the brain sends orders to the sinews, agitating the body; the brain palpitates, dilating and contracting, even pouring forth tears (Screech 1970, 220-1). More generally, comic theory has to interpret these contrasting movements in the body, as we have already seen with Fracastorio and Vives at the end of the preceding section. Joubert (1579, 87-8) thus analyzed the *matière* of laughter. It consists of two contrasting movements. The ridiculous thing moves us to pleasure and sadness: pleasure, as it does not deserve pity and is not harmful, and thus the heart rejoices and opens up to true joy (*le coeur s'an rejouït, & s'elargit*); sadness, as this ridiculousness derives from hoax and depravity, and therefore the heart closes up in pain (*le coeur . . ., comme santant douleur, s'etressit & resserre*). Laughter embodies the contrasting movement of these emotions. Mancini (1591, 101, 139) dubbed it as *duplici ratione motus, atque impulsus*: laughter, a passion proper of humankind, is an involuntary dilatation of the heart, following a constriction of the praecordium and of those muscles that are at the sides of the mouth; it is performed by the rational soul through the apprehension of a species of turpitude devoid of pain.

And yet this is still moderate laughter, a twofold movement that cannot be controlled because of its suddenness. In excessive laughter, the alterity of the risible destabilizes all theoretical constraints and legitimizations. Laughter is natural, involuntary: yet it can be contained by usage and reason, preventing the excessive kind that shakes up all the body (*concutiens corpus universum*, Vives 1555, 203). In fact, laughter was eschewed as one the most suspicious movements affecting the body, as the permanent deformation of the physical traits in the excessive laugher conveyed the corruption of virtuous mediocrity.[22] The Rule of St. Benedict (7:56) quoted the Bible (Eccl 21.20) to the effect of the loud deformity induced by laughter: "Stultus in risu exaltat vocem suam" ["A foole lifteth up his voyce with laughter"] (LeGoff 1990). One of the major distinctions between the liberal jester and the immoderate fool imported on the deformity caused by excessive laughter: the ever-laughing fool distorts his face, signifying through his facial ugliness the moral depravity deep-seated in unrestrained derision. In *The Ship of Fools*, mockers and scorners were subsumed under the example of Cham, "the son of Noy / Whiche laughyd his Father vnto derysyon" (Barclay 1874, 214). Laughter naturally bears on the "disordred and vngoodly maners," offering a panorama of fools reveling in laughing and moral corruption, whose distorted, grinning faces in the original edition testify to both kinds of deformity, in the body as well as the soul: "Some starynge some cryeng some haue great slace / In rybawde wordes, some in deuysyons / Some them delyte in scornes and derysons" (64). In terms of the ilk Alan of Lille (1955, 7.102:76r) described the right type of laughter that originally adorned our body: before its corruption, laughter did not deform the mouth (*nullo deformans ora cachinno*). Excessive laughter befits the fatuous person: the laughing mouth aptly signifies the man that, in the throes of laughter, contorts himself in derision (*la bocca che ridendo se storze per derision d'altri*, Scotus 1555, 76). Analogously, Castiglione (1900, 157, 160) enjoined the Courtier to refrain from scurrilous, continuous laughter; nor is it comely for him "to make weepinge and laughing faces, to make soundes and voices."

Politianus (1606) offered a compact theory of excessive laughter. After having performed the division of the object, laughter, into its several branches, Politianus proceeds to the description of the subject, the figure of the laugher. Laughter is inherently associated with an inordinate movement; for good measure, Politianus describes it in its most violent form, which utterly discomposes the laugher's body. The mouth has become a gulf, almost breaking ajar the jaws; the lips are unnaturally contracted until showing the *gelasini*, the teeth of laughter; the eyebrows are contracted or corrugated; the region encircling the mouth, called *peripheria* by the Greeks, is especially commoved by laughter. The face looks distorted and depraved. All parts of the body, including head, arms and legs, act inordinately. The whole body, alongside the distortion of the mouth, seems almost to have dissolved its pristine form. Movements become irregular and disorderly, as laughers alternatively start to run on the spot or even lie down on the ground as taken by a seizure. The whole body becomes disarranged: it suffers from a sort of ludicrous erection owing to the copious affluence of spirits, which release their flux through the limbs until the apotheosis of self-consumption, and then falls back on comparative quietness, shedding tears that are said to be warmer than those deriving from pain (Politianus's distinctive addition to the tradition). The voice is impeded, as the laugher, almost unable to talk, utters inchoate repetitions or tremulously whispers half-formed words (41-2, 45).

By all standards, this was a benign report. One is usually treated to more revealing epithets for the absence of the orthodox human figure in the excessive laugher. Animal features convey moral corruption, in a constant relation between excessive laughter and the physical signs of the distorted visage. The courtier should not "make il fauoured gestures, distorting his countenance, and disfiguring his bodie . . . It is an yll noyse to heare a man rayse his voyce highe, lyke to a common Cryer" (Della Casa 1576, 70-1, 86). Laughter was ironically compared to other bathetic ways of discharging the body while sitting at table: "You so should sometimes laugh, that meate, which in your mouth doth lie, / Might sodainely from out the same into the platter flie" (Dedekind 1605, 66). Preceptors often reprobated the immoderate laughter that shakes up the human figure, "lo smoderato riso & crollante la persona"; one should not produce neighing sounds when laughing, nor corrugate the mouth until showing the teeth of laughter—for this is sardonic laughter, which rather befits dogs (*Operetta utile* 1515, A4r).

Speaking of the laughing man's best friends, even liberal jesting was commonly compared to biting. No doubt hilarity is opposed to the rusticity of those who never laugh or smile. The good jester, however, bites with discretion, and the abuse in urbane laughter is vividly conveyed by the distorted usage of the mouth: "There be some Iestes that bite, and some that bite not at all . . . . Iestes must bite the hearer like a sheepe, but not like a dogge." Immoderate laughers often "cannot forbeare their laughing, but laughe in spyte of their teeth, from whom as from our right and lawfull Iudges, we must not appeale to our selues" (Della Casa 1576, 66, 70). On the other hand, the moderate bites given by lawful jesting can provoke sympathetic laughter and pleasure even in their object. Jests should not cause pain. Having to reply to jests coming from persons of higher rank, one will reply to their bites without any bite ("senza morso alcuno"), only acknowledging the first offense with moderate defense (Parravicino 1615, 44, 48). This tradition reprimanded open scoffing: "We must neither reproue the blemishes of nature in other men, nor make a sport to counterfeit their imperfections" (*Rich Cabinet* 1616, 174v-175r). And the legitimacy of such tender bites was extended to comedy as well. A posthumous praise of a famous Italian actress eulogized her biting (*mordace*) ability in scourging the vices (Pandolfi 1957-8, 2:145). Reporting the performance of a *Comedia all'improuiso* in Germany, Troiano added that the ladies, although incapable of understanding the Italian actors, were brought to the extreme of laughter, so much so that all beholders graciously incurred in the violation of etiquette and generously showed the *gelasini*: "Incominciarono a mostrare i denti delle risa" (Troiano 1569, 3.2: 146v, 147v).

Comic theory favored the instinctive connection between the screeching sound of excessive laughter and its animal connotations. This was most explicitly clear in the conventional distinction between good actors and fools. Discussing the aptest delivery of lines, Cecchini (Pandolfi 1957-8, 4:85) uncannily commented that the abrupt pronunciation of words like laughter (*riso*), especially when the untrained actor dwells upon its first letter one instant too many, is an invitation to barking: "Fanno quella r. così lunga, che par proprio ch'invitino i cani a latrare." As Malvolio will learn because of his unnatural smiling, the courtier must avoid excessive smiling when he pays homage to his lord, for this can be mistaken for derision: "Like as some doe, who by their continuall grining and shewing of their teethe, make men doubt whether they honour them, or laugh at them" (Guazzo 1581, 26r). Fools are the best examples of how these abrupt distempers in the human body can be counterfeited to generate more laughter. Garzoni (1587, 119:815-16) described the mongrelized show of a *buffone* who usually distorts his lips like a monstrous mask, "con le labbra torte, che par un mascherone contrafatto," juts out his tongue like a dog exhausted with thirst and by means of his wild convulsions induces contagious laughter in the beholders. Instead, the graceful actor of the Commedia dell'Arte strives to provoke delight. Barbieri (1971, 33-4), the author of a celebrated apology of acting, reported that, on a bodily level, there is a hiatus between virtuous laughter (*riso*) and devilish grin (*ghigno*). Both actors and fools arouse laughter: yet, in the former, laughter stems from pleasant wit and equivocation, in the latter from *trabbochevole prontezza*, excessive quickness. If delight is not moved by profit, laughter itself is derided, since the grin does not always bubble up out of sheer joy: "Resta il riso deriso; atteso che il ghigno non gorgoglia sempre per lo gaudio."[23] The fool cannot control himself, nor can he counterfeit gravity, "for as soone as euer hee setleth his countenance, he discouers a change; and in the very restraint, bursts out into ridiculous action in one manner, or other" (*The Rich Cabinet* 1616, 61r).

Aristotle's reference to the distorted visage of the ridiculous person was hardly a peripheric remark. For Avicenna (1974, 3.5.14:75), the Aristotelian restriction of the risible to a definite genus of evil calling for ridicule and mocking are summed up by the comic mask, where the three attributes of ugliness, bad temper and freedom from any sign of grief change its appearance: ugliness, "because it is necessary to change from the natural shape to contempt"; bad temper, "because it is meant to portray a general lack of esteem towards someone and an appearance of prejudice against him"; and freedom from any sign of grief, because this is not an angry man's facial expression. In Averroes' interpretation (1986, 3.18:72), Aristotle posits a deeper definitory analogy between ugliness, viciousness and absence of pain and the very nature of the risible. The sign that what is ridiculous must combine these three characteristics is that they are present in the face of the ridiculous person, in the ugliness of its face, its mis-shapenness, and the indifference to its ridiculousness, whereas the face of the angry man betrays the presence of something ugly and anxious in his soul.[24]

The facial distortion caused by laughter also admits of a mirror effect: one may be induced into laughter even by seeing somebody else's deformity. The natural movement of lips may reveal the teeth to the extent of violating the grace of laughter and provoking a sense of deformity that will beget laughter among strangers and reprobation among friends (Pesserl 1602, A4r). Maggi (1970, 302), the champion of sudden surprise, interprets Aristotle's precept on painless deformity as extended to the face of the comic object, which must be deformed and distorted without pain. For there is an analogy between laughter and its object: apart from the laughter occasioned by the presence of sons or friends or by physical stimuli like titillation, the presence of *peccatum & turpe sine dolore* causes legitimate laughter in us when we laugh and distort our mouth (*cum deformitate, vel distortione oris*); yet, nobody would legitimately laugh at the face of a person contracted in sincere pain (Berrettari 1603, 19r, 20r).

It is my point that the temporary absence of the human in the laugher's body is as an iconic rendering of diversion, the very element that, to the eyes of the Renaissance, most bespoke laughter. Beneath the theoretical tiers of good and bad laughter, the debatable property of humankind constantly elides the human in a moment of protracted absence, leaving the scene to the emergence of beastly contortion. Much of the critical effort at containment derived from the paradox of laughter as a typical beacon of human nature and yet something that escapes our control. The Renaissance enhanced the sense of temporary diversion from the rule as well as from our expectations and concerns.

Albeit placed in our body, laughter is not confined to the corporeal mansion, nor is it only an operation of the body alone (*risus non est corporis operatio tantum*). As soon as it takes place, some kind of cognition is granted as well (Iossius 1580, 45). The precepts on the diverting nature of laughter are to be coupled with the recreation it may legitimately offer to princes and audiences alike. Scotus (1608, 4.1:190) saw in the *ludus liberalis* a healthy diversion from the scholar's continuous application, which, as *Middlemarch*'s Dr. Casaubon should have known, would otherwise dry up all his spirits: if the soul is always bent on study, vehemently applied to the task of saying or doing something, its vital spirits will be dissipated. As a virtuous exercise for the courtier and the gracious actor, laughter enables the recreation of spirits. Aquinas had established the point: mirth and entertainment are necessary forms of rest, offering a temporary recess from the continuous exercise of virtue (*ST* 2-2.168.3 ad 3). Glossing the passage in his self-advertising manifesto, Andreini (Pandolfi 1957-8, 3:336) averred that recreation and pastimes are necessary to human commerce, since our soul craves rest and relaxation, the kind it gets from the sport and entertainment occasioned by jests and merry actions.[25] Jest-books and treatises likewise attested the medicinal powers of laughter, and many Italian actors called themselves doctors. Laughter is lawful inasmuch it occurs now and then as a *tempestiva laboris intermissione* before one hastens back to business as usual (Barlandus 1529, A1v). Erasmus summed up the distinctive quality of good jesting in its occasional, diverting nature: "Nether doe I esteme it a thyng worthye blame euer now and then with laughter to refreshe the mynde with cures and maters of charge." Furthermore, the apparent simplicity of laughter conceals a deeper meaning. Under the pretence of the witty joke or jest, laughter diverts us to the true image of man, as in the famous example of Diogenes:

> For what could bee a more fond thyng to laugh at then Diogenes geoying from place to place with a candle in his hande at high noonetid saiying still & he did seeke a manne: But in y[e] meane tyme by laughying, wee learne that he is not by & by in all the halfe a name, that hath the figure and shape of a manne (whiche images also of wood & stone haue,) but to fynd out a manne, the botome of the herte and mynde must bee found out. (Erasmus 1542, 7r-v)

Also because of their intellectual momentum, jests must be carefully planned and performed. Being "no other thing but deceites," they demand "subtilnes and craft" and "quicken the notions of the minde" (Della Casa 1576, 67-8). However, the quickness of jests might also be prone to unwanted diversion from the main thread of the narration. Cecchini (Pandolfi 1957-8, 4:87) exhorted the good actor and playwright to refrain from lending too much importance to humor: for the ridiculous parts often threaten to disrupt the order of the whole comedy, offering useless digressions that make the audience forget the plot and thus relinquish the thread of the comedy (*rompono il filo della Comedia*). The appropriate brand of jesting is never disjoined or set apart from the path (*sentiero*) of the comedy.

By offering a diversion from continuous exercise, laughter also diverts the sequence of our expectations. Drawing on Cicero, Castiglione (1900, 168, 172, 178) argued that a pleasant jest occurs "when we give eare to heare one thinge, and he that maketh answere, speaketh an other and is alleaged contrarye to expectacion." Thanks to witty turns of phrase and sentence, the merry jesting "maketh a man laughe muche, bicause it bryngeth wyth it other maner answeres then a manne looketh for to heare." The dynamics of jesting represents diversion even in its form, for instance when "woordes placed contrarywyse give a great ornament" or when "a contrarye clause is sett agaynste another." Jesting practises a certain kind of "dissimulacion, whan a man speaketh one thinge and privilie meaneth another." The good sort of jesting lies on understatement, "that who so heareth and seeth us, may by our wordes and countenances imagin much more then he seeth and heareth, and upon that take occasion to laughe" (161). The good jester responds to this ideal of diversion in his own figure, since he is encouraged to "turne all his thoughtes and force of minde to love, and (as it were) to reverence the Prince he serveth above al other thinges" (122-23). The straight man for others' jests, he must act as an indirect "inciter to discouer and reason" and therefore "propound questions easie to be answered, laying them sometimes neare the professions or knowledge of those with whom we are" (Scotus 1614, 234-5).

As a further constituent of diversion, laughter takes away time and takes place in time. One of the endemic objections raised against acting was time-wasting. In their apologetical replies, the Italian actors inverted the argument: laughter buys up time. Courtesans complain that their usual customers now spend their pastime at the theater: the hours previously allotted to the ladies, who are no longer "accosted," have been now given up to such virtuous performances. A simple ticket allows for the representation of diverse scenes from real life, buying up that time that would be devoted to other forms of entertainment: "Con il qual prezzo si compra ancora quel tempo, che da molti potrebbe esser speso in quei trattenimenti" (Cecchini 1616, 15, 22).[26] Not only this: laughter also takes away time, drawing away the attention from other concomitant things. It bars simultaneity through an unconscious dip into the temporary absence of reason, says Castiglione (1900, 156): "Whatsoever therfore causeth laughter, the same maketh the minde jocunde and geveth pleasure, nor suffreth a man in that instant to minde the troublesome greefes that our life is full of."

The pleasure associated with the diverting nature of laughter derives from our inherent relish for variety. Quintilian had argued that the talent for the *ridiculum* assuages the judge by exciting his laughter and frequently diverts his attention from the case: "Animum ab intentione rerum frequenter avertit" (*Institutio Oratoria* 6.3.1). Resting on Cicero's doctrine of the comical salts that the orator may use to spice up his talk and entertain the audience, Robortello (1548, 52, 53) observes that the audience is greatly affected by the masterful shift from piety to mirth and hilarity (*ad commiserationem & lacrimas cieamus, ad laetitiam & hilaritatem reuocemus*), and hilarity itself is another means of affecting the souls of the listeners. Since "the naturall inclination of our corrupt affections . . . is inamored of nothing so much as of Variety," and "since of all the varieties with which we feaste and surfeit our mindes, Iests (though cloated in foolish, filthy, or unfit garments) haue got the most eminent and precedent place in mens soules" (Copley 1614, A2r), laughter responds to our taste for variety and appeases our desire for recreation.

Transformation, vicissitude, and constant interchange between elements *à la Barabas* informed the Renaissance tradition on pleasure. For the four elements are in a pattern of "continual change both amongst themselves togither, and eche of them seuerally." The human being embodies the greatest token of variety: "During the time while he liueth from the infancy, euen til his old age, he hath neuer the same things in him, neither is the same: but is stil renewed, subject to change as wel in his body, . . . as in his minde." Variety produces, and both responds to, a pleasure principle: "it seemeth that nature taketh pleasure, to supply the indigence of man, not only producing euery one more apt for something then another . . . but also making the people borne in diuers parts of the habitable earth, to differ in inclinations, and complexions" (Le Roy 1594, 5v, 11r-v; cf. Norden 1600).

An explicit association of laughter with vicissitude and general diversion within the fabric of the cosmos occurs in a chapter devoted by the Italian polymath Anton Francesco Doni to the "risible world," the scene of our frail passions and inane longings. For Doni, the variety of ludicrous things derives from our insatiable appetite for curiosity. Striving to embrace its object, desire chases it away from day to day: "la cosa se ne va d'oggi in domani." At the end of our relentless endeavors, we are exhausted by our own internal engine, which is transfixed by Doni (1994, 132-3, 135 – my translation) into the image of a perpetual mill:

> After we have turned the mill for a long time, here, the wheel of our brain stops, the water of fury is stopped dry and there is nothing else to grind. For don't we turn the mill of time? Continuously one hour goes by and there comes another; when you reach the bottom, here you start again. Discharging and filling your body, now isn't this yet another mill to turn? The letters of the alphabet are a mill turning through all books, and we turn our lives along them. Generation and corruption is a giant mill to turn. And is there a more beautiful mill than when we want or want not to, we are satisfied or not, we like or dislike something? And what about another beautiful mill, crying and laughter?

Laughter is a prodigious mill that takes time away from other things and represents the human nature in its continuous quest for variety and diversion. While taking place in time, it is also an absence from time that temporarily unframes the human figure and ultimately blurs any comic theory. Frye (1965, 139) saw the comical movement between the reversals of the original postulates of the comedy, which mark its conclusion as a "turning around."[27] It is time to lend an ear to Feste's miniatured report of Malvolio's ominous theory of laughter, near the end of *Twelfth Night*: "'Madam, why laugh you at such a barren rascall. / and you smile not, he's gagged'? And thus the whirligig / of time brings in his revenges" (*TN* 5.1.373-6).

"Accosting" *Twelfth Night* through Renaissance comic theory often narrows the focus onto violations against the rules of good laughter (Barber 1986). Then again, this amounts to falling back on laughter *in* Shakespeare, also gelling into the hardly surprising hiatus between the virtuous precepts of Renaissance comic theory and the outrageous practice launched by Feste and Maria—so what?

In fact, both the virtuous application of Renaissance comic theory and the Bakhtinian exaltation of inversive laughter are enslaved to a similar marginalization of laughter: comic theory is never accepted as a legitimate discourse *per se*. It accompanies recreation and purging, and its diversion is not the subject, but the instrument by which the virtuous exercise of recreation can take place. On the other hand, when we emphasize the allegedly inversive powers of laughter, we likewise use laughter as an accompanying cause that prompts more general descriptions of society. In either case, laughter is inserted back into the margins of critical discourse as an illustrative appendage.

The diverting nature of laughter I have tried to etch out explodes both the poetics of gracious constraint exemplified by Renaissance comic theory and the poetics of enfranchisement vindicated by Bakhtin. My hypothesis is that Renaissance comic theory envisioned laughter in ways widely different from its virtuous or inversive usage. Laughter is manifold diversion: it is a diversion from the things that becomes a diversion itself, also responding to an inner diversion within the human being as well. My intention is to juxtapose (accost) the similarity of representation between absence, diversion and laughter. And here one needs images rather than words. The best intimations of the flickering, volatile nature of laughter in the Shakespearean text are interpretative devices that might be likened to the allegorical interpretation of the images of pagan deities. I will present four characters (since pages and comedies must contain characters) which respectively impersonate four topics of interpretation of laughter and *Twelfth Night*: *if, where, presence* and *absence*.

The "if" (Orsino), taken from the incipit of the comedy, embodies comic theory, the belief that good laughter can restore the dissipated spirits. The "where" (Viola) is the effort to visualize the play's recurrent references to the construction of the comic scene as a virtual place whereby characters, depending on their presence either on the margins or inside the picture, are led back to the production of laughter. As to the "presence" and "absence," they are conveyed by the contrasting characters of Malvolio, much too present in the scene of laughter, and Feste, continuously deferred and diverted to its margins.

My first image is the "if." Music was advocated as a remedy against melancholy even by the harshest censors of public entertainment. Northbrooke (1843, 109) allowed for the use of music on the basis of the Biblical example of Saul's (1 Sam 16.23): "They used then to recreate the mindes, and to comfort such as were pensiue, heauy and sad for the deade: as Saule being heauie . . . caused Dauid to play upon the harpe to refresh him."[28] The first twenty lines of *Twelfth Night* encompass the whole theory of recreational laughter in a nutshell. The play is launched by the recreational premise stated by Orsino in the opening speech: "*If* music be the food of love, play on, / Give me excess of it, that, surfeiting, / The appetite may sicken, and so die" (*TN* 1.1.1-3). Mirth, much like that "if," envisions a place where music, as a form of diversion, takes away time, recreating and diverting the spirits and alternating between repetition and satisfaction: "Enough, no more" (7).[29] The production of music, and its attendant effects on the ruler's belabored spirits, follow an intermittent pattern, praising the quickness of love: for whatever enters there, "falls into abatement and low price, / Even in a minute" (1.1.13-4).

Much as the volatile nature of laughter, music mirrors the incessant fatigue occasioned by Orsino's desire, the agency of change and impossible pursuit that the "if" tries to accommodate: "My desires . . . [e]'er since pursue me" (1.1.22-3). Music and the recreation later afforded by Feste's songs offer a temporary diversion away from this incessant trajectory towards self-consumption.

The theme of courteous love in *Twelfth Night* is attuned to the constant intimation of the characters being diverted somewhere else, to the failure in checking the concomitant flow of spirits. It will be remembered that two of the comical staples listed by Castelvetro were the encounter with long-lost characters and the amorous deception. Olivia's love has been truly diverted from its veritable source as well: if such a noble heart can pay this debt of love to a brother, "[h]ow will she love, when the rich golden shaft / Hath kill'd the flock of all affections else" (1.1.35-6). Olivia's report of the quickness with which the fire of love can catch, its "invisible and subtle stealth" (1.5.301), is also keyed on a poetics of misplacement, an intimation of aiming constantly off the true target, hence embracing the wrong object of desire, the messenger instead of the master.[30] The other absent characters (like Orsino) are likewise diverted from the scene. Much as his opening lines seem to undermine the pretence of the theory of recreation, Orsino himself is placed into virtual existence. Olivia "supposes" him virtuous and noble, yet she cannot love him (262-3, 66). The "if" also informs the representation of novel pleasures aroused by the unknown. As a messenger, Viola uses the "if" to question the identity of Olivia, much as if her message could risk consumption: "I pray you tell me if this be the lady of the house, for I never saw her. I would be loath to cast away my speech" (172-4). The "if" is the theory of presence, what might have well been if all the characters had fallen in love and accordingly directed their spirits to the true object of their desire, if the apprehension of the future good bestowed by the sense of elation had been directed towards the right target.

Inherent in this theory of correct love in *Twelfth Night* is the intimation that desire never places its object. Laughter was said to precede the apprehension of some future good, either had or about to be had. What *Twelfth Night* shows is the presence of the topic I dubbed "where," the constant effort to visualize characters as complying with a position in the symbolic topography of the comedy. If the theory of laughter were generally good, and spirits could be restored either by music, jesting and love, then the scene would be complete and the object would be there. What we do have instead is that even the cheap laughter of practical jokes diverts the object away from the scene: only jesters can say where it is. The objects of carping are meticulously assigned to exact roles limited by honest mirth. Maria, the mastermind of jesting in all its upshots, prescribes Sir Toby to adhere to the conventions of laughter, "the modest limits of order" (1.3.8-9). Malvolio, often described by scholars as a bookish advocate of the Puritan distaste for wit, imaginatively translates this requirement into impossible self-division, again prefaced by the "if," the convention of good laughter: "If you can separate yourself and your misdemeanours, you are welcome to the house" (2.3.98-9).

The misplacing of the object of desire also underscores the recreation of amorous laughter through Viola's intermittent envoys. It has been noted that *Twelfth Night* festively inverts the figure of Viola as the conventional go-between that had to arrange marriages, turning her into the false go-between who woos for herself rather than for her master (Cook 1991, 113-4). I would like to add that, as the messenger of amorous laughter, Viola enacts the pleasure of diversion precisely through such a liminal existence. She is conspicuously described almost in the capacity of a liminal god, a "divinity" (*TN* 1.5.221) that, like the god of cheer, Comus, waits at the door for the fulfillment of the festive promises of mirth.[31] As the young messenger of love, Viola would have been expected to be "more prompt to laugh then other," for "Yoong women are under the safegard and tuition of Venus, the Goddesse of laughter, and so they doe easily laugh . . . they haue tender and delicate bodies, and laughter is no other thing then a spice of Ioy, wantonnesse, or tickling" (Chartier 1596, 11). Raised to the status of Orsino's conscience ("I have unclasp'd / To thee the book even of my secret soul"), Viola performs liminal, unwavering duties for him at Olivia's gate: "stand at her doors" (*TN* 1.4.13-4, 16).

"There's one at the gate" (126-7)—while denouncing Viola's ungainly attributes as a messenger, Malvolio underscores her stubborn presence on the margins of the *hortus conclusus* where the encounters with Olivia will take place.[32] Viola will "stand at your door like a sheriff's post, . . . but he'll speak with you" (149-51). From her pristine status as a messenger, Viola turns into the message for Olivia, an agency constantly diverted away to the place of emission and then recalled to the garden, even with perfunctory devices such as the non-existing ring Olivia professes to give back to Viola. All this happens while Viola is taking away time for the recreation of Olivia's spirits dissipated by protracted mourning. The clock upbraids Olivia "with the waste of time" (3.1.132), in yet another moment of suspension: the lady has enjoyed thorough recreation by perusing the object of her desire: "Why then methinks 'tis time to smile again" (128). Viola receives "entertainment," diverted from the main trajectory that should unite Orsino and Viola. She has egressed from the margins of her master's commission to negotiate with Olivia's face—"You are now out of your text" (1.5.235-6). "Yet come again" (3.1.165): Viola lives in her being diverted away and made to come back to the garden, out of the text of Orsino's original commission and into the scene construed by Olivia.

Malvolio is the "presence" of the play. In this sense, the subplot of *Twelfth Night* ad-libs the Renaissance theory of correct mirth. Resting on the millennial tradition which originated from Aristotle, Wilson (1909, 136) claimed that, while it is impossible to ascertain the causes of the risible, yet "we laugh alwaies at those things, which either onely or chiefly touch handsomely, and wittely, some especiall fault, or fond behauiour in some one body, or some one thing," two types of deformity admirably embodied by Malvolio. And his salience for Shakespeare's comic theory has been duly underlined in criticism.[33]

Yet what Malvolio portends in his antifestivity is precisely the "presence" of the theory of correct laughter. Olivia voices the law of urban jesting in her defense of Feste: "There is no slander in an allowed fool, though he do nothing but rail" (*TN* 1.5.93-4). Drawing on the confessional language, Barbieri (1971, 107) contended that laughter is not sinful in its nature, but rather because of the circumstances: "Le circostanze del ridere sono quelle che possono far il riso peccabile." Malvolio advocates a similar casuistry over the virtuous brand of mirth in his reprobation of the excessive laughter and the inhuman sounds produced by Sir Toby and Sir Andrew. In the process, while invoking the respect of the circumstances of civil laughter, Malvolio himself becomes much too conspicuous in his presence as a comical butt: "Is there no respect of place, persons, nor time in you?" (*TN* 2.3.92-4). Malvolio offers his ludicrous "presence" as a foil to the marginal activity of the jesters. He is framed inside the comic scene, easily hemmed in by the beholders while he fabricates the incongruity of his self-love. From an Aristotelian viewpoint, his moral deformity adamantly calls for purgation at Maria's hands: "The best persuaded of himself, so crammed (as he thinks) with excellencies, that it is his grounds of faith that all look on him love him" (149-52).

Laughter is a cage—*Twelfth Night* rings with this constant intimation of characters that are, like Viola, temporarily put out of the text and those that conversely are continually framed into a structure of interpretation. The letter scene, staging the literality of Malvolio's reading, juxtaposes his apparent faculty of construing the other characters and marginalizing them in his apprehension, with his actual process of being marginalized and construed into present laughter. While acting in their beholding, he makes the jesters marginal, absent, placing them into his talk and even extending his hand to the image of Sir Toby his bloated *philautia* has ghosted (2.5.66). In Maria's stage-managed show, contemplation only foments laughter by the act of filling the scene from the margins of the presence: "I will plant you two, and let the fool make a third, where he shall find the letter: observe his construction of it" (2.3.173-5).[34]

In his observation of the literal sense of Olivia's message, Malvolio becomes the presence created by the laughers on the margins of the scene. An internal theater of passions displays the effects of his vices, which are the cause of his ludicrous deformity: "Now he's deeply in: look how imagination blows him" (2.5.42-3). Malvolio visibly offers a sign of continuous presence, subjected to an entertainment that resolves itself into what the letter prescribes, a passage rendered by the eclipse of the human, the unnatural, protracted smiling that, hardly befitting the good courtier, transforms him into a grinning brute. Malvolio's folly consists of the belief in the magical correspondence between the letter and the events: "This concurs directly with the letter" (3.4.65-6). Yet his adherence belies the belief in the everlasting presence of something unchangeable, removed from the vicissitude of things. While he does nothing but smile, he professes to be looking for the innermost element of his soul, afar from the wild misrule of jesters—he asks to be allowed to enjoy his private (90), for he, like Barabas, is not of their element (125). Owing to his unnatural permanence in the midst of the transient nature of elements, Malvolio offers a cause for breaking one's sides with laughter. The notoriousness of the wrong he suffered testifies to his continuous presence in the beholders' eyes to make him ludicrous.

Although it is often argued that the lampooning of Malvolio is a striking violation of liberal jesting, it is also devoid of the element of surprise and *admiratio* that the Renaissance theories of laughter unanimously ascribed to the promptness of successful jesting. Such is Malvolio's compliance with the planned jest that he becomes a device for testing the theory to the upshot (4.2.73), artificially diverted to new scenes of derision until being confined and bound into a dark room. Far from being the simple recreation of spirits, laughter seems to imply the obliteration of a something or somebody, not merely to be derided but to be laughed out of existence (Poole 1994, 85). As the beacon of presence, a point-to-point adherence to the letter of jesting, Malvolio is safely maneuvered and diverted by the revelers, who pursue their entertainment to the apotheosis, until the purgation of all humors salutes Maria as the discoverer of human follies, like Diogenes in Erasmus's interpretation: "We may carry it thus for our pleasure, and his penance, till our very pastime, tired out of breath, prompt us to have mercy on him" (*TN* 3.4.138-40). Lacking *admiratio*, Malvolio's derision is a scene of presence conducted from the margins right to the upshot, no matter how dangerous and illiberal that could prove. Malvolio tests the letter of jesting. Yet jesting is precisely the art of diverting an object from its own internal theatre of passions into the central scene of derision. Thus the whirligig of time brings in his revenges, says Feste. Let it be not thought excessive to surmise that Malvolio, alongside ridiculing Puritan antifestivity, might well be a good example of the self-contained reading that juxtaposes the theory of laughter with its violations in order to argue either violation or confirmation of the rules on Shakespeare's part.

In *Twelfth Night* laughter sits on the margins, as befits the continuous "absence" of Feste, the main agency of diversion. For him to be a good, canonical jester, Feste has to be a marginal observer of the presence of others: "He must observe their mood on whom he jests, / The quality of persons, and the time" (3.1.63-4). Malvolio aptly captures the infectious quality of jesting, the fool's need to sponge on his neighbor and receive the clue from him, much as the good courtier was asked to deflect from direct taunting and rather target the mark close to the Prince. His description renders Feste's comic skill an absence by close proximity, a rascal who is undone if nothing viable is sent to him: "Look you now, he's out of his guard already: unless you laugh and minister occasion to him, he is gagged" (1.5.84-6). As a further token of his constant proximity, Feste puns on his whereabouts, for he lives "by" the church (3.1.5). This, and other quips by Feste, usually buttresses his ability as a corrupter of words, his skill in turning outward the wrong side of a sentence as if it were a glove (12). Seen from the vantage point of comic theory, such a brilliant self-advertisement of Feste's skill, together with rephrasing the Ciceronian praise of the unexpected turns in meaning and sentence structure which are favored by the audience, provides yet another sign of absence. Diverting the structure of words, living parasitically on the odds and ends that occasion serves him, refraining from being pinpointed in the topography of *Twelfth Night*—the fool, much as he should be as oft with the master as with the mistress, is never to be placed.

Where is Feste? Maria drops a tantalizing hint about his continuous absence, shortly after the beginning: "Tell me where thou hast been," for Olivia "will hang thee for thy absence. . . . Yet you will be hanged for being so long absent; or to be turned away—is not that as good as a hanging to you?" (1.5.1, 3-4, 16-8). "He is not here, so please your lordship, that should sing it" (2.4.8-9): Feste is absent also at the Duke's, where he should offer the solace of musical recreation and thus relieve the amorous passion through his song, vicariously recreating the pleasure and, like doctors-actors, being paid for that. For Orsino's offer to pay for his pleasure (69) is yet another embodiment of the vicarious principle of the "if," the theory of recreation through the diversion offered by fools. Asked to dodge the dissipation of spirits in Orsino, Feste evokes the final dissolution of all spirits by summoning what Orsino constantly tries to dispel and divert from the scene and that conversely occupies the center of Olivia's mourning: "*Come away, come away death, | And in sad cypress let me be laid. . . . | My part of death no one so true | Did share it*" (51-2, 57-8). As the agency of diversion and absence in the play, Feste envisions the ultimate destination of the other characters' as an indifferent diversion from their follies and vices which, much like the "good voyage of nothing" he wishes to Orsino, heads for nowhere(78-9).

Freund (1986, 475) questioned the "powerful waywardness of interpretive operations" in *Twelfth Night* by analyzing the relevance of absence as a constitutive component. I would like to add that absence, especially Feste's, is yet another term for the inherent diversion by which the play deploys its actions, from the recreation of amorous spirits to the lampooning of Malvolio. While Viola acts as the in-between that mediates between different instances of the "if," the theory of love and recreation—if music be the food of love, if the recreation of spirits exists—Feste reconstructs the presence of the others in terms of constant diversion. Seeing Sir Andrew and Sir Toby, he puts himself into the picture of "we three" (*TN* 2.3.17). As a good dialectician, he denies Viola any intellectual operation that might escape his wits: "I will conster to them whence you come; who you are and what you would are out of my welkin" (3.1.57-9).

For Feste is always diverted. In constant delay like the amorous messenger at Olivia's gate, Feste is always sent for: "Will you make me believe that I am not sent for you?" (4.1.1). In all his appearances on stage, Feste betrays the impossibility to tarry longer in a place. Even in his bogus manifestation as Sir Topas, Feste is desperately asked to go and report Malvolio's affliction to Olivia (4.2.24-5). While Malvolio, in his presence, offers a safe turf for practising the diverting nature of jesting right to the upshot, and thereon above it by all standards of courteous biting, Feste represents an idea of diversion where no upshot is available. He moves on the margins of laughter, on the limit where the theory of conventional laughter locates the "if's": "I am gone, sir, and anon, sir, / I'll be with you again" (4.2.125-6).

Feste performs the final clearing of the Malvolio affair by giving Olivia his letter. Through his fabricated appearance as an ever-smiling courtier, Malvolio is the artificial construction of the inhuman peeping through the odd nature of laughter. Even Feste wields a powerful flair of absence of humanity in his constant diversion—he is just as inhuman as laughter. He lives on the thresholds of the presence of laughter where Malvolio and the jesters are reabsorbed into the ear of comical theory:

> *O mistress mine, where are you roaming?*
> *. . . What is love? 'Tis not hereafter,*
> *Present mirth hath present laughter:*
> *What's to come is still unsure.*
> *In delay there lies no plenty.*
>
> (2.3.40, 48-51)

In delay and diversion lies Feste. Like laughter in Parravicino's description as a flickering entity that continuously becomes in becoming, in a flux of interrupted sounds that diverts our soul and body from the normal flow of conscience and self-constraint, Feste stays in staying, "sta in starsi."

Asking Berowne to visit "the speechless sick" and enforce them to smile, a task that Berowne dubs as "to move wild laughter in the throat of death," Rosalind thus enounces the theory of the birth of jesting: "A jest's prosperity lies in the ear / Of him that hears it, never in the tongue / Of him that makes it" (*LLL* 5.2.843, 847, 853-5). To escape, disarticulate the preinscribed terms used by "him that hears it," comic theory should restore some of its recondite images, the "if," "where" and the "presence" and "absence" exemplified by *Twelfth Night*, the first rudiments of a Shakespearean grammar of laughter. "Shakespeare in laughter" is the impossible desire to get, in a suspension, to the tongue that articulated those images and envisioned laughter as absence and diversion. "Shakespeare in laughter" also suggests that laughter is not a sign of other social, literary or political discourse, but a god of his own: Garzoni (1600, 63-4) described the ridiculous fools as those who, executing "follies for the most part, foppish and ridiculous," worship "the image of god *Risus*, adored of the ancients, they being recommended unto him, as their peculiar godhead and patrone"; it is to him that they move the petition, quite similar to the tenets of good laughter, to "remooue from their mindes that discontentment, which they receiue from humours phrenticall, delirant, melancholike, and sauage . . . wherefore many men are not a little bound unto thee, in perceiving by thy meanes, their hearts exhilarated, and mindes replenished with exceeding alacritie." Feste's diversion offers a radiant scrutiny of these fading margins of Renaissance laughter, a suspended walk on the neighboring purlieus of Shakespearean lustre where theory really matters.

Notes

Chapter One: A Descent Into Richard

1. See Mathieu-Castellani (1988). On confession as a contract, see Legendre (1986, 402). On anticlerical parody in literature, see McKinley (1993).

2. On the relation between Shakespeare, Hall and Holinshed, see Churchill (1970, 173-207, 211-13) and Neill (1976). More's history of Richard III, another source for Shakespeare, reports that the priest hid them "in such place, as by the occasion of his deathe, whiche onely knew it could never synce come to light" (More 1963, 2:86).

3. On providentiality in history, see Hassel (1987), Kelly (1970, 276-95) and Rackin (1990, 62-75). See also Hassel (1986) and Knapp (1994). One of the maledictions spat out at Richard explicitly invokes Biblical examples of the hollowing out performed by the worm of conscience (*R3* 1.3.222). Mason (1994) traces back the reference to Is 66.24 and Mk 9.44, 46, 48.

4. Lancashire and Warwickshire saw the resilience of a very active Catholicism, thanks to the work of both Marian and seminars priests (Trimble 1964, 139-55).

5. A Paul's Cross sermon in 1618 referred to those "Romanists who creep into great houses to lead captive simple women laden with sinnes"; still in 1642, the Jesuit confessor is a shrewd manipulator of conscience: "Confession is his engine by which he Skrews himselfe into acquaintance with all Affairs, all Dispositions; which he makes the best conducing to his ends, that is, the worst use of" (Sibthorpe 1618, A2v, A3r). See Morey (1978).

6. See Allison & Rogers (1994, 68 n. 329). Other Catholic figures who might have had some bearing on Shakespeare's religious background were Robert Persons, whose *Resolutio* (1582) offered an analysis of the various elements of sin and penance that bears analysis in relation to Hamlet and Othello; Jasper Heywood, the translator of Seneca, took Persons's position as superior of the few Jesuits in England; Robert Southwell dedicated *Mary Magdalen's Funeral Tears* and *Saint Peter's Complaint*, two works which gave rise to the "literature of tears" of the nineties, "to my worthy cousin, Master W. S." (Millward 1973, 43-67).

7. See McNeill (1951, 163-9). Lorenzo Valla similarly criticized the translation: the Latin term involves weariness or annoyance, whereas the Greek embeds more positive meanings such as "reconsidering one's judgment" or "concern to become better" (Bentley 1983, 64).

8. Whiting argues that by 1570 only a limited minority could have been classified as staunch Catholics, and that only a small percentage of the population could have been labeled as "committed Protestants"; the Reformation could thus be seen as "a decline from religious commitment into conformism and indifference," rather than a simple shift from Catholicism to Protestantism (1989, 267).

9. "Let everyone of the faithful of both sexes, after he has arrived at the years of discretion, alone faithfully confess all his sins at least once a year to his own priest, and let him strive to fulfill with all his power the penance enjoined" (Denzinger 1957, 173 n. 437). See Bériou (1983).

10. Analogous conclusions are in Tentler (1977, 82-133), Braswell (1983, 25-6) and Gallagher (1991, 80). On the *summae* as a guide to conduct, see Turrini (1991).

11. The English Catholic manuals of rhetorical theory are studied in Sullivan (1995). For a contextualization of casuistry, see Jonsen and Toulmin (1988).

12. Hopkins (1990, 32) observed that "penance in the romances bears a greater resemblance to the 'solemn penance' meted out in the Middle Ages only very occasionally and only to sinners whose offences had caused public scandal."

13. Braeckmans (1971, 191) argued that "nulle part le Concile n'affirmé que l'obligation de confesser les péchés mortels avant de célébrer ou avant de communier serait d'origine divine." Cf. Duval (1974).

14. For Ozment (1975, 156) "it is an irony still to be appreciated by many scholars that by so maximizing sinfulness (before God every man is guilty of every conceivable sin) Protestants tried to minimize its psychological burden (no man is required to ponder and recite his every actual sin)."

15. The proposition that seemed to regard confession *in absentia* as licit was condemned by Pope Clement VIII in 1602 (Fazzalaro 1950, 49).

16. A founding case is the episode of Zacharias, who was made dumb for his unbelief and then was forced to reveal his acquiescence to the name of John for his newborn sons by making signs and asking for writing tables (Lk 1.20). See Reginaldus (1622, 5, 33).

17. The ideal confessor will also welcome the sinner in a symbolical embrace that iterates the figure of Christ on the Cross: the sinner receives a hug from Him who stretched out his arms to embrace all humankind ("in omnium amplexus brachia sua expandit in cruce") and who let open his heart for being pierced by his persecutors, for whom he also prayed (Robert of Flamborough 1971, 1.1.3).

18. Cf. Faren (1485, A2r): "La premiere consideracion sera de regarder se le temps passe on a este toujours bien confesse."

19. A seventeenth-century French preacher described Lazarus's resurrection by exhorting his audience to a vivid representation of their mortal condition. They are enclosed into the tomb, unable to swing open the ponderous door: "il faut que vous reconnoissiez la grandeur de vostre maladie: & le danger où vous estes: mais ceste lumiere doit venire du Ciel, où vous ne levez jamais les yeux" (Godeau 1667, 312).

20. The genre of Calvinist passions is studied in Sunger (1994). For the general contexts of Biblical interpretation in this period, see Steinmetz (1990).

21. Ambrose refers to St. Peter's tears after having denied Christ: "flevit ut lacrimis suum posset lavare delictum" (*Exp. Ev. Sec. Luca* 10.90, *PL* 15.1826).

22. Besides, the *fletus* was a measure of time that originally indicated in the ancient Church one of the stages in the separation of the sinner from the body of believers before full acceptance (Morin 1682, 205.1.c-d).

23. Even the killers, bemoaning the Princes' fate, "Wept like two children, in their deaths' sad story" (*R3* 4.3.8).

24. Brooks thus reconstructs Shakespeare's inference from the sources behind the scene: "The corpse of Henry VI was taken to Chertsey, a journey fifteen miles out of London, for burial, and (according to Holinshed and Stow), while at rest at St. Paul's and further on at Blackfriars, it bled, traditionally a sign of murder. It was in the presence of the murderer that such corpses were

ordinarily supposed to bleed afresh: so these incidents would readily suggest an encounter between Richard and the funeral procession" (Brooks 1980, 728).

25. Zumthor (1987) argues that the practice of auricular confession enlarged itself with the rise of both a penitential theology constructed on writing and a predicatory art based on oral examples and local diffusion.

26. "For the abundance of the heart the mouth speaketh" (Mt 12.34). Cf. Mk 7.14-5. One of the earliest references in doctrinal writing to the heart as the original source of confession occurs in *The Shepherd of Hermas*, an apocalypse whereby repentance after baptism is granted only once: all sins will be forgiven "to all the saints who have sinned up to this day, if they repent with their whole heart and put aside double-mindedness from their heart" (2.2.4).

27. Augustine is commenting on Rom 10.10: "For with the heart man beleeueth vnto righteousnes, and with the mouth man confesseth to saluation."

28. Vincenzo Bruno expediently sums up the tripartite theory of satisfaction: "Al the sortes of Satisfactions are reduced vnto these three onely, Fasting or other corporall asperities: Almes, and Prayer, which are correspondent vnto three good things of a man: that is, the goodes of the Soule, the goods of the Body, and Exterior goodes" (1597, 59).

29. Either in its direct or indirect form of transmission, the Senecan scenario is still taken for granted (Boas 1914, 130-1; Brooks 1980, 727-33; Arkins 1995).

30. Remarking the similarity to the analogous in *Phaedra*, a passage which Shakespeare also adapted in *Titus Andronicus*; Whitaker (1953, 66) also observed that the same combination of elements was present in Thomas Legge's *Richardus Tertius*, a Latin play probably staged at St. John's College, Cambridge, in 1579. See also Deianira offering her breast to Hyllus in *Hercules Oetheus* (1000-2). Cf. the 1581 translation of the passage: "My foltring tong doth in my mouth my tale begun denye"; Hippolitus exhorts his stepmother: "the griefe that galles your heart come whisper in mine eare" (Seneca 1927, 1:158).

31. Seneca does not refer to crying: "Cecidere fratres: arma non servant modum, / Nec temperari facile: nec reprimi potest / Stricti ensis ira: bella delectat cruor" (*Hercules Furens*, 403-5, 13v).

32. The Folio text appends the passage with a revealing stage-direction for Richard's confession: *"[Kneels] he lays his breast open, she offers at [it] with his sword."*

33. On confession and the *artes moriendi*, see Doebler (1974), Ariès (1981) and Gurevic (1982).

34. While couched in the classical analogues of the encounter between Aeneas and Palinurus (Jones 1977, 207-11), as well as of Juno's descent into Hades in Ovid (Brooks 1979, 145-7), the scene hosts the confessional vision of the last things (Narkin 1967, 147-50).

35. Iser (1993) notes the presence of prophetic dreams and the "protracted curses" as permeating a rise and fall pattern.

36. On the killing of sleep, see *R3* 1.3.225-27, 4.1.83-4, 5.3.161-62.

37. Colley (1986) detected here an intimation of the Herod figure.

Chapter Two: What the Matter Is With Barabas

1. The episode, originally reported in 1503, was hinted at in the chapters 7 and 8 of the *Prince*, of which there existed at least three English translations

before 1585. For the progression from the simple *notitia* to the status of *exemplum*, see Godorecci (1993).

2. Wealth is dismissed as a candidate for happiness on the grounds "that it is sought only for the sake of further goods. In this respect . . . the other goods mentioned—pleasure, honor, and virtue. are more plausible candidates for happiness, since they are loved for themselves"; even these candidates are however dismissed in the end (Krant 1989, 226). *Teleion,* the Greek word usually translated as perfect, means literally "endy": something is more *teleion* if chosen for its own sake, not for anything else (Kenny 1991, 71). See also Kaye (1998).

3. For the rise of the merchant-financier and the decline of the image of the merchant as a usurer, see Miskinin (1979) and Stevenson (1984).

4. On Barabas as the prehistory of capitalism, see Thurn (1994) and Halpern (1991).

5. For Garber, this famous line introduces the theme of the constant attempt, performed by all the characters, to exercise control one over another (1977, 7).

6. See Gill (1989, 83-107) and Cohen 1996. For the ancient theories of matter, see Vidal (1977).

7. For the influence of Lucretius on the Renaissance, see Minadeo (1969).

8. On cosmogony in Ovid, see Myers (1994). For the relationship between Marlowe and Ovid, see Pearcy (1984).

9. "All things doo chaunge. But nothing sure dooth perish. This same spright / Dooth fleete, and fisking heere and there dooth swiftly take his flyght / From one place to another place" (*Shakespeare's Ovid* 1961, 15.183-4).

10. "Neyther dooth there perrish aught . . . / In all the world, but altering takes new shape. For that which wee / Doo terme by name of being borne, is for too gin too bee / Another thing than that it was" (*Shakespeare's Ovid* 1961, 15.278-81).

11. Giordano Bruno's *Heroici furori* was printed in London in 1585, round about the time Marlowe was a student in Cambridge; Marlowe's connection with the 'School of Night', championed by Harriot and Warner, was another term of comparison; one point of their indictment for heresy, both compiled round 1593, respectively reported their alleged scathing animadversions against biblical figures like Moses and Jesus as mere jugglers. See Gatti (1989) and McNulty (1960). For Marlowe's likely knowledge of the works of Bruno, see Mebane (1989). For Pythagorism in Bruno, see Centamore (1997). An analysis of the relationship between Marlowe and Bruno on the theme of hermeticism may be found in Howe (1976).

12. Greenberg (1950, 33) contends that, whereas for Aristotle prime matter cannot be known unless by analogy (the famous example of the bronze statue in *Physics* 1.7.191a7-12), for Bruno "matter is not non-being; it is not unintelligible in itself. In its own right is an intelligible Principle, on an equal level with the formal Principle, the Universal Form."

13. For Védrine (1967, 274), "d'après la *Physique* d'Aristote la substance est tout ce qui est sujet et posséde en soi le principe de son mouvement. Bruno appelle, au contraire substance ce qui persiste à travers un éternel changement . . . Aristote réduit le réel aux êtres qui possèdent une existence actuelle, Bruno le réduit au substrat."

14. Barabas has been often reduced to the character of a tragic farce, resting on Eliot's famous remark (Mahood 1970). Barabas's accumulating wealth

would be thus an example of extreme infantile narcissism (Kuriyama 1980, 159).

15. Sanders (1986) noted the continuous inversion of the Jew-Christian antithesis. For the motif of Barabas as a travesty of Christ, see Goldberg (1992).

16. See the note by Gill (Marlowe 1995, 124). Sims (1966, 18) noted the similarity between the scenes with Barabas and the other Jewish merchants and the encounters between Job and his friends.

17. Kermode (1995, 220) sees in Barabas's acting as an outsider a parallel to the critical act of "communal fashioning" experienced by the spectators, a "'resemblance' of the personal character that exists without the structure and stricture of the city law.

18. For Machiavellism in Marlowe's play, see Ribner (1954) and Cheney (1997). For the rendition of Barabas as a Machiavellian villain, see Bawcutt (1970). Minshull (1982) has noted that Barabas's appetite for wealth may be rather traced to Gentillet's *Discours contre Machiavel*, since Machiavelli barely mentions financial matters.

19. Plato would aim to defend the view that there exist both true and false names, since in his theory of Forms the existence of errors is instrumental to the progress from ignorance to knowledge (Sprague 1962, 46-50). Without indicating what the ideal language is, Socrates' consciously strained etymologies are a parody of those philosophic arguments that make the names more epistemologically important than the nominatum itself in their apparent stableness over flux-ridden things (Baxter 1992, 87). Socrates' paradoxical conclusion is, however, that the existence of such stable natures is contradicted by the result of these etymologies, overtly inadequate in getting to the nature of things when compared with dialectic (Gonzalez 1998, 73-6). See also Robinson (1969).

Chapter Three: The Invention of Perdita

1. I refer to Todorov's analysis of Columbus's frequent references to "le désir de s'enrichir," pointing not quite to the "cupidité vulgaire" but to his dream of new crusades and the accompanying intimation of the "découverte de la nature" (1982, 14-6).

2. An intriguing interpretation could be that this myth is compared to a mirage (*sarab*): the root *s-r-b* has two groups of meanings, "to go freely for one's own way" and "to flow" the idea of going for one's own way would be akin to that of an island floating in the sea (Arioli 1989, 122-3).

3. Columbus was also said to have met in 1484 a man from the island of Madeira who had asked the King "for a caravel in order to go to this land that he saw. He swore that each year he saw it and always in the same way" (Las Casas 1988, 2v).

4. For the coinage, see Dash (1976). Frey sees in it associations that "deepen and universalize the story" (1980, 61).

5. On the point of the Bohemia seacoast, see Hoenselaars (1994, 241-4).

6. See also Turner (1971), Blissett (1971), Roberts (1975) and Ewbank (1995).

7. Aristotle had distinguished between spontaneity (*to automaton*) and chance (*tyche*): chance only can befall those beings that are capable of purposive action, while the "spontaneous" can befall children, animals and inanimate objects (Else 1967, 331 n. 106).

8. The contrast between past and present may not exceed the status of a commonplace, as the experience of time is presented as a duality that borders on the paradox: "If the present in *The Winter's Tale* is the realm of an almost prelapsarian joy, time is the province of memory and anticipation, nostalgia and eagerness, regret and foreboding" (Garner 1985, 349).

9. Cavell (1987, 204) thus comments on the adaptation of the discovery myth to Hermione: "The matter of drama, by contrast, is to investigate the finding of a wife not in empirical fact lost, but . . . transcendentally lost, lost just because one is blind to her—as it were conceptually unprepared for her—because that one is blind to himself, lost to himself."

10. The epithet for Apollo, *hekebolos*, uniting *ekas* ("far from," "far away from"), might also mean "shooting a hundred *bele*." Perhaps it originally meant "hitting the mark at will," as instanced by the similar word *hekaergos*, another epithet of Apollo that "may have originally contained the stem *eknt*—'at will'." See *hekatebolos* and *hekebolos* in Liddell (1968) s.v.

11. On the Greek sources, see Miller (1986) and Hanna (1994).

12. For the topic of the journey by sea as both a search for a missing person and the prelude of the return to a changed world, see Sowa (1984).

Chapter Four: Inducting Pocahontas

1. Some objections were formulated in Febvre (1968, 423, 386) and in Scammell (1969, 394).

2. This identification is summed up by Martire (1612, 140v): "They lyve without any certayne dwelling places, and without tyllage or culturyng of the grounde, as wee read of them whiche in old tyme lyved in the golden age." Cf. Levin (1969, 61) and Honour (1975).

3. Albeit differing from first theology (ontology) in its non-scientific character, "it is dialectic alone that can examine the special foundations of each science" (Evans 1977, 49).

4. Weinberg underlines the requirement of sense perception for knowledge: "universals can only be grasped by induction from particulars and only by perception do we grasp the particulars" (1965, 123).

5. Evans rephrases this distinction as the one separating what is "more intelligible *absolutely*" from "that which is more intelligible *to us*" (1977, 52).

6. In demonstrative science this can be translated into the basic distinction that McKiraham establishes between essential and derivative facts (1992, 111).

7. It was probably this reference that prompted Woodward's intuition (1969, 179): Jonson "questioned her rapidly for five minutes and then for the next forty-five minutes sat staring at her curiously until Pocahontas finally withdrew silently to her quarters upstairs, leaving Jonson to his bottle of sherry." For the "colonizing discourse of the settlers," see Robertson (1996).

8. On the posthumous fortune of Pocahontas, see Bell (1994) and Tilton (1995).

9. Hulme instanced the Pocahontas story as the first ever (1986, 138). An historical antecedent is, however, reported by Young (1962, 397).

10. A more disturbing account comes from Strachey (1953, 113, 72), who described Pocahontas as "a well featured but wanton young girle . . . [who would] gett the boyes forth with her into the markett place and make them wheele, falling on their handes turning their heeles vpwardes, whome she would follow, and wheele so her self naked as she was all the Fort over."

11. One single objection is the bilious billet that Chamberlain sent to Dudley Carleton, understandably coming as it did from a worried shareholder of the sponsoring Virginia Company: "Here is a fine picture of no fayre Lady and yet with her tricking up and high stile and titles you might thincke her and her worshipfull husband to be sombody" (Chamberlain 1939, 2.57.259).

12. Orgel noted that this two-fold look found a scope also in the distinction between the performers: "The characters in Jonsonian antimasques, played by professional actors, are nearly always unaware that there are spectators; but his masquers, court ladies and gentlemen, regularly conclude their revels by joining the spectators in a dance" (1965, 14).

13. Chamberlain (1939, 2.50.257) records Pocahontas's privileged place during the performance of *Christmas His Masque*: "The Virginian woman Poca-huntas, with her father Counsaillor hath ben with the King and graciously used, and both she and her assistant well placed at the maske." Pocahontas probably sat on the royal dais at the monarch's right, while the Queen and the Prince of Wales were at his left (Mossiker 1977, 250).

14. Janicka sees in *Christmas His Masque* "a whole gallery of grotesque and burlesqued personification," drawing on the Bruegelian festive tradition (1969, 197-98).

15. In *The Vision of Delight* Jonson would show "an intriguing susceptibility to Italian theory and practice" (Peacock 1991, 92).

Chapter Five: The Likes of Viola

1. Miola detects the reference to Donatus's and Evanthius's "analysis of the comic plot in terms of *errores*, i.e. mistakes of identity, resolved through recognition" (1994, 19).

2. Riehle (1990, 134-40) sees in the interplay of questions and persuasions the indebtedness to Renaissance rhetoric. Cf. Freedman (1997).

3. For the diffusion of place-logic, see McNally (1968). Medieval narrative often responded to the rationale of the topic "from kind," filling up the gaps left by the logical question *unde locus* (whence the place?). See Vance (1987) and Hunt (1979).

4. The "Aristotelicians" quoted by Viola (*TN* 1.5.244) explicitly refer to a dispute on method (Ong 1968, 64). Although there was no English edition of Aristotle's *Organon* before 1594, logic was a popular subject, as is also evident in Shakespeare's use of logical terms, especially in the *Sonnets* (Craig 1929). Two example of Renaissance compilations are Périon and Grouchy (1556) and [Bede? 1592]. Aristotelian philosophy more at large was widely available through translations, summaries and *tabulae* (Schmitt 1983, 63). See also Reulos (1976) and Ashworth (1988). Whereas the early sixteenth-century curriculum in Cambridge was mostly based on the *Summulae logicales* by Peter of Spain, the latter half saw the extensive usage of Agricola, Melanchton and Ramus's *Dialecticae Institutiones* (Jardine 1974). It has been even conjectured that John Florio's English translation of Ramus might have been seen in manuscript by Shakespeare (Jacobus 1992, 2). The Ramist popularization of dialectics is analyzed in Craig (1952, 142-52). See also Whitaker (1969, 14-44) for the probable knowledge of Aristotle's *Topics*. Cf. Trousdale (1982, 14-21, 31-8) on method and place-logic; see also Schwartz (1990).

5. "The name 'merchant' is being extended to cover those who buy knowledge . . . But what is then named further and divided is a couple of

branches or parts, or kinds, in view of common functions" (Moravcsik 1973, 161).

6. His invention of a formal logic also responded to a strong metaphysical, epistemological motivation: "One can exhaustively partition the truths of some science into those that are known through themselves, and those that are known through other things (i.e., things other than themselves) that are their causes" (Code 1987, 128-9).

7. For Weil (1975), Aristotle is proposing two equally scientific techniques (one of which for scientific arguments only), rather than a scientific and a non-scientific theory.

8. The Renaissance hosted more lenient views on definition as an indication of genus and differentia (Kuhn 1997, 325-30).

9. Not only does it express the very essence (*ousia*), but it does so more clearly than any other component of the definition, says Slomkowski: "Genus is that which is predicated in the category of essence of several things which differ in their species" (1997, 81). The genus is "a highly structured collection," which is to be considered "as a network of subjects and attributes than as an unordered set" (McKiraham 1992, 60). The analysis by genus and differentia "singles out, first, the element an object has in common with other objects (thus in humanity, animality is common to man and to other creatures), and secondly the characteristic that the object alone possesses (in humanity, rationality is the specific difference)" (LeBlond 1979, 67).

10. Among the editions of Ramus published in England, see Ramus (1574). For the diffusion of Ramism, see Howell (1956), Gilbert (1960), Adams (1990) and Oldrini (1997).

11. According to Walton (1970), Ramus laid an emphasis on invention instead of categories. See also Robinet (1969, 12-49).

12. For Ong (1958), Ramus's theory of dialectic is far from being either consistent in time or strictly deducted from the classic sources he said to be quoting. However, Vickers (1988, 475-6) criticizes Ong's emphasis on method and on the bracketed tables as a means of "spatializing of consciousness," for they already existed in manuscripts. See Bruyère (1984, 203-10).

13. Fraunce (1960, 4-9) accordingly introduces the "Metonymia of the cause" ("A trope which useth the name of one thing for the name of another that agreeth with it"), the "Metonymia of the subject" and the Metonymia of the adiunct ("When by the adiunct we expresse the subiect").

14. For the sake of comparison, here is how Macilmaine's translation of Ramus (1574) renders these points. By the use of similitude "we knowe what kynde of one eache thing is, whether lyke or unlyke. These are sayde to be lyke which be of one qualitie" (46); as to the distribution from the effects, "heere the distribution of the generall argumente into the speciall dothe excell. The generall is the whole, of one essence with the partes: The speciall or kynde is a parte of the generall" (57); the "generall" and the "speciall" are in fact "notes and signes of the causes & the effects. For the generall containeth the cause, which dothe equally appartaine to his specialles: and agayne the speciall containethe the effecte of their generall" (58).

15. See Ong (1968, 203-4). In *Republic* 510B, 511B-C, 533C, Plato introduces the image of the divided line, whereby dialectic (inductive) is contrasted with mathematical reasoning (deductive). As Sayre argues, dialectic starts "from assumptions [*hypotheseon*]" and goes "travelling, not up to a principle, but down to a conclusion." The hypotheses are to be taken "in the

literal sense, things 'laid down' like a flight of steps up which [dialectic] may mount all the way to something that is not hypothetical, the first principle of all" (1969, 42).

Chapter Six: A Poem On the Tube

1. The painting was probably intended as a wedding gift for the Vespucci family, referred to by the wasps that fly out of the helmet. The playing satyrs may derive from Lucian's description of Aetion's painting of the *Nuptials of Alexander and Roxana* (Lightbown 1989, 164-70).

2. See Ludovici (1976) and Fuchs (1983, 97-128). According to Rosemann, Augustine sees in procreation "les traces d'un élan fondamental qui traverse le monde crée tout entier: celui de surmonter la différence entre l'identité et la différence pour se rapprocher de l'unité du Dieu un et trine" (1994, 170).

3. For the relevance of *kinesis* and *klonesis* to the separation of elements, see Louie's commentary to Hippocrates (1981, 99-103). On Aristotle, see Preus (1975).

4. For the several meanings of *pneuma*, see Clark (1975, 202-5). Galen glosses the Aristotelian theory of the *pneuma* transmitted with the male semen by arguing that the intense pleasure of sexual ecstasy is concomitant with its discharge: "Whenever, therefore, there is not only a moisture of this sort [serous and acrid humors] needing to be evacuated and hence stimulating and provoking its own evacuation, but also a great deal of warm pneuma requiring to be exhaled, we must consider that there is an extraordinary, excessive pleasure" (1968, 14:640-1). See Jacquart and Thomasset (1985).

5. Because of the memory associated to such an excessive pleasure, many incur in the profligate usage of coitus, "pour l'appetence excitee pour la memorie du plaisir & de la volupté" (Paré 1598, 911-12). Parè was translated in English in 1634 by T. Johnson. See also Banister (1578, 85r-88v).

6. Dodds analyzes the madness of Eros in Plato as "one mode of experience which brings together the two natures of man, the divine self and the tethered beast. For Eros is frankly rooted in what man shares with the animals, the physiological impulse of sex . . . yet Eros also supplies the dynamic impulse which drives the soul forward in its quest of a satisfaction transcending earthly experience" (1968, 218). See also Rutherford (1995).

7. Allen observes that "the providential care the gods extend to the lower world lacks the element of appetitive desire present in the concept of 'generation' . . . it also implies caring for and sustaining in the paternal sense (as opposed to the erotic yearning and longing of the lover for the higher" (1984, 95).

8. For the tradition on marriage literature, see Hagstrum (1992). The diffusion of similar medical beliefs occurred in England thanks to the *Aristotle's Masterpiece, or the Secrets of Generation* (1583; 1595). See Blackman (1977).

9. This befits the work that would represent Donne's "most elaborate attempt to describe that something that was neither merely visible beauty nor merely 'vertue of the minde'" (Leishman 1962, 225). The poem is also a moment of self-recognition and wholeness, effected in the postcoital languor while the body drifts back toward sleep (Shullenberger 1992, 46-62).

10. Baumlin (1991, 203-11) reads this poem as Donne's retreat to an Augustinian rhetoric of transcendence.

11. The poem has been alternatively vindicated as either a defense or a critique of Neoplatonism, an apology for bodily pleasures or a spiritualized interpretation of ecstasy. "The Extasie" would thus be a "remarkable fantasia on Neoplatonic love theory and casuistry" (Vickers 1972, 158), or "a parody, almost a burlesque, of Neoplatonic conventions" (Roston 1974, 137).

12. Empson saw the presence of "annihilating lines" in this poem for "an adequate success in love is a kind of knowledge that transcends the barriers of the ordinary kind" (1935, 133-36).

Chapter Seven: Shakespeare in Laughter

1. See also Stearns (1972), Boston (1974), Holland (1982), Glasgow (1997), Berger (1997).

2. In similar terms, Hawkes underlined the risk lurking behind this usage *of* Shakespeare's plays: "For us, the plays have the same function as, and work like, the works of which they are made. We *use* them in order to generate meaning. [. . .] Shakespeare doesn't mean: *we* mean *by* Shakespeare" (Hawkes 1992, 3). For the study of the risible in Shakespeare, see Muir (1979), Nevo (1980), Berry (1984), and Slights (1993).

3. Menager (1995, 5) observes that Bakhtin's work "ignorait dangereusement l'importance des débats ouverts à cette époque sur la nature et le bon usage du rire."

4. Levin (1976, 53) noted the substantial failure of comic definitions when applied to Shakespeare, "perhaps because they tend to emphasize the spectatorial attitude of ridicule. Shakespeare's emphasis falls on playfulness, man at play." For Leech, *TN* does not abound with much laughter, arguably offering the best example of the type of profitable comedy envisaged by Sidney (1965, 31).

5. For Weimann, Feste "embodies the spirit of festive comedy" (1978, 43).

6. See Salingar (1986), Barber (1986) and Charney (1978). For Hartmann, *Twelfth Night* stages "a turning away of the evil eye" which averts Malvolio's "malevolent interpretation of life" (1985, 49).

7. For Plato's reuse of comic techniques in the dialogues, see Brock (1990).

8. For Else (1967, 186), "the limitation of comedy to the 'ugly', and to that part of the ugly which causes no pain or damage, signifies a greater refinement of feeling, but also an objectification of the poet's attitude. Instead of hating and berating, he depicts." For Golden (1992, 385), "the 'ridiculous' must generate the same emotion we experience toward any other dimension of 'the inappropriate', and this, then, would be that form of *nemesan* [indignation] which, like the constitutive elements of *to geloion*, "error" and "ugliness," is "painless and not destructive."

9. On humor and expectation, see Haury (1955) and Jensen (1994).

10. See also Janko (1984, 156-60) on Aristotle's description of the emotions aroused by the risible action.

11. A list of comical causes also appears in Scaligero (1964, 1.5:10-11, 1.13:20-2).

12. See also Minturno (1559, 1:2-3, 2:106-8, 124).

13. On the collection of literary trivia and memorable anecdotes, see Bowen (1988, xv) and Speroni (1964).

14. See also *Institucion of a Gentleman* (G6r) and *Nevv Yeeres Gift* (1582).

15. *Kinesis*, the word regularly used by Aristotle to indicate change, includes *energeia* in the wide sense, "an actuality as opposed to potentiality. While the *kinesis* refer to single activities like walking or house building, the *energeiai* refer to more continuous, perfect actions: "An action that has a limit is not itself an end (*telos*) but is directed to an end or goal which is not yet in existence during the course of the action. Such an action is not perfect. On the other hand, an action that has no limit is one which is an end, or one in which the end is present; this is a perfect action" (Ackrill 1997, 143).

16. On Shakespeare and medical knowledge, see Hoeniger (1992).

17. Jests offer "a civilized response to paradoxes and injustices that might otherwise have made life painful" (Grudin 1974, 199). Falvo (1992, 58) sees in *facetudo* "an art, a dangerous but necessary activity that requires at all times the use of *sprezzatura* in order to attain social success." For the interplay between "facetious self-fashioning" and the exposure of the courtly code of conduct, see Korda (1994).

18. See Whigham (1984) and Bryson (1990).

19. On the graced actor in the Commedia dell'Arte, see Coronato (2000).

20. See also *Parts of Animals* 3.10.672b and *Movement of Animals* 8.11.702a-703b.

21. Cf. Ricci (1995, 86): "Col vedere e udire cose piacevoli e facete, il sangue e quelli spiriti vengono ad assomigliarsi, e la natura sollevata ne fa apparir tosto i segni per occulte rispondenze nel dilatamento dei muscoli della bocca, degl'occhi e della faccia tutta, il quale si esprime col riso."

22. "Pour Aristote, comme pour les ouvrages latins ou arabes du Moyen Age, le sage se reconnaît à la 'médiocrité' des signes" (Courtine 1988, 215-6). Menager notes that "avant d'être le signe d'un sentiment . . . , le rire apparaît alors comme un mouvement du corps, surtout dans sa variante extrême: le fou rire" (1995, 7).

23. Perrucci (1699, 2.11: 139) reported the usage of *derisio* in Horatius and Persius as a comical way of distorting the mouth and showing the teeth ("*storcere la bocca, dimostrare i denti*"). See Lea (1962).

24. Vettori (1560, 48) notes that the deformed face without any sign of grief ("*facies . . . distorta sine dolore*") of the ridiculous person bespeaks no pain, for we would not laugh at a man beset with torments ("*si namque ea res, quae faciem partemve aliquam corporis deformat, dolorem ipsi inureret: aut hominem ad interitum perduceret, non rideremus*").

25. Commenting on the same passage, Cecchini (1616, 11) concludes that comedy can be performed as a lawful pastime, necessary to human recreation ("*giuoco necessario per ricreazione della vita humana*").

26. Cf. Barbieri (1971, 120): two or three comedies suffice to dispel all the idle hours of the year ("*due o tre comedie portano via l'ore oziose di tutto l'anno*").

27. Leggatt underlined the "sense of enclosure" marked by the respective houses of *Twelfth Night* (1974, 225).

28. Yet, if recreation is good for the health, the more so is the unflinching exercise of virtue, argues Rainolds: "As recreation is needfull in regard of the body, so vertuous recreation in regard of the minde: and vertue more necessarie much then recreation, by how much the minde is of more excellencie then the body" (1600, 24). See also Hoeniger (1984).

29. Music, a symbol for recreation and yet for the mutability of fortune in love, easily offers "a symbolic reflection of its themes of sexual discord and harmony" (Wells 1994, 208).

30. For Girard, Malvolio's self-love is extended to other characters as well: Olivia will be purged of her folly only through the "mimetic theory" detected in her "shift from herself to Viola" (1991, 107-9).

31. Comus, the god of festive intoxication, was described by the Greek sophist Philostratus as a youth stationed at the doors of a chamber, all but asleep under the sway of drink, while peals of laughter resonate (Philostratus 1931, 1.2:8-10).

32. The counterpart of Viola's liminality is the presence of the mock-fighter, Sir Toby: "Thy intercepter, full of despite, bloody as the hunter, attends thee at the orchard-end" (*TN* 3.4.224-26). In the making up of the practical joke, Toby is described as an impending menace dangling on the margins, much as Viola-Cesario defies containment: "Fabian can scarce hold him yonder" (3.4.286-87).

33. See O'Connor (1978). Logan (1982) defines the comedy as an anatomy of festivity. Shakespeare adds to the pastoral theme of amorous equivocation the duping of Malvolio, chastening his "anti-festive *diskolia*" (Miola 1994, 39, 44). Malvolio is also the killjoy who resists assimilation (Beiner 1993), the agelast who is reconciled with the community by forced integration (Suhanny 1995; Labriola 1975). Yet the ridicule exceeds the limits of urbanity: the return to normalcy in the end does not completely reconcile the characters with the disruption of norms (Daphinoff 1990). For Coddon (1993), it tests the limits of theatrical license and ultimately confounds holiday and history in an almost contestatory dimension.

34. Cf. the lines by Olivia: "Under your hard construction must I sit, / To force that on you in a shameful cunning / Which you knew none of yours" (*TN* 3.1.117-9).

Bibliography

Ackrill, J.L. 1997. Aristotle's Distinction Between *Energeia* and *Kinesis*. In *Essays on Plato and Aristotle*. Oxford: Clarendon Press. 142-62.

Adams, John Charles. 1990. Gabriel Harvey's *Ciceronianus* and the Place of Peter Ramus' *Dialecticae Libri Duo* in the Curriculum. *Renaissance Quarterly* 43(3):551-69.

Agricola, Rudolph. 1539. *De Inuentione Dialectica libri tres*. Lyon.

Alan of Lille. 1955. *Anticlaudianus*. Ed. R. Bossuat. Paris: Vrin.

———. 1965. *Liber Poenitentialis*. Ed. J. Longère. Louvain: Nauwelaerts; Lille: Giard. Volume 2.

Allen, Michael J.B. 1984. *The Platonism of Marsilio Ficino*. Berkeley, Los Angeles and London: Univ. of California Press.

———. 1989. *Icastes: Marsilio Ficino's Interpretation of Plato's Sophist*. Berkeley, Los Angeles and Oxford: Univ. of California Press.

Allison, A. F. and D.M. Rogers, 1994. *The Contemporary Printed Literature of the English Counter-Reformation Between 1558 and 1640*. Vol. 2, *Works in English*. Aldershot: Scolar Press.

Angelica, Summa. 1578. [Angelo Carletti]. Venice.

Apollonius of Tyre. 1991. Ed. E. Archibald. Cambridge: D. S. Brewer.

Aquinas. Thomas. 1954. *De regimine principum ad regem Cypri*. In *P. Thomae Aquinatis Opuscula Philosophica*. Ed. R. Spiazzi. Turin-Rome.

Arias, Francisco. 1602. *The Litle Memorial*. Roan.

Ariès, Philippe. 1981. *The Hour of Our Death*. Trans. H. Weaver. New York-Oxford: Oxford Univ. Press.

Arioli, Angelo. 1989. *Le isole mirabili*. Turin: Einaudi.

Arkins, Brian. 1995. Heavy Seneca. *Classics Ireland* 2:1-16.

Ashworth, E.J. 1988. Changes in Logic Textbooks from 1500 to 1650. In *Aristotelismus und Renaissance*. Ed. E. Kessler, C. H. Lohr and W. Sparn. Wiesbaden: Otto Harrassowitz. 75-87.

Averroes. 1986. *Averroes' Middle Commentary on Aristotle's Poetics*. Ed. and trans. by C. E. Butterworth. Princeton: Princeton Univ. Press.

L'aveu. Antiquité et Moyean Age. 1986. Ecole Française de Rome.

Avicenna. 1974. *Avicenna's Commentary on the Poetics of Aristotle*. Ed. and trans. I. M. Dahiyat. Leiden: Brill.

Azpilcueta, Martín. 1592. *Manuale de' confessori et penitenti*. Trans. C. Camilli. Venice.

Bacon, Francis. 1962. *Novum Organon*. In *The Works of Francis Bacon*. Stuttgart-Bad Cannstatt: Friedrich Frommann Verlag Gunther Holzboog. Vol. 4.

Balduin, Friedrich. 1654. *Tractatus Luculentus Posthumus*. Frankfurt.

Baldwin, John W. 1994. *The Language of Sex*. Chicago and London: The Univ. of Chicago Press.

Banister, John. 1578. *The Historie of Man*. London.

Barber, C.L. 1986. Testing Courtesy and Humanity in *Twelfth Night*. In *Twelfth Night – Critical Essays*. Ed. S. Wells. New York and London: Garland Publishing. 107-29.

Barbieri, Nicolò. 1971. [1634]. *La supplica*. Ed. F. Taviani. Milan: Il Polifilo.

Barclay, Alexander. 1874. *The Ship of Fools*. Translation of Sebastian Brant, *Narrenschiff*. Edinburgh: William Paterson; London: Herny Sotheran & Co.

Barlandus, Hadrianus. 1529. *Iocorum veterum ac recentium libri tres*. Antwerp.

Bartholomeus Anglicus. 1601. *Bartholomei Anglici de genuinis rerum colestium, terrestrium et inferarum proprietatibus*. Frankfurt.

Baumlin, James S. 1991. *John Donne and the Rhetoric of Renaissance Discourse*. Columbia and London: Univ. of Missouri Press.

Bawcutt, N.W. 1970. Machiavelli and Marlowe's *The Jew of Malta*. *Renaissance Drama* n.s. 3:3-50.

Baxter, Timothy M. S. 1992. The Etymologies of the *Cratylus*. Chap. 4 in *The Cratylus*. Leiden, New York and Cologne: Brill. 86-106.

Beattie, James. 1779. *Essays on Poetry and Music*. London.

Becon, Thomas. 1844. *Jewel of Joy* (1553). In *The Catechism With Other Pieces*. Ed. J. Ayre. Cambridge: Cambridge Univ. Press.

———. 1990. *A Potation for Lent*. 100-1. Quoted in G. Rowell, "The Anglican Tradition". In *Confession and Absolution*, ed. M. Dudley and G. Rowell (London: SPCK, 1990). 93-4.

[Bede?] 1592. *Aristotelis Philosophica Venerabilis Bedae*. London.

Beiner, G. 1993. "Twelfth Night". Chap. 8 in *Shakespeare's Agonistic Comedy*. Rutheford, Madison and Teaneck: Fairleigh Dickinson Univ. Press; London and Toronto: Associated Univ. Presses. 203-34.

Bell, B.L. 1994. Pocahontas. *Studies in American Indian Literatures* 6(1):63-70.

Belleforest, François de. 1578. *Le quatriesme tome des histoires tragiqves*. Lyon.

Belton, Francis George. 1949. *A Manual for Confessors*. London and Oxford: Mowbray.

Bembo, Pietro. 1991. *Gli Asolani*. Ed. G. Dilemmi. Florence: Accademia della Crusca.

Bentley, Jerry H. 1983. *Humanists and Holy Writ*. Princeton: Princeton Univ. Press.

Berger, Peter L. 1997. *Redeeming Laughter*. Berlin and New York: Walter de Gruyter.

Bériou, N. 1983. Autour de Latran IV (1215). In Groupe de la Bussière (1983). 73-93.

Berrettari, Elpidio. 1603. *Tractatu de Risu*. Florence.

Berry, Edward. 1984. *Shakespeare's Comic Rites*. Cambridge: Cambridge Univ. Press.

Bertrand, Dominique. 1995. *Dire le rire à l'âge classique*. Aix-en-Provence: Publications de l'Université de Provence.

Betussi, Giuseppe. 1975. *Il Raverta*. In *Trattati d'amore* (1975).

Biller, P. 1998. Confession in the Middle Ages. In *Handling Sin*. Ed. P. Biller and A.J. Minnis. York: York Medieval Press.

Bishop, T.G. 1996. *The Winter's Tale*; or, filling up the graves. In *Shakespeare and the Theatre of Wonder*. Cambridge: Cambridge Univ. Press. 125-75.

Blackman, J. 1977. Popular Theories of Generation. In *Health Care and Popular Medicine in Nineteenth Century England*. Ed. J. Woodward and D. Richards. New York: Homes & Meyer. 56-88.

Blanchard, Joël. 1995. Le corps du roi. In *Répresentation, pouvoir et royauté à la fin du Moyen Age*. Ed. J. Blanchard. Paris: Picard. 199-211.

Blissett, William. 1971. "This Wide Gap of Time". *English Literary Renaissance* 17(1):52-70.

Boas, Frederick S. 1914. *University Drama in the Tudor Age*. Oxford: Clarendon Press.

Book of Curtesye, The. 1907. [1477]. Cambridge: Cambridge Univ. Press.

Bossy, John. 1975. The Social History of Confession in the Age of the Reformation. *Transactions of the Royal Historical Society*, 5th ser., 25:21-38.

———. 1976. *The English Catholic Community, 1570-1850*. New York: Oxford Univ. Press.

Boston, Richard. 1974. *An Anatomy of Laughter*. London: Collins.

Bowen, Barbara C., ed. 1988. *One Hundred Renaissance Jokes*. Birmingham, Al.: Summa Publications.

———. 1998. *Enter Rabelais, Laughing*. Nashville and London: Vanderbilt Univ. Press.

Boyle, Leonard E. 1974. The Summa for Confessors as a Genre. In Trinkans (1974). 126-30.

———. 1982. Summae Confessorum. In *Les genres littéraires dans les sources théologiques et philosophiques médiévales*. Louvain-la-Neuve: Publications de l'Institut d'Etudes Médiévales. 227-37.

Braeckmans, L. 1971. *Confession and Communion au Moyen Age et au Concile de Trente*. Gembloux: J. Duculot.

Braswell, Mary Flowers. 1983. *The Medieval Sinner*.London and Toronto: Associated Univ. Presses.

Braudel, F. 1977. *La Méditerranée*. Paris: Arts et métiers graphiques.

Brendan, The Anglo-Norman Voyage of St. 1928. Ed. E.G.R. Waters. Oxford: Clarendon Press.

Briggs, R. 1989. *Communities of Belief*. Oxford: Clarendon Press.

Broc, Numa. 1980. *La Géographie de la Rénaissance, 1420-1620*. Paris: Bibliothèque Nationale.

Brock, R. 1990. Plato and Comedy. In *Owls to Athens*. Oxford: Oxford Univ. Press. 39-49.

Brooks, Harold F. 1979. "Richard III": Antecedents of Clarence's Dream". *Shakespeare Survey* 32(1979): 145-50.

———. 1980. "Richard III", Unhistorical Amplifications. *Modern Language Review* 75(4): 721-37.

Brouwsma, W.J. 1980. Anxiety and the Formation of Early Modern Culture. In *After the Reformation*. Ed. B.C. Malamont. Philadelphia: Univ. of Pennsylvania Press, 1980. 215-46.

Brown, Bonaventure A. 1948. *The Numerical Distinction of Sin*. Washington: The Catholic Univ. of America Press.

Bruno, Giordano. 1973. *De la causa, principio et uno*. Ed. Giovanni Aquilecchia. Turin: Einaudi.

Bruno, Vincenzo. 1597. *A Short Treatise of the Sacrament of Penaunce*. [London].

Bruyère, N. 1984. *Méthode et dialectique dans l'oeuvre de Ramée*. Paris: Vrin.

Bryson, Anna. 1990. The Rhetoric of Status. In *Renaissance Bodies*. Ed. L. Gent and N. Llewellyn. London: Reaktion Books. 136-53.

Buonamici, Francesco. 1597. *Discorsi poetici nella Accademia Fiorentina in difesa d'Aristotile*, 34. Quoted. in Bernard Weinberg, *A History of Literary*

Criticism in the Italian Renaissance (Chicago: Univ. of Chicago Press, 1961), 691.

Caizzi, Fernanda Decleva. 1988. La "materia scorrevole". In *Matter and Metaphysics*. Ed. J. Barnes and M. Mignucci. Naples: Bibliopolis. 425-70.

Calvin, Jean. 1559. *Institutio Christianae Religionis*. Genève.

———. 1960. *Institution de la Religion Chrestienne*. Ed. Jean-Daniel Benoit. Paris: Librairie Philosophique J. Vrin.

Cameron, Evan. 1991. *The European Reformation*. Oxford: Clarendon Press.

Castelvetro, Ludovico. 1971. *Poetica d'Aristotele vulgarizzata e sposta*. Ed. W. Romani. Bari: Laterza.

Castiglione, Baldassarre. 1900. [1561]. *The Booke of the Courtier*. Trans. T. Hoby. London: David Nutt.

Castro, Rodriguez. 1603. *De universa mulierum medicina*. Hamburg.

Cavell, Stanley. 1987. *Disowning Knowledge in Six Plays of Shakespeare*. Cambridge: Cambridge Univ. Press.

Cecchini, Pier Maria. 1616. *Brevi discorsi intorno alle comedie*. Naples.

———. 1622. *Lettere Facete e Morali*. Venice.

Centamore, F. 1997. "Omnia Mutantur, Nihil Interit". *Bruniana & Campanelliana* 3(2): 231-44.

Chamberlain, John, 1939. *The Letters*. Ed. N.E. McClure. Philadelphia: The American Philosophical Society.

Chapman, George. 1874. *The Mask of the Middle Temple and Lincoln's Inn*. In *Works. Plays*. London: Chatto & Windus.

Charney, Maurice. 1978. Comic Premises of *Twelfth Night*. *New York Literary Forum* 1: 151-65.

Chartier, A. 1596. *Delectable demaundes . . . in matters of Loue*. London.

Chemnitz, Martin. 1596. *Examinis Concilii Tridentini . . . quatuor partes*. Frankfurt.

Cheney, Patrick. 1997. Machiavelli and the Play of Policy in *The Jew of* Malta. In *Marlowe's Counterfeit Profession*. Toronto, Buffalo and London: Univ. of Toronto Press. 136-56.

Chiappelli, Fredi, M. J. B. Allen and R. L. Benson, eds. 1976. *First Images of America*. Berkeley, Los Angeles and London: Univ. of California Press. Vols. 2.

Churchill, George B. 1970. *Richard the Third Up to Shakespeare*. Dursley: Alan Sutton; Towota, NJ: Rowman & Littlefield.

Cicero. 1556. *Marcus Tullius Ciceroes thre bokes of duties*. Trans. N. Grimalde. London

Clark, Stephen R.L. 1975. *Aristotle's Man*. Oxford: Clarendon Press.

Cobain, Kurt. 1994. The Rolling Stone interview with David Fricke. In *Cobain. By The Editors of Rolling Stone*. Boston, New York, Toronto and London: Little, Brown & Company.

Cochrane, A.C. 1977. The Act of Confession-Confessing. *The Sixteenth Century Journal* 8(4): 61-84.

Code, Alan. 1987. Metaphysics and Logic. In *Aristotle Today*. Edmonton, Alberta: Academic Printing & Publishing. 127-50.

Coddon, K.S. 1993. "Slander in an Allow'd Fool": *Twelfth Night's* Crisis of the Aristocracy. *Studies in English Literature* 33. 309-25.

Cohen, Sheldon. 1995. Aristotle's Doctrine of the Material Substrate. In *Aristotle. Substance, Form and Matter*. Ed. T. Irwin. New York and London: Garland Publishing. 95-118.

Cohen, Sheldon 1996. Elemental Transformation and the Persistence of Matter. Chap. 3 in *Aristotle on Nature and Incomplete Substance*. Cambridge: Cambridge Univ. Press. 55-100.

Coislinianus.1922. *An Aristotelian Theory of Comedy With an Adaptation of the Poetics and a Translation of the "Tractatus Coislinianus"*. Ed. Lane Cooper. New York: Harcourt, Brace & Company.

Cole, Douglas. 1970. Barabas the Jew. In *The Jew of Malta. Text and Major Criticism*. Ed. I. Ribner. New York: The Odissey Press. 128-45.

Colie, Rosalie L. 1973. Inclusionism. Chap. 3 in *The Resources of Kind*. Ed. B. K. Lewalski. Berkeley, Los Angeles and London: Univ. of California Press. 76-102.

Colley, Scott. 1986. Richard III and Herod. *Shakespeare Quarterly* 37(4): 451-8.

Colombo, Cristoforo. 1988. Tercer Viage du Colón. In *The Four Voyages of Columbus*. Trans. and ed. Cecil Jane. New York: Dover Publications.

Contarini, Giovanni Matteo. 1924. [1506]. *A Map of the World*. London.

Conti, Natale. 1567. *Natalis Comitis Mythologiae*. Venice.

Cook, Ann Jennalie. 1991. Agents and Go-Betweens. In *Making a Match*. Princeton: Princeton Univ. Press. 104-19.

Copley, Anthony. 1614. *Wits, Fits, and Fancies*. London.

Cordano, Franca. 1992. *La geografia degli antichi*. Bari: Laterza.

Coronato, Rocco. 2000. *The Italian Job*. In *Shakespeare and His Contemporaries in Performance*. Ed. E. J. Esche. Aldershot: Ashgate. 177-90.

Cotrugli, Benedetto. 1990. [1573]. *Libro dell'arte di mercatura*. Ed. Ugo Tucci. Venice: Arsenale.

Courtine, J.-J. and C. Haroche. 1988. *Histoire du visage*. Paris: Rivages/Histoire.

Craig, Hardin. 1929. Shakespeare and Formal Logic. In *Studies in English Philology*. Ed. K. Malone and M. B. Ruud. Minneapolis: Univ. of Minnesota Press. 380-96.

———. 1952. *The Enchanted Glass*. Oxford: Basil Blackwell.

Crinò, Sebastiano. 1941. *La scoperta della carta originale di Paolo dal Pozzo Toscanelli*. Florence.

Da Cagli, Bernardino Pino. 1970. [1572]. *Breve considerazione intorno al componimento de la comedia de' nostri tempi*. In *Trattati di Poetica e Retorica del Cinquecento*. Vol. 2.

Daphinoff, Dimiter. 1990. "None Can Be Called Deformed but the Unkind". In *On Strangeness*. Ed. M. Bridges. SPELL 5: 99-112.

D'Aragona, Tullia. 1975. *Della infinità di amore*. In *Trattati d'Amore* (1975).

Dash, Irene G. 1976. Bohemia's "Sea-Coast" and the Babe Who Was Lost Forever. *Literary Onomastics Studies* 3: 102-9.

De Butrio, Antonius. (ca. 1477). *Speculum de Confessione*. Louvain.

De Chaimis, Bartholomaeus. [1474?]. *Interrogatorium sive [con]fessionale*. Strasbourg.

Dedekind, F. 1605. *The School of Slovenrie*. London.

Defecerunt. 1499. *Defecerunt scrutantes scrutinio*. [St. Antoninus of Florence]. Venice.

De Léry, Jean. 1994. *Histoire d'un voyage fait en la Terre du Brésil*. Paris: Le Livre du Poche.

Della Casa, Giovanni. 1576. *Galateo of Maister Iohn della Casa*. London.

Delumeau, Jean. 1983. *Le péché et la peur*. Paris: Fayard.

———. 1990. *L'aveu et le pardon*. Paris: Fayard.

De Medina, Bartolomé. 1584. *Breve istruttione de' confessori*. Bergamo.

Demetrius on Style. 1979. Ed. W. Rhys Roberts. New York: Arno Press. 1902. Reprint.

Denis, P. 1983. Remplacer la confession. In Groupe de la Bussière (1983). 165-76.

Denzinger, Henry. 1957. *The Sources of Catholic Dogma*. Trans. R. J. Deferrari. St. Louis, Mo., and London: B. Herder Book.

De Odendorff, Henricus. 1490. *Repetitio de capituli Omnis utriusq[ue] sexus de Poenitentiis et remissionibus*. Memmingen.

DeRocher, G. 1979. *Rabelais' Laughers and Joubert's 'Traité du Ris'*. University. Univ. of Alabama Press.

Derrida, Jacques. 1982. Tympan. In *Margins of Philosophy*. Trans. A. Bass. Chicago: Univ. of Chicago Press. 9-29.

De Sivry, Louis Poinsinet. 1986. [1768]. *Traité des causes physiques et morales du rire*. Ed. W. Brooks. Exeter: Univ. of Exeter.

De Tarrega, Gabriel. 1524. *Opera brevissima*. Bordeaux.

Deyermond, Alan David. 1984. "¡Muerto soy! ¡Confesion!". In *De los romances-villancico a la poesia de Claudio Rodriguez*. Ed. J.-M. Lopez de Abiada and A. Lopez Bernasocchi. [n.p.] José Esteban. 129-39.

Didache, The. 1912. In *The Apostolic Fathers*. Vol. 1. Trans. K. Lake. Loeb Classical Library.

Diekstra, F.N.M. ed. 1991. *The Middle English "Weye of Paradys" and the Middle French "Voie de Paradis"*. Leiden: Brill.

Doebler, Bettie Anne. 1974. "Despair and Dye". *Shakespeare Studies* 7: 75-86.

D'Oddo, Sforza. 1578. *L'Erofilomachia*. Venice.

Dodds, E. 1968. *The Greeks and the Irrational*. Berkeley and Los Angeles: Univ. of California Press.

Doni, Anton Francesco. 1994. Mondo Risibile. In *I mondi e gli inferni*. Ed. P. Pellizzari. Turin: Einaudi.

Donne, John, 1955. *The Sermons of John Donne*. Ed. G.R. Potter and E. Simpson. Berkeley and Los Angeles: Univ. of California Press.

Duggan, L.G. 1984. Fear and Confession on the Eve of the Reformation. *Archiv fuer Reformationsgeschichte* 75: 153-75.

Duval, André. 1974. Le Concil de Trente et la Confession. *La Maison-Dieu* 118: 131-80.

Early English Tracts on Commerce. 1954. Ed. J.R. McCulloch. Cambridge: Cambridge Univ. Press.

Eisengrein, M. 1577. *Confessionale*. Ingoelstadt.

Else, Gerard F. 1967. *Aristotle's Poetics*. Cambridge, Mass.: Harvard Univ. Press.

Empson, William. 1935. *Some Versions of Pastoral*. London: Chatto & Windus.

Erasmus, 1542. *Apophthegmes*. Trans. N. Udall. London.

———. 1972a. *Confessio militis (De militaribus)*. In *Opera Omnia*, vol. 1.3. Amsterdam: North-Holland Publishing Company.

———. 1972b. *Adagia*. In *Opera Omnia*, vol. 2.2. Amsterdam: North-Holland Publishing Company.

Eruditorium Penitentiale. 1490. Paris.

Evans, J.D.G. 1977. *Aristotle's Concept of Dialectic*. Cambridge: Cambridge Univ. Press.

Ewbank, Inga-Stina. 1995. The Triumph of Time in *The Winter's Tale*. In *The Winter's Tale: Critical Essays*. Ed. M. Hunt. New York: Garland. 139-55.

Falvo, J.D. 1992. *The Economy of Human Relations*. New York: Peter Lang.

Faren, Antoine. 1485. *La pratique de soy bien confesser*. Paris.

Farley-Hills, David. 1981. *The Comic in Renaissance Comedy*. Totowa, NJ: Barnes & Noble Books.

Faure, Alain, ed. 1988. *Rires et sourires littéraires*. Université de Nice Sophia Antipolis.

Faure, François. 1970. Langage religieux et language petrarquiste dans *Richard III* de Shakespeare. *Etudes Anglaises* 23: 23-37.

Fazzalaro, F.J. 1950. *The Place for the Hearing of Confessions*. Washington: The Catholic Univ. of America Press.

Febvre, Lucien, 1968. *Le problème de l'incroyance au 16ᵉ siècle*. Paris: Editions Albin Michel. Reprint. 1942.

Ficino, Marsilio. 1973. [1469]. *Sopra lo amore over' Convito di Platone*. Ed. G. Ottaviano. Milan: Celuc.

Fifteenth-Century Courtesy Book, A (MS. Addl. 37969). 1914. Ed. R.W. Chambers. London, Early English Text Society: Oxford Univ. Press.

Formularies of Faith Put Forth by Authority During the Reign of Henry VIII. 1856. Oxford: Oxford Univ. Press.

Foucault, Michel. 1980. *A History of Sexuality*. Transl. R. Hupley. New York: Vintage Books.

Fracastorio, Gerolamo. 1546. *De sympathia et antipathia rerum*. Venice.

Franck, Sebastian. 1534. *Weltbuch: Spiegel und Bildtniss des ganzten Ertbodes*. Tuebingen.

Fraunce, Abraham. 1960. [1589]. *Arcadian Rhetorike*. Ed. E. Seaton. Oxford: Basil Blackwell.

Freedman, Barbara. 1991. Naming Loss. In *Staging the Gaze*. Ithaca: Cornell Univ. Press. 192-235.

———. 1997. Reading errantly. In *The Comedy of Errors. Critical Essays*. Ed. R. S. Miola. New York and London: Garland Publishing. 261-97.

Fregoso, Antonio. 1511. *Riso de Democrito: et Pianto de Heraclito*. Milan.

Freund, Elizabeth. 1986. *Twelfth Night* and the Tyranny of Interpretation. *English Literary History* 53(3): 471-89.

Frey, Charles. 1980. *Shakespeare's Vast Romance*. Columbia and London: Univ. of Missouri Press.

Frye, Northrop. 1965. *A Natural Perspective*. New York: Harcourt, Brace & World.

Fuchs, Eric. 1983. *Sexual Desire and Love*. Trans. M. Daigle. Cambridge: James Clarke & Co; New York: The Seabury Press.

Fulke, William. 1583. *A Defense of the Sincere and True Translations of the Holye Scriptures into the English Tongue*. London.

Gabrielli, Lodovico. 1561. *Metodo di confessione*. Venice.

Gadamer, H. G. 1980. Plato's Educational State. Chap. 4 in *Dialogue and Dialectic*. Ed. P. Christopher Smith. New Haven and London: Yale Univ. Press. 73-92.

Galen. 1968. *On the Usefulness of the Parts of the Body*. Ed. M. Tallmadge May. Ithaca, New York: Cornell Univ. Press.

Gallagher, L. 1991. *Medusa's Gaze*. Stanford: Stanford Univ. Press.

Galvano, Antonie. 1601. *The Discoveries of the World.* London.

Garber, Marjorie. 1977. "Infinite Riches in a Little Room". In *Two Renaissance Mythmakers*. Ed. A. Kernan. Baltimore: Johns Hopkins Univ. Press. 3-21.

Garner, Stanton B. jr.. 1985. Time and Presence in *The Winter's Tale*. *Modern Language Quarterly* 46(4): 347-67.

Garzoni, Tomaso. 1587. *La piazza universale di tutte le professioni del mondo.* Venice.

⸺. 1600. *The Hospitall of Incurable Fooles.* London. Translation of *L'ospidale dei pazzi incurabili.* 1589.

Gatti, Hilary. 1989. Bruno and Marlowe. Chap. 4 in *The Renaissance Drama of Knowledge.* London and New York. Routledge. 74-113.

Gerard, John. 1951. *John Gerard. The Autobiography of an Elizabethan.* Trans. P. Caraman. London, New York and Toronto: Longmans, Green & Co.

Gerson, Jean. [1487?]. *Opusculum Tripartitum.* [Antwerp?].

Gilbert, Neal W. 1960. Echoes of the Methodological Controversy in England. Chap. 9 in *Renaissance Concepts of Method.* New York: Columbia Univ. Press. 197-212.

Gilby, Thomas. 1958. Personal and Common Good. Chap. 7.5 in *The Political Thought of Thomas Aquinas.* Chicago: The Univ. of Chicago Press. 237-50

Gilchrist, J. 1969. The Economic Doctrines of the Canonists and Theologians. Chap. 4 in *The Church and Economic Activity in the Middle Ages.* London, Melbourne and Toronto: Macmillan; New York: St. Martin's Press. 48-82.

Gill, M. Louise. 1989. *Aristotle on Substance* Princeton: Princeton Univ. Press.

Gillies, John. 1994. Of Voyages and Exploration. Chap. 2 in *Shakespeare and the Geography of Difference.* Cambridge: Cambridge Univ. Press. 40-69.

Giraldi, Lucio Olimpio. 1961. [1566]. *Ragionamento in difesa di Terentio.* Quoted in Bernard Weinberg, *A History of Literary Criticism in the Italian Renaissance* (Chicago: Univ. of Chicago Press:1961), 289.

Girard, René. 1991. *A Theater of Envy.* New York and Oxford: Oxford Univ. Press.

Glasgow, R.D.V. 1997. *Split Down the Sides.* Lanham, New York and London: Univ. Press of America.

Goclenius, Rodolphus [Rudolp Goeckel]. 1597. *Physiologia de risu ac lacrymis.* Marburg.

⸺. 1607. *Physiologia Crepitus Ventris, et Risus.* Frankfurt.

Godeau, Antoine. 1667. *Les Tableaux de la pénitence.* Paris.

Godorecci, Barbara J. 1993. Machiavelli's Re-Writing of Himself. In *After Machiavelli.* West Lafayette, Indiana: Purdue Univ. Press. 103-20.

Goldberg, Dena. 1992. Sacrifice in Marlowe's *The Jew of Malta. Studies in English Literature* 32: 233-45.

Golden, Leon. 1992. Aristotle on the Pleasure of Comedy. In *Essays on Aristotle's Poetics.* Ed. A. Oksenberg Rorty. Princeton: Princeton Univ. Press. 379-86.

Goldstein, Thomas. 1976. Impulses of Italian Renaissance Culture Behind the Age of Discoveries. In Chiappelli (1976). Vol. 1. 27-35.

Gonzalez, Francisco J. 1998. The *Cratylus* on the Use of Words. Chap. 3 in *Dialectic and Dialogue.* Evanston, Il.: Northwestern Univ. Press. 62-93.

Goodman, John. 1684. *A Discourse Concerning Auricular Confession.* London.

Graf, Arturo. 1964. *Miti, leggende e superstizioni del Medioevo.* Bologna: A. Forni.

Graham, William A. 1993. Holy Writ and Holy Word. Chapter 5 in *Beyond the Written Word*. 1987. Reprint. Cambridge: Cambridge Univ. Press. 58-66.

Gransden, K.W. 1969. *John Donne*. Hamden, CT: Archon Books.

Grant, M.A. 1924. *The Ancient Rhetorical Theories of the Risible*. Univ. of Wisconsin Studies in Language and Literature, n. 21.

Grantley, Darryll. 1986. *The Winter's Tale* and Early Religious Drama. *Comparative Drama* 20: 17-37.

Greenberg, Sidney. 1950. *The Infinite in Giordano Bruno*. New York, Columbia Univ.: King's Crown Press.

Greenblatt, Stephen. 1980. Marlowe and the Will to Absolute Play. In *Renaissance Self-Fashioning*. Chicago and London: The Univ. of Chicago Press. 193-221.

———. 1991. *Marvellous Possessions*. Oxford: Clarendon Press.

Green-Pedersen, Niels Jørgen. 1984. *The Tradition of the Topics in the Middle Ages*. Muenchen and Wien: Philosophia Verlag.

Groupe de la Bussière. 1983. *Pratiques de la confession*. Paris: Les Editions du Cerf.

Grudin, Robert. 1974. Renaissance Laughter. *Neophilologus* 58(2):199-204.

Grynaeus, Simon. [Simon Gruener] 1532. *Novus Orbis Regionum ac Insularum Veteribus incognitarum*. Paris.

Guazzo, Stefano. 1581. *The Ciuile Conuersation*. Trans. G. Pettie. London.

Gurevic, A. 1982. Au Moyen Age. *Annales ESC*. 37(2): 255-75.

Guss, D.L. 1966. *John Donne, Petrarchist*. Detroit: Wayne State Univ. Press.

Hagstrum, J.H. 1992. *Esteem Enlivened by Desire*. Chicago and London: The Univ. of Chicago Press.

Hakluyt, Richard. 1985. *Voyages and Discoveries*. Ed. J. Beeching. Harmondsworth: Penguin.

Hall, Edward. 1548. *The Union of the Two Noble and Illustrate Famelies of Lancastre and York*. London.

Halpern, Richard. 1991. *The Poetics of Primitive Accumulation*. Ithaca: Cornell Univ. Press.

Hamlin, William. Attributions of Divinity in Renaissance Ethnography and Romance. *Journal of Medieval and Renaissance Studies* 24(3): 415-47.

Hamor, R. 1615. *A True Discourse of the Present Estate of Virginia*. London.

Hanna, Sara. 1994. Voices Against Tyranny. *Classical and Modern Literature* 14(4):335-44.

Hariot, Thomas. 1888. [1590]. *A Briefe and True Report of the New Found Land of Virginia*. Manchester: Holbein Society.

Hartmann, Geoffrey. 1985. Shakespeare's Poetical Character in *Twelfth Night*. In *Shakespeare and the Question of Theory*. Ed. P. Parker and G. Hartmann. New York: Methuen. 37-53.

Hassel, Chris. 1986. Providence and the Text of *Richard III*. *The Upstart Crow* 6(1): 84-93.

———. 1987. Perceptions of Providence in *Richard III*. In *Songs of Death*. Lincoln and London: Univ. of Nebraska Press. 89-121.

Haury, Auguste. 1995. *L'ironie et l'humour chez Cicéron*. Leiden: Brill.

Hawkes, Terence. 1992. *Meaning by Shakespeare*. London and New York: Methuen.

Heawood, Edward. 1921. *The World Map Before and After Magellan's Voyage*. Reprinted from *The Geographical Journal*. June 1921. 431-46.

Heidegger, Martin. 1987. *Plato's Sophist*. Trans. R. Roicewicz and A. Schuwer. Bloomington and Indianapolis: Indiana Univ. Press.

Herrick, Marvin. 1950. *Comic Theory in the Sixteenth Century*. Illinois Studies in Language and Literature 34(1-2).

Hippocrates, 1981. On Generation. Ed. I. M. Louie. Berlin and New York: Walter de Gruyter.

Hobbes, Thomas. 1994a. Discourse on Human Nature. In *The Elements of Law Natural and Politic*. Oxford and New York: Oxford Univ. Press.

Hoeniger, F.D. 1984. Musical Cures of Melancholy and Mania in Shakespeare. In *Mirror Up to Shakespeare*.Ed. J.C. Gray. Toronto, Buffalo and London: Univ. of Toronto Press. 55-67.

———. 1992. How Did Shakespeare Gain His Medical Knowledge? Chap. 3 in *Medicine and Shakespeare in the English Renaissance*. Newark: Univ. of Delaware Press; London and Toronto: Associated Univ. Presses. 32-53.

Hoenselaars, A.J. 1994. Mapping Shakespeare's Europe. In *Reclamations of Shakespeare*. Ed. A.J. Hoenselaars. Amsterdam and Atlanta: Rodopi. 223-48.

Holinshed, Raphael. 1966. *Shakespeare's Holinshed*. Ed. W.G. Boswell-Stone. New York: Benjamin Blom.

Holland, Norman N. 1982. *Laughing*. Ithaca and London: Cornell Univ. Press.

Hollander, John. 1986. *Twelfth Night* and the Morality of Indulgence. In *William Shakespeare. Comedies & Tragedies*. Ed. H. Bloom. New York, New Haven and Philadelphia: Chelsea House Publishers. 133-46.

Honour, H. 1975. *The New Golden Land*. London: Allen Lane.

Hopkins, Andrea. 1990. *The Sinful Knights*. Oxford: Clarendon Press.

Horton, Ronald A. 1991. The Argument of Spenser's *Garden of Adonis*. In *Love and Death in the Renaissance*. Ed. K.R. Bartlett, K. Eisenbichler and J. Liedl. Ottawa: Dovehouse. 61-72.

Howe, James Robinson. 1976. Tamburlaine, Magic and Bruno. Chap. 11 in *Marlowe, Tamburlaine, and Magic*. Athens: Ohio Univ. Press. 39-85.

Howell, Wilbur Samuel. 1956. The English Ramists. Chap. 9 in *Logic and Rhetoric in England, 1500-1700*. Princeton: Princeton Univ. Press. 146-281.

Huarte, Juan. 1594. *The Examination of mens Wits*. Trans. M. C. Camilli and R. Carew. London.

Hulme, Peter, 1986. *Colonial Encounters*. London and New York: Methuen.

Hunt, Tony. 1979. Aristotle, Dialectic, and Courtly Literature. *Viator* 10: 95-129.

Hunter, Gail K. 1964. The Theology of Marlowe's *Jew of Malta*. *Journal of the Warburg and Courtauld Institutes* 27: 211-40.

Hymn to Apollo. 1976. In *The Homeric Hymns*. Ed. A. N. Athanassakis. Baltimore and London: The Johns Hopkins Univ. Press.

Jacobus, Lee A. 1992. *Shakespeare and the Dialectics of Certainty*. New York: St. Martin's Press.

Jacquart, Danielle, and Claude Thomasset. 1985. La physiologie ou les étapes d'une purification. Chap. 2 in *Sexualitè et savoir médical au Moyen Age*. Paris: Presses Universitaires de France. 67-120.

Jameson, Fredric. 1977. Of Islands and Trenches. *Diacritics* 7(2): 2-21.

Janicka, Irena. 1969. The Popular Background of Ben Jonson's Masques. *Shakespeare-Jahrbuch* 105:183-208.

Janko, R. 1984. *Aristotle on Comedy*. Berkeley and Los Angeles: Univ. of California Press.

Jardine, Lisa. 1974. The Place of Dialectic Teaching in Sixteenth-Century Cambridge. *Studies in the Renaissance* 21: 31-62.

Jensen, Ejner J. 1994. "Knowing Aforehand". In *Acting Funny*. Ed. F. Teague. Rutheford, Madison and Teaneck: Fairleigh Dickinson Univ. Press; London and Toronto: Associated Univ. Presses. 72-84.

Institucion of a Gentleman, The. 1568. London.

Johnson, Hildegard Binder. 1976. New Geographical Horizons. In Chiappelli (1976). Vol. 2. 615-33.

Johnson, R. 1612. *The New Life of Virginia*. London.

Jones, Emrys. 1977. *The Origins of Shakespeare*. Oxford: Clarendon Press.

Jonsen, Albert R. and S. Toulmin. 1988. *The Abuse of Casuistry*. Berkeley, Los Angeles and London: Univ. of California Press.

Iossius, Nicandrus. 1580. *De risu, & Fletu*. Rome.

Joubert, Laurence. 1579. *Traité du Ris*. Paris.

————. 1989. *Popular Errors*. Trans. G. D. De Rocher. Tuscaloosa and London: The Univ. of Alabama Press.

Isaac the Jew [Ishak Ibn Sulzaiman]. 1515. *Liber de elementis*. In *Omnia Opera Ysaac*. Lyon.

Iser, Wolfgang. 1993. The End of the First Tetralogy: *Richard III*. Chap. 3 in *Staging Politics*. New York: Columbia Univ. Press. 44-68.

Judic, Bruno. 1986. *Confessio* chez Grégoire Le Grand. In *L'aveu* (1986). 169-90.

Ingram, Martin. 1984. Religion, Communities and Moral Disciplines in Late Sixteenth- and Early Seventeenth-Century England: Case Studies. In *Religion and Society in Early Modern Europe, 1500-1800*. Ed. K. von Greyerz. London, Boston and Sydney: The German Historical Institute. 177-93.

Kaye, Joel. 1998. The Aristotelian Model of Money and Economic Exchange. In *Economy and Nature in the Fourteenth Century*. Cambridge: Cambridge Univ. Press. 37-55.

Kelly, Henry Ansgar. 1970. *Divine Providence in the England of Shakespeare's Histories*. Cambridge, Mass.: Harvard Univ. Press.

Kennedy, William J. 1984. Comic Audiences and Rhetorical Strategies in Machiavelli, Shakespeare, and Molière. *Comparative Literature Studies* 21(4): 363-82.

Kenny, Anthony. 1991. The Nicomachean Conception of Happiness. In *Aristotle and the Later Tradition*. Ed. H. Blumenthal and H. Robinson. Oxford: Clarendon Press. 67-80.

Kermode, Lloyd Edward. 1995. "Marlowe's Second City". *Studies in English Literature* 35: 215-27.

Ketterer, Robert C. 1990. Machines for the Suppression of Time. *Comparative Drama* 24(1): 3-23.

Knapp, Robert S. 1994. Resistance, Religion, and the Aesthetic. *Research Opportunities in Renaissance Drama* 33(1-2): 143-52.

Korda, Natasha. 1994. Mistaken Identities. In *Desire in the Renaissance*. Ed. V. Finucci and R. Schwartz. Princeton: Princeton Univ. Press. 39-66.

Krant, Richard. 1989. *Aristotle on the Human Good*. Princeton: Princeton Univ. Press.

Kuhn, Heinrich C. 1997. Non-Regressive Methods. In *Method and Order in Renaissance Philosophy of Nature*. Ed. D. A. DiLiscia, E. Kessler and C. Methuen. Singapore and Sydney: Ashgate; Aldershot: Brookfield. 319-36.

Kuriyama, Constance Brown. 1980. *Hammer or Anvil*. New Brunswick: Rutgers Univ. Press.

Labriola, Albert C. 1975. *Twelfth Night* and the Comedy of Festive Abuse. *Modern Language Studies* 5(2): 5-20.

Lange, Marjory E. 1996. *Telling Tears in the English Renaissance*. Leiden, New York and Cologne: Brill.

Las Casas, Bartolomé de. 1988. *The Diario of Christopher Columbus's First Voyage to America 1492-1493*. Trans. O. Dunn and J. E. Kelley jr. Norman and London: Univ. of Oklahoma Press.

Laurent, Sylvie. 1989. *Naître au Moyen Age*. Paris: Le Léopard d'Or.

Lea, H.C. 1896. *A History of Auricular Confession and Indulgences in the Latin Church*. Vol. 1. Philadelphia: Lea Brothers.

Lea, K.M. 1962. *Italian Popular Comedy*. New York: Russell & Russell.

LeBlond, J.M. 1979. Aristotle on Definition. In *Articles on Aristotle. 3. Metaphysics*. Ed. J. Barnes, M. Schofield and R. Sorabji. London: Duckworth. 63-79.

Leech, Clifford. 1965. *Twelfth Night and Shakespearean Comedy*. Toronto: Univ. of Toronto Press.

Legendre, Pierre. 1986. *De Confessis*. In *L'aveu* (1986). 401-8.

Leggatt, Alexander. 1974. *Shakespeare's Comedy of Love*. London: Methuen.

Legge, Thomas. 1979. *Richardus Tertius*. Ed. R. J. Lordi. New York-London: Garland Publishing.

LeGoff, Jacques. 1990. Le rire dans les règles monastiques du haut Moyen Age. In *Melanges Pierre Riché*. Paris: Ed. Erasme. 93-104.

Leishman, J.B. 1962. *The Monarch of Wit*. London: Hutchinson.

Leo the Jew [Judah Abrabanel]. 1929. *Dialoghi d'amore*. Ed. S. Caramella. Bari: Laterza.

Lever, Ralph. 1573. *The Art of Reason*. London.

Levin, Harry. 1952. *The Overreacher*. Cambridge, Mass.: Harvard Univ. Press.

———. 1969. *The Myth of the Golden Age in the Renaissance*. London: Faber & Faber.

———. 1976. The Underplot of *Twelfth Night*. In *De Shakespeare à T.S. Eliot*. Ed. M.-J. Durry, R. Ellrodt, M.-T. Jones-Davies and A. Roussin. Paris: Didier. 53-9.

Lewalski, Barbara K. 1965. Thematic Patterns in *Twelfth Night*. *Shakespeare Studies* 1: 168-81.

Lewes, Robert. 1954. [1641]. *The Treasure of Traffike, or a Discourse of Forraigne Trade* In *Early English Tracts on Commerce* (1954).

Liber Exemplorum. 1908. Ed. A.G. Little. London: British Society of Franciscan Studies 1.

Liddell, Henry George. 1968. *A Greek-English Lexicon*. Oxford: Oxford Univ. Press.

Liébault, Jean. 1649. *Trois livres de maladies et infirmites des femmes*. Rouen.

Lightbown, Ronald. 1989. *Sandro Botticelli*. London: Thames & Hudson.

Little, L.K. 1981. Les techniques de la confession. In *Faire Croire*. Ecole française de Rome. 87-99.

Logan, T. Jenkins. 1982. *Twelfth Night:* The Limits of Festivity. *Studies in English Literature* 22(2). 223-38.

Le Roy, Louis. 1594. *Of the Interchangeable Course.* Trans. R. Ashley. London.

Ludovici, Emanuele Samek. Sessualità, matrimonio e concupiscenza in Sant'Agostino. In *Etica sessuale e matrimonio nel cristianesimo delle origini.* Milan: Vita & Pensiero. 212-72.

Luther, Martin. 1520. *Confitendi ratio.* Augsburg.

Machiavelli. Niccolò. 1550. Descrizione del modo tenuto dal Duca Valentino, nello ammazzare Vitellozzo Vitelli, Oliverotto da Fermo, il Signor Pagolo & il Duca di Grauina Orsini. In *Tutte le opere di Nicolo Machiavelli cittadino et secretario fiorentino.* Florence. Seconda Parte. 92-7.

McKinley, Mary B. 1993. Telling Secrets. In *Critical Tales.* Ed. J. D. Lyons and M. B. McKinley. Philadelphia: Univ. of Pennsylvania Press. 146-71.

McKiraham, Richard D. 1992. *Principles and Proofs.* Princeton: Princeton Univ. Press.

McNally, James Richard. 1968. *Prima Pars Dialectica:* The Influence of Agricola's *Dialectica* Upon English Accounts of Invention. *Renaissance Quarterly* 21: 166-77.

McNeill, John T., ed. 1938. *Medieval Handbooks of Penance.* New York: Columbia Univ. Press.

———. 1951. *A History of the Cure of Souls.* New York: Harper Brothers.

McNulty, Robert. 1960. Bruno at Oxford. *Renaissance News* 13(4): 300-05.

Maggi, Vincenzo. 1970. *De ridiculis.* In *Trattati di Poetica e Retorica del Cinquecento.* Vol. 2. 91-125.

Mahood, M.H. 1970. The Jew of Malta as Tragic Farce. In *The Jew of Malta. Text and Major Criticism.* Ed. I. Ribner. New York: The Odissey Press. 80-6.

Mancini, Celso. 1591. *De risu, ac ridiculis.* Ferrara.

Mandeville. 1968. *Mandeville's Travels.* Ed. M.C. Seymour. London, New York and Toronto: Oxford Univ. Press.

Mangan, Michel. 1996. Laughter and Elizabethan Society. Chap. 1 in *A Preface to Shakespeare's Comedies, 1594-1603.* London and New York: Longman. 19-49.

Mannyng, Robert. 1983. *Handling Synne.* Ed. I. Sullens. Binghamton: Medieval and Renaissance Texts and Studies. A

Manns, Frédéric. 1984. "Confessez vos péchés les uns aux autres". *Revue de Sciences Réligieuses* 58: 233-41.

Mansfield, Mary C. 1995. *The Humiliation of Sinners.* Ithaca and London: Cornell Univ. Press.

Manuale per confessori del Quattrocento inglese, Un. 1993. Ed. M. L. Maggioni. Milan: Vita e Pensiero.

Marchi, D.M. 1993. Montaigne and the New World. *Modern Language Studies* 23(4): 35-54.

Marlowe, Christopher. 1995. *The Jew of Malta.* In *The Complete Works of Christopher Marlowe.* Ed. R. Gill. Oxford: Clarendon Press.

Martianus Capella. 1977. *The Marriage of Philology and Mercury. [De nuptiis Mercurii et Philologiae]* Trans. W. H. Stahl, R. Johnson, and E.L. Burge. New York: Columbia Univ. Press. Vol. 2.

Martin, H. Confession et contrôle social à la fin du Moyen Age. In *Pratiques de la confession* (1983). 117-36.

Martire, Pietro. 1612. *De novo orbe.* Trans. R. Eden. London.

Marx, Groucho. 1959. *Groucho and Me.* New York: Bernard Geis Associates.

Mason, Shirley Carr. 1994. Queen Margaret's Christian Worm of Conscience. *Notes & Queries* 41(239[1]): 32-3.

Mathieu-Castellani, Gisèle. 1988. La Parole entr'ouverte. *Revue d'histoire littéraire de la France* 88(5): 974-82.

Mebane, John S. 1989. Vision and Illusion in Marlowe's *Dr Faustus*. In *Renaissance Magic and the Return of the Golden Age*. Lincoln and London: Univ. of Nebraska Press. 113-36.

Menager, Daniel. 1995. *Le Renaissance et le rire*. Paris: Presses Universitaires de France.

Mercator, Gerard. 1961. *Gerard Mercator's 'Map of the World' (1569)*. Rotterdam/'s-Gravenhage.

Michaud-Quantin, Pierre. 1962. *Sommes de casuistique*. Louvain: Nauwelaerts, Analecta Mediaevalia Namurcensia.

Miller, Andrew M. 1986. *From Delos to Delphi*. Leiden: Brill.

Milner, G.B. 1972. Homo Ridens. *Semiotica* 5: 1-30.

Millward, Peter. 1973. *Shakespeare's Religious Background*. Chicago: Loyola Univ. Press.

Minadeo, Richard. 1969. *The Lyre of Science*. Detroit: Wayne St. Univ. Press.

Minois, George. 1988. Absolutisme et conflits réligieux. Chap. 9 in *Le confesseur du roi*. Paris: Fayard. 241-74.

Minshull, Catherine. 1982. Marlowe's "Sound Machevill". *Renaissance Drama* 13: 35-55.

Minturno, Anton Sebastiano. 1559. *De poeta*. Venice.

Miola, Robert S. 1994. New Comedic Errors. Chap. 2 in *Shakespeare and Classical Comedy*. Oxford: Clarendon Press. 19-61.

Miraval, Raimon de. 1971. Chansoneta farai, vencut. In *Les Poésies du Troubadour Raimon de Miraval*. Ed. L.T. Topsfield. Paris: Nizet. 8.1.9.

Mirk, John. 1974. *Instruction for Parish Priests*. Ed. G. Kristensson. Lund: Cwk Gleerup.

Mirror for Magistrates, The. 1938. Ed. L. B. Campbell. Cambridge: Cambridge Univ. Press.

Miskinin, Harry A. 1979. The Impact of Credit on Sixteenth-Century English Industry. In *The Dawn of Modern Banking*. New Haven and London: Yale Univ. Press. 275-89.

Montaigne, Michel de. 1587. Des Cannibales. In *Essais de Messire Michel, Seigneur de Montaigne*. Paris. 1.31.

Montalboddo, Fracanzano da. 1507. *Paesi nuovamente retrovati*. Vicenza.

Moravcsik, J.M.E. 1973. Plato's Method of Division. In *Patterns in Plato's Thought*. Ed. J.M.E. Moravcsik. Dordrecht, Holland; Boston: D. Reidel Publishing Company. 158-80.

More, Thomas. 1963. The History of King Richard. In *The Complete Works*. Ed. R. S. Sylverster. Vol. 2. New Haven and London: Yale Univ. Press.

Morin, Jean. 1682. *Commentarius Historicus de disciplina in administratione sacramenti poenitentiae*. Antwerp.

Morey, Adrian. 1978. Jesuits. Chap. 11 in *The Catholic Subjects of Elizabeth I*. Totowa, N.J.: Rowman and Littlefield. 191-98.

Morreall, John. A New Theory of Laughter. In *The Philosophy of Laughter and Humor*. Ed. John Morreall. State Univ. of New York Press. 128-38.

Mossiker, F. 1977. *Pocahontas*. London: Victor Gollancz.

Muir, Kenneth. 1977. *The Sources of Shakespeare's Plays*. London: Methuen.

———. 1979. *Shakespeare's Comic Sequence.* Liverpool: Liverpool Univ. Press.

Mun, Thomas. 1954. [1621]. *A Discourse of Trade from England unto the East Indies* In *Early English Tracts on Commerce* (1954).

Myers, K. Sara. 1994. Pythagoras, Philosophy, and Paradoxography. Chap. 4 in *Ovid's Cause.* Ann Arbor: The Univ. of Michigan Press. 133-66.

Myers, W.D. 1996. *"Poor, Sinning Folk".* Ithaca and London: Cornell Univ. Press.

Narkin, Anthony P. 1967. Day-Residue and Christian reference in Clarence's Dream. *Texas Studies in Literature and Language* 9: 147-50.

Neill, M. 1976. Shakespeare's Halle of Mirrors. *Shakespeare Studies* 8:99-129.

Nevo, Ruth. 1980. *Comic Transformations in Shakespeare.* London and New York: Methuen.

Nevv Yeeres Gift, A. The Covrte of Ciuill Courtesie. 1582. London.

Nichols, A. Eljenholm. 1986. The Etiquette of pre-Refomation Confession in East Anglia. *The Sixteenth Century Journal* 17(2): 145-63.

Nichols, Stephen G. 1991. Voice and Writing in Augustine and in the Troubadour Lyric. In *Vox Intexta.* Ed. A.N. Doane and C. Brawn Pasternak. Madison: Univ. of Wisconsin Press. 137-61.

Nobili, Flaminio. 1895. *Il Trattato dell'Amore Humano.* Ed. P. D. Pasolini. Rome: Loescher.

Norden, John. 1600. *Vicissitudo Rerum.* London.

Northbrooke, John. 1843. [1577]. *A Treatise Against Dicing, Dancing, Plays, and Interludes.* London: Shakespeare Society.

Novarini, Luigi. 1637. *Risus sardonicus.* Verona.

Novarr, David. 1972. "The Extasy". In *Just So Much Honor.* Ed. P.A. Fiore. Univ. Park and London; The Pennsylvania State Univ. Press. 219-44.

Nugae venales, sive, Thesaurus ridendi & iocandi. 1648. Amsterdam.

O'Connor, J.J. 1978. Physical Deformity and Chivalric Laughter in Renaissance England. In *Comedy. New Perspectives.* Ed. M. Charney. New York Literary Forum 1. 59-71.

Oecolampadius, Johannes. [Johann Husschin] 1521. *Quod non sit onerosa Christianis confessio: Paradoxon.* Augsburg.

O'Gorman, Edmundo. 1961. *The Invention of America.* Bloomington: Indiana Univ. Press.

Oldrini, Guido. 1997. Le particolarità del ramismo inglese. Chap. 3 in In *La disputa del metodo nel Rinascimento.* Florence: Le Lettere. 225-308.

Olson, Glending. 1982. *Literature as Recreation in the Later Middle Ages.* Ithaca and London: Cornell Univ. Press.

Ong, Walter J. 1958. *Ramus.* Cambridge, Mass.: Harvard Univ. Press.

———. 1968. Tudor Writings on Rhetoric. *Studies in the Renaissance* 15:39-69.

Operetta utile del costumare i fanciulli. 1515. Modena.

Orgel, Stephen. 1965. *The Jonsonian Masque.* Cambridge, Mass.: Harvard Univ. Press.

———. 1987. Shakespeare and the Cannibals. In *Cannibals, Witches, and Divorce.* Ed. M. Garber. Baltimore-London: The Johns Hopkins Univ. Press. 40-66.

Ortelius, Abraham. 1968. *The Theatre of the Whole World, London 1606.* Amsterdam: Nico Israel.

Osborne, Kenan B. 1990. *Reconciliation and Justification.* New York and Mahwah: The Paulist Press.

Ouy, Gilbert. 1985. Quelques conseils de Gerson aux confesseurs. In *Codes in Context.* Ed. A. Gruijs. Nijmegen: Alfa. 289-312.

Ozment, S. E. 1975. *The Reformation in the Cities.* New Haven: Yale Univ. Press.

Pacifica. 1509. *Summa Confessionis Intitulata Pacifica Conscientia.* Venice.

Paden, William D. jr. 1979. "Utrum Copularentur": Of *Cors. L'Esprit Créateur* 19(4) :70-83.

Pancirolli, Guido. 1612. *Raccolta breve d'alcune cose piu segnalate c'hebbero gli antichi, e d'alcune altre trouate da Moderni.* Venice. Vol. 2.

———. 1622. *Rerum Memorabilium Libri Duo.* Frankfurt. Vol. 1.

Pandolfi, V. Ed. 1957-8. *La commedia dell'arte.* Florence: Sansoni.

Paré, Ambroise. 1598. *Oeuvres.* Paris.

Parker, Barbara C. 1987. *A Precious Seeing.* New York and London: New York Univ. Press.

Parravicino, Basilio. 1615. *Discorso del riso vera proprietà dell'huomo.* Como.

Patrizi, Francesco. 1963. *L'amorosa filosofia.* Ed. J. C. Nelson. Florence: LeMonnier.

———. 1970. [1587]. *Della poetica.* Ed. D. Aguzzi Barbagli. Florence: Istituto Nazionale Studi sul Rinascimento. Vol. 2.

Peacock, John. 1991. Ben Jonson's Masques and Italian Culture. In *Theatre of the English and Italian Renaissance.* Ed. J.R. Mulryne and M. Shewring. New York: St. Martin's Press. 73-94.

Pearcy, Lee T. 1984. Marlowe: Inexcusable Pythagorisme. Chap. 2 in *The Mediated Muse.* Hamden, Ct.: Archon Books, 1984. 21-36.

Périon J, and N. Grouchy, eds. 1556. *Aristotelis Logica.* Paris.

Perkins, William. 1966. *A Discourse of Conscience.* Ed. T.F. Merrill. Nieuwkoop: B. De Graaf.

Perrucci, Andrea. 1699. *Dell'arte rappresentativa.* Naples.

Pesserl, Jonas. 1602. *Theses de Risu.* Wittenberg.

Peter of Poitiers. 1980. *Summa de confessione.* Ed. J. Longère. Brussels: Brepols.

Peter of Spain. 1990. *Summulae Logicales.* Trans. F. P. Dinneeu. Amsterdam and Philadelphia: John Benjamins Publishing Company.

Peterson, Douglas L. 1973. *Time, Tide and Tempest.* San Marino, Cal.: The Huntington Library.

Pettazzoni, R. 1936. La confession des péchés dans l'histoire des religions. *Melanges Franz Cumont* 4: 893-901.

Pfister, Mandred. 1987. Comic Subversion. In *Deutsche Shakespeare.* Verlag Ferdinand Kamp Bochum. 27-43.

Philostratus. 1931. [1532]. *Icones, transl. Stephani Nigri.* Loeb Classical Library.

Piccolomini, Enea Silvio. 1973. *Historia de duobus amantibus.* Ed. M.L. Doglio. Milan: TEA.

———. 1996. [1553]. *The Goodli History of the Ladye Lucres and her lover Eurialus.* Ed. E.S. Morall. Oxford: Oxford Univ. Press.

Pico Della Mirandola. 1994. *Commento sopra una canzone d'amore [1486].* Ed. P. Angelis. Palermo: Novecento.

Valeriano Bolzani, Giovanni Pierio. 1587. *Hieroglyphica.* Lyon.

Platt, Peter G. 1992. "Not Before Either Known or Dreamt of". *Review of English Studies* 43(171): 387-94.
Poe, Edgar Allan. 1843. The Murders in the Rue Morgue. In *The Prose Romances of Edgar Allan Poe.* Philadelphia: William H. Graham.
Politianus, Antonius Laurentius. 1606. *Dialogus de risu.* Marburg.
Poole, A. 1994. Laughter, Forgetting, and Shakespeare. In *English Comedy.* Ed. M. Cordner, P. Holland, and J. Kerrigan. Cambridge: Cambridge Univ. Press. 85-99.
Preus, Anthony. 1975. Science and Philosophy in Aristotle's *Generation of Animals.* Chap. 2 in *Science and Philosophy in Aristotle's Biological Works.* New York: Georg Olms Verlag Hildesheim. 48-107.
Pryor, John H. 1988. *Geography, Technology, and War.* Cambridge: Cambridge Univ. Press.
Purchas, Samuel. 1625. *Purchas his Pilgrimes in Five Books.* London.
Pusey, E.B. 1878. Preface to *Advice for Those Who Exercise the Ministry of Reconciliation Through Confession and Absolution.* London.
Puteanus, Erycius. 1644. *Democritus, sive de Risu.* In *Dissertationum ludicrarum, et annitatum, scriptores varij.* Leiden.
Puttenham, George. 1589. *The Arte of English Poesie.* London.
Quesnel, C. 1991. *Mourir de rire d'apres et avec Rabelais.* Paris: Urin; Montreal: Bellarmin.
Quia Non Pigris. In *Trois Sommes de Pénitence de la première moitié du XIIIe siècle.* Ed. J.-P. Renard. Louvain-la-Neuve: Centre Cerfaux-Lefort.
Quinones, Ricardo J. 1972. Shakespeare's Comedies and Last Plays. In *The Renaissance Discovery of Time.* Cambridge, Mass.: Harvard Univ. Press. 413-43.
Rackin, Phyllis. 1990. *Stages of History.* London: Routledge.
Rainolds, John. 1600. *Th'Overthrow of Stage-playes.* Middleburgh.
Raleigh, Walter. 1966. [1601]. *Observations Touching Trade and Commerce With the Hollander.* In *Scarce and Valuable Tracts on Commerce.* Ed. J. R.McCullouch. New York: Augustus M. Kelley.
Ramus. 1555. *Dialectique.* Paris.
———. 1574. *The Logike of the Moste Excellent Philosopher P. Ramus Martyr.* Transl. M. Macilmaine. London.
Randolph, B.W. 1911. *Confession in the Church of England Since the Reformation.* London.
Razzi, Serafino. 1585. *Cento casi di coscienza.* Venice.
Raymund of Peñafort. 1500. *Summula sacramentorum,* Cologne.
Reginaldus, Valerius. 1622. *Compendiaria praxis difficiliorum casorum conscientiae.* Cologne.
Resnick, I.M. 1987. "Risus Monasticus". *Revue Bénédictine* 97:90-100.
Reulos, M. 1976. L'enseignement d'Aristote dans les collèges du XVIe siècle. In *Platon et Aristote à la Renaissance.* Paris: Vrin. 147-54.
Ribner, Irving. 1954. Marlowe and Machiavelli. *Comparative Literature* 6: 348-56.
Ribner, Irving, ed. 1970. *The Jew of Malta.* New York: The Odissey Press.
Ricci, Bernardino. 1995. *Il Tedeschino.* Ed. T. Megale. Florence: Le Lettere.
Rich Cabinet, The. 1616. London.
Richmond, Hugh M. 1984. *Richard III* and the Reformation. *Journal of English and Germanic Philology* 83(4): 509-21.

Riehle, Wolfgang. 1990. *Shakespeare, Plautus and the Humanist Tradition.* Cambridge: D.S. Brewer.

Robert of Flamborough. 1971. *Liber Poenitentialis.* Ed. J. J. F. Firth. Toronto: Pontifical Institute of Mediaeval Studies.

Roberts, David A. 1975. Mystery to Mathematics Flown. *The Centennial Review* 19(3): 136-56.

Robertson, Karen, 1996. Pocahontas at the Masque. *Signs* 21(3): 551-83.

Robinet, André. 1969. *Aux sources de l'esprit cartésien.* Paris: Vrin.

Robinson, Richard. 1969. The Theory of Names in Plato's *Cratylus.* In *Essays in Greek Philosophy.* Oxford: Clarendon Press. 100-17.

Robortello, Francesco. 1548. *De Arte Poetica Explicationes.* Florence.

Rolfe, J. 1951. *A True Relation of the State of Virginia.* New Haven: Yale Univ. Press.

Root, J. 1990. Vernacular Confessional Literature and the Construction of the Medieval Subject. Chapter 3 in *"Space to Speke".* Ann Arbor: Univ. Microfilms International. 66-124.

Rosemann, Philipp W. 1994. "Homo Hominem Generat". In *Actualité de la pensée médiévale.* Ed. S. Follon and J. McEvoy. Louvain and Paris: Editions Peeters. 159-70.

Roston, M. 1974. *The Soul of Wit.* Oxford: Clarendon Press.

Rule of Saint Benedict, The. 1983. Transl. J. B. Hasbrouck. Kalamazoo, Mich.: Cistercian.

Rusconi, Roberto. 1996. Immagini della confessione sacramentale. In *Dalla penitenza all'ascolto delle confessioni.* Spoleto: Centro Italiano di Studi sull'Alto Medioevo. 263-85.

Rutherford, R.B. 1995. The *Phaedrus.* Chap. 9 in *The Art of Plato.* Cambridge, Mass.: Harvard Univ. Press. 241-71.

Ryan, M.T. 1981. Assimilating New Worlds in the Sixteenth and Seventeenth Centuries. *Comparative Studies in Society and History* 23: 519-38.

Sale, Kirkpatrick. 1989. What Columbus Died Believing. *Terrae Incognitae* 21: 9-16.

Salingar, Leo. 1986. The Design of *Twelfth Night.* In *Dramatic Forms in Shakespeare and the Jacobeans.* Cambridge: Cambridge Univ. Press. 53-77.

Salman, Phillips. 1979. Instruction and Delight in Medieval and Renaissance Criticism. *Renaissance Quarterly* 32: 303-22.

Sanders, B. 1995. *Sudden Glory.* Boston: Beacon Press.

Sanders, Wilbur. 1986. Dramatist as Realist. In *Modern Critical Views. Christopher Marlowe.* Ed. H. Bloom. New York-Philadelphia: Chelsea House Publishers. 55-76.

Savonarola, Girolamo. [1496?]. *Introductorium confessor[um].* Florence.

Sayre, Kenneth M. 1969. *Plato's Analytical Method.* Chicago and London: The Univ. of Chicago Press.

Scaligero, Giulio Cesare. 1964. [1561]. *Poetices libri septem.* Stuttgart and Bad Cannstatt: Friedrich Frommam Verlag.

Scaltsas, Theodore. 1994. *Substance and Universals in Aristotle's Metaphysics.* Ithaca and London: Cornell Univ. Press.

Scammell, G.V. 1969. The New Worlds and Europe in the Sixteenth Century. *Historical Journal* 12(3): 389-412.

Scarsella, Marco. 1592. *Giardino di Sommisti.* Venice.

Schaffer, Neil. 1981. *The Art of Laughter.* New York: Columbia Univ. Press.

Schmitt, Charles B. 1983. *Aristotle and the Renaissance*. Cambridge, Mass.: Harvard Univ. Press.

Schwartz, Robert S. 1990. Misprision in the Highest Degree: *Twelfth Night*. Chap. 4 in *Shakespeare's Parted Eye*. New York: Peter Lang. 101-22.

Scotus, Michael. 1555. *Del riso*, cap. 76. Quoted in Nuccio Ordine, *Teoria della novella e teoria del riso nel Cinquecento* (Naples: Liguori: 1996), 17.

———. 1608. *Mensa Philosophica*. Frankfurt.

———. 1614. *Philosophers Banqvet, The*. Transl. W. B. Esquire. London.

Screech, M.A. 1980. *Ecstasy and the Praise of Folly*. London: Duckworth.

Screech, M.A. and R. Calder. 1970. Some Renaissance Attitudes to Laughter. In *Humanism in France*. Ed. A.H.T. Levi. Manchester: Manchester Univ. Press.

Seneca. 1927. [1581]. *His Tenne Tragedies*. London: Constable & Co.; New York: Alfred A. Knopf.

Shaheen, Naseeb. 1989. *Biblical References in Shakespeare's History Plays*. Newark: Univ. of Delaware Press; London and Toronto: Associated Univ. Presses.

Shakespeare's Ovid. 1961. *Shakespeare's Ovid Being Arthur Golding's Translation of the Metamorphoses*. Ed. W.H.D. Rouse. London: Centaur Press.

Shepherd of Hermas, The. 1924. In *The Apostolic Fathers*. Trans. K. Lake. The Loeb Classical Library.

Sherwood, T.G. 1984. *Fulfilling the Circle*. Toronto, Buffalo and London: Univ. of Toronto Press.

Shullenberger, William. 1992. Love as a Spectator Sport in John Donne's Poetry. In *Renaissance Discourses of Desire*. Ed. C.J. Summers and T. L. Pebworth. Columbia and London: Univ. of Missouri Press. 46-62.

Sibthorpe, Robert. 1618. *The Jesuits Character*. London. Quoted in Arthur F. Marotti, Alienating Catholics in Early Modern England, in *Catholicism and Anti-Catholicism in Early Modern English Texts* (New York: Macmillan, 1999), 15-16.

Sidney, Philip. 1973. *An Apology for Poetry*. Ed. G. Shepherd. Manchester: Manchester Univ. Press.

Sims, James H. 1966. *Dramatic Uses of Biblical Allusions in Marlowe and Shakespeare*. Gainesville: Univ. of Florida Press.

Slights, Camille Wells. 1993. *Shakespeare's Comic Commonwealths*. Toronto: Univ. of Toronto Press.

Slomkowski, Paul. 1997. *Aristotle's Topics*. Leiden, New York and Cologne: Brill.

Smith, A.J. 1985. *The Metaphysics of Love*. Cambridge: Cambridge Univ. Press.

Smith, John. 1986. *The Generall History of Virginia [1624]*. In *The Complete Works*. Ed. P.L. Barbour. Chapel Hill and London: The Univ. of North Carolina Press. Vol. 2.

Solmsen, Friedrich. 1968. Dialectic Without the Forms. In *Aristotle on Dialectic*. Ed. G.E.L. Owen. Oxford: Clarendon Press.

Sowa, Cara Angier. 1984. The Journey. Chap. 8 in *Traditional Themes and the Homeric Hymns*. Chicago: Bolchazy-Carducci Publishers. 212-35.

Speroni, C. 1964. *Wit and Wisdom of the Italian Renaissance*. Berkeley and Los Angeles: Univ. of California Press.

Spicciani, Amleto. 1977. *La mercatura e la formazione del prezzo nella riflessione teologica medioevale.* Rome: Accademia Nazionale dei Lincei.

Sprague, Rosamund Kent. 1962. *Plato's Use of Fallacy.* London: Routledge & Kegan Paul.

Spykman, Gordon J. 1955. The Doctrine of Penitence in Thomas Aquinas. In *Attrition and Contrition at the Council of Trent.* N.V. Kampen, J.H. Kok. 51-70.

Starnes, DeWitt T. 1964. The Figure Genius in the Renaissance. *Studies in the Renaissance* 11: 234-44.

Stearns, Frederic R. 1972. *Laughing.* Springfield, Ill.: Charles C. Thomas.

Steinmetz, David C., ed. 1990. *The Bible in the Sixteenth Century.* Durham-London: Duke Univ. Press.

Stevenson, L. Caroline. 1984. *Praise and Paradox.* Cambridge: Cambridge Univ. Press.

Stracca, Benvenuto. 1553. *De mercatura, seu Mercatore Tractatus.* Venice.

Strachey, William. 1953. [1612]. *The Historie of Travell into Virginia Britannia.* Ed. L.B. Wright and V. Freud. London: Hakluyt Society.

Suhanny, Henry. 1995. Malvolio et la comédie du trouble-fête. *QWERTY* 5:21-5.

Sullivan, Ceri. 1995. *Dismembered Rhetoric.* Madison: Teaneck Fairleigh Dickinson Univ. Press; London: Associated Univ. Presses.

Sylvestrina. 1518. [Mazzolini, Silvestro]. *Suma sumarum quae Sylvestrina dicitur.* Strasbourg.

Szafran, A. Willy, and A. Nysenholer, eds. 1994. *Freud et le rire.* Paris: Éditions Métailié.

Tentler, Thomas N. 1974. The Summa for Confessors as an Instrument of Social Control. In Trinkans (1974). 103-26.

———. 1977. *Sin and Confession on the Eve of the Reformation.* Princeton: Princeton Univ. Press.

Ravisius, Joannes. 1588. *Officina.* Venice.

Thirty-Nine Articles, The. 1854. Cambridge: Cambridge Univ. Press.

Thomas, K. 1977. The Place of Laughter in Tudor and Stuart England. *Times Literary Supplement,* 21 January, 77-81.

———. 1997. *Religion and the Decline of Magic.* 1971. Reprint. London: Weidenfeld & Nicolson.

Thompson, W. N. 1975. *Aristotle's Deduction and Induction.* Amsterdam: Rodopi.

Thurn, David H. 1994. Economic and Ideological Exchange in Marlowe's *Jew of Malta. Theatre Journal* 46: 157-70.

Tilton, R.S. 1995. *Pocahontas.* New York: Cambridge Univ. Press.

Todorov, Tzvetan. 1982. *La conquête de l'Amerique.* Paris: Seuil.

Trattati d'amore del Cinquecento. 1975. Ed. M. Pozzi. Bari: Laterza.

Trattati di Poetica e Retorica del Cinquecento. 1970. Ed. B. Weinberg. Bari: Laterza. Vols. 4.

Trimble, William Raleigh. 1964. *The Catholic Laity in Elizabethan England 1558-1603.* Cambridge, Mass.: Harvard Univ. Press, Belknap Press.

Trinkans, C., and H. A. Oberman, eds. 1974. *The Pursuit of Holiness in Late Medieval and Renaissance Religion.* Leiden: Brill.

Trissino, G.G. 1970. [ca. 1549] *La quinta e la sesta divisione della poetica.* In *Trattati di Poetica e Retorica del Cinquecento.* Vol. 2.

Troiano, Massimo. 1569. *Dialoghi.* Venice.

Trousdale, Marion. 1982. *Shakespeare and the Rhetoricians*. London: Scolar Press.

True Relation of Such Occurrences and Accidents of Note as Hath Hapned in Virginia, A. 1608. London.

True Tragedy of Richard the Third. The. 1594. London.

Tucci, Hannelore Zug. 1993. "Negociare in omnibus partibus per terram et per aquam". In *Mercati e mercanti nell'Alto Medioevo*. Spoleto: Centro Italiano di Studi sull'Alto Medioevo. 51-79.

Turner, Frederick. 1971. *Shakespeare and the Nature of Time*. Oxford: Oxford Univ. Press.

Turrini, Miriam. 1991. *La coscienza e le leggi*. Bologna: Il Mulino.

Tyndale, William. 1548. *The Obedience of a Christen man*. London.

Valgiglio, E. 1980. *Confessio nella Bibbia e nella letteratura cristiana antica*. Turin: Giappichelli.

Vance, Eugene. 1987. "Si est homo, est animal". In *From Topic to Tale*. Minneapolis: Univ. of Minnesota Press. 53-79.

Van den Keere, Pieter. 1980. *The World Map of 1611*. Amsterdam: Nico Israel.

Védrine, Hélène. 1967. *La conception de la nature chez Giordano Bruno*. Paris: Vrin.

Vettori, Pietro. 1560. *Commentarii in Primum Librum Aristotelis de Arte Poetarum*. Florence.

Vickers, Brian. 1972. "The 'Songs and Sonets' and the Rhetoric of Hyperbole". In *John Donne*. London: Methuen. 132-74.

———. 1988. *In Defence of Rhetoric*. Oxford: Clarendon Press.

Vidal, Bernard. 1977. *Evolution des théories sur la structure de la matière*. Paris: Centre National de la Recherche Scientifique.

Villeneuve, Arnauld de. 1512. *S'ensuit le trésor de poures qui parle des maladies*. Paris.

Vives, Juan Luis. 1555. *De anima et vita libri tres*. Basel.

Waghenaer, Lucas Jansz. 1964. [1584-85] *Spieghel der Zeevaerdt*. Amsterdam, Nico Israel Publ.: Theatrum Orbis Terrarum.

Waller, G.F. 1971. Transition in Renaissance Ideas of Time and the Place of Giordano Bruno. *Neophilologus* 55: 3-15.

Walton, Craig. 1970. Ramus and the Art of Judgment. *Philosophy and Rhetoric* 3: 152-64.

Watkins, Oscar D. 1920. *A History of Penance*. London: Longmans, Green & Co.

Weeler, John. 1931. [1601]. *A Treatise of Commerce*. Ed. G. Burton Hotchkiss. New York: The New York Univ. Press.

Weil, E. 1975. The Place of Logic in Aristotle's Thought. In *Articles on Aristotle. 1. Science*. Ed. J. Barnes, M. Schofield and R. Sorabji. London: Duckworth. 88-112.

Weill, J.T. 1923. *The Celtic Penitentials and Their Influence on Continental Christianity*. Paris: Librairie Ancienne Honoré Champion.

Weimann, Robert. 1978. *Shakespeare and the Popular Tradition in the Theater*. Baltimore and London: The Johns Hopkins Univ. Press.

Weinberg, Bernard. 1961. *A History of Literary Criticism in the Italian Renaissance*. Chicago: Univ. of Chicago Press.

Weinberg, Julius R. 1965. Historical Remarks on Some Medieval Views of Induction. In *Abstraction, Relation, and Induction*. Madison: Univ. of Wisconsin Press. 121-53.

Wells, Robin Headlam. 1994. "Ydle Shallowe Things". In *Elizabethan Mythologies*. Cambridge: Cambridge Univ. Press. 208-24.

Westerweel, Bart. 1993. The Dialogic Imagination. In *Renaissance Culture in Context. Theory and Practice*. Ed. J. R. Brink and W. F. Gentrup. Cambridge: Scolar Press. 54-74.

Whigham, F. 1984. *Ambition and Privilege*. Berkeley, Los Angeles and London: Univ. of California Press.

Whitaker, A. 1613. *Good Newes from Virginia*. London.

Whitaker, Virgil K. 1969. *Shakespeare's Use of Learning*. San Marino: The Huntington Library.

Whiting, Robert. 1989. *The Blind Devotion of the People*. Cambridge: Cambridge Univ. Press.

Whitney, George. 1584. *Choice of Emblemes*. Leiden.

Wilson, Thomas. 1909. [1560]. *Arthe of Rhetorique*. Ed. G.H. Mair. Oxford: Clarendon Press.

Wilson, Richard. 1997. Shakespeare and the Jesuits. *The Times Literary Supplement*, 19 December, 11-3.

Wood, Thomas. 1952. *English Casuistical Divinity During the Seventeenth Century*. London: SPCK.

Woodward, G.S. 1969. *Pocahontas*. Norman: Univ. of Oklahoma Press.

Wyclif, J. 1845. Trialogus. In *Tracts and Treatises*. Ed. R. Vaughan. London.

Young, P. 1962. The Mother of Us All. *Kenyon Review* 24: 391-415.

Zumthor, Paul. 1987. La parole fondatrice. Chap. 4 in *La lettre et la voix*. Paris: Seuil. 83-106.

Index